Intuition in
Organizations

*To my colleagues
at FIT.*

Wes Agn

To Carol Mottinger,
my best friend.

Intuition in Organizations
LEADING AND MANAGING PRODUCTIVELY

Edited by
Weston H. Agor

SAGE PUBLICATIONS
The Publishers of Professional Social Science
Newbury Park   London   New Delhi

For information address:

SAGE Publications, Inc.
2111 West Hillcrest Drive
Newbury Park, California 91320

SAGE Publications Ltd.
28 Banner Street
London EC1Y 8QE
England

SAGE Publications India Pvt. Ltd.
M-32 Market
Greater Kailash I
New Delhi 110 048 India

Printed in the United State of America

Library of Congress Cataloging-in-Publication Data

Intuition in organizations : leading and managing productively /
  edited by Weston H. Agor.
     p.   cm.
  Bibliography: p.
  Includes index.
  ISBN 0–8039–3562–5. — ISBN 0–8039–3563–3 (pbk.)
  1. Intuition (Psychology) 2. Leadership. 3. Management.
  I. Agor, Weston H., 1939–
  HD38.I58   1989   *F A C U L T Y   C O L L .*
  658.4'09—dc20   89–10216
                                                              CIP

FIRST PRINTING, 1989

Contents

Acknowledgments

There are many people to thank for their help in preparing this book. First, special thanks go to my graduate students in public administration at the University of Texas at El Paso and elsewhere, who stimulated my thinking and often aided me, without even knowing it, by challenging my basic assumptions about intuition. Some thanks also go to all the executives whom I have tested, worked with in workshops around the world, and often spent other countless hours with discussing this subject. Finally, let me personally thank Ann West, my editor, for having the foresight to publish this book. Her vision, observations, and critiques of my various submissions helped to improve this book in countless ways.

Introduction

Purpose of This Book

This book is the first collection of readings that I am aware of on the role of intuition in leadership and management available anywhere in the world. Hopefully it will not be the last you will see or read in your unfolding future.

Being the first such book, I have a special obligation to make it a "good start" in what is presently a relatively open field in the management literature just now beginning to be explored more fully by researchers and other writers. Accordingly, I have tried to make this book *special* in a number of ways.

First, I have brought together in one convenient place for you not only the best available theoretical research on this topic but also the best available literature at the moment on how the brain skill intuition can be "mainstreamed." By that I mean how the skill can be practically used to increase productivity (a combination of effectiveness and efficiency) at both the individual and the organizational level.

Second, I have selected as many articles as possible for inclusion that not only make an important contribution to the literature on this topic but are also easy to understand. All too often academic research loses the power it could potentially have on "the real world" of organizational life because it is written in a jargon that is likely to destine it to a dusty back shelf somewhere. I want this book to be on your desk, not just for show but to be used in all aspects of your life every day.

Third, I have picked articles about the use of intuition in leadership and management that are balanced, reasonable, and help to make clear how this emerging literature can be well integrated into what already exists. It is not my objective to start another management fad.[1] It is not my objective to try to encourage every prospective leader/manager to have "exactly the right quotient" of intuitive skills in order to succeed in the future. I am not a guru—the guru is within you! Rather it is my objective to try to strike a *better balance* than we presently have between what is available in the literature and management training programs on one aspect of the "art of the leadership/management" process as compared (*not opposed*) to the science of the process. It is my contention that intuitive skill assessment and training (what I call a Brain-Skill Management Program) should be an *important part* of any education and training program in every organization at every level beginning with K-12 on up to wherever you are or are going to be in your lifetime.[2] Accordingly, I advocate *integrating* intuitive skill assessment and training into the management curriculum of universities (whether they are located in programs in business, public administration, education, health administration, nursing, and so on).[3] I advocate *integrating* intuitive skill assessment and training in the management of all types of organizations (whether we are talking about a school system, a university, a government agency, or the private sector).

I also believe that an important part of intuitive decision making has a factual and experience base to it. In my view, it is not a magical or paranormal skill. I seek here in this book to show how and why this is so and why, then, it is important to *merge* our more traditional management skills/styles/literature with the new, emerging literature of which intuitive decision making is an important part. Whether we are speaking of the individual, the organizational, the global, or the universal context/setting, our future survival and general well-being demand it.

Fourth, I would like to encourage you to see and feel the potential value of getting more proactive about your intuition as a useful resource in organizational life and life in general. By this I mean it is my purpose to give you some hints about how this skill can be practically used to increase your productivity, help guide your most important decisions, and help to achieve happiness in your personal life. Toward this end, I have included selections that help to demystify what intuition is and make clearer to you what the brain skill in fact is/can be. I have included selections that demonstrate how the skill varies by management level and by sex, ethnic group, and occupational specialization. I try to outline some of the practical implications of these recent research findings. I have also included selections that demonstrate that successful executives use intuition to guide their most critical decisions and how they go about strengthening this skill for future use. You will also find several articles that will outline how your present level of intuitive skills can be enhanced still further and some of the techniques that have proven effective in this process.

As I have worked toward fulfilling this fourth objective, I have tried to also include articles that would make this book a "crossover" book. By this I mean that the book should be practically relevant and useful to a lateral as well as a vertical array of persons, groups, and organizations. The message of this book should be felt at every one of these "stations" in executive life. Professors and students of leadership/management-related programs at every level should find this book practically useful to them. Trainers in whatever organization in whatever state and nation should find that this book rings a responsive chord.

My fifth goal is to encourage interdisciplinary research on the use of intuition in leadership and management. When I set out to prepare this book, I found that there was very little available on the subject—especially pieces showing in a meaningful way how intuition could be used in practical settings to help guide decision making. The last selection in this book outlines in detail the gaps in our present literature on this subject and the direction I think research should take to fill it. I also outline there ways this research can be focused and coordinated for practical payout, and the appendix contains a form for you to complete should you wish to actively engage in this process yourself and network with others interested in the same research or practical application.

Finally, it is my hope that this book will help to contribute to a "global literature on management," which is now also emerging. We all know the megatrends worldwide that have been identified by other authors. It is clear that we are seeing a merging of the East and the West in the management world today and tomorrow. It is my belief that intuition is one brain skill that is going to help facilitate the smooth flow of this process in a productive and peaceful way. I see intuition as a skill that will grow in importance in the emerging climate we all face. It is clearly a skill we need to cultivate for use in today's and tomorrow's world if we are to survive and prosper.

What makes me say this? Just look at and think about the organizational environment we are in today. It is characterized by crisis and rapid change. Traditional analytical techniques such as straight-line projections are not as useful as they once were for guiding major decisions. For example, if you as a buyer continued to stock for next year what sells today, you would probably soon run out of business. One has to have the skill to sense new trends that are emerging and come up with practical ways to capitalize on them. Intuition is one brain skill that will serve you most effectively in this context.

Top leaders of organizations that I have tested and/or interviewed find that intuition is particularly useful to help guide their major decisions in settings that are becoming increasingly more common today:

- where there is a high level of uncertainty
- where there is little previous precedent
- where reliable "facts" are limited or totally unavailable
- where time is limited and there is pressure to be right
- where there are several plausible options to choose from, all of which can be plausibly supported by "factual" arguments

If you hope to be better prepared for tomorrow, then it only seems logical to pay some attention to the use and development of intuitive skills for decision making. Even if you yourself don't want to pursue this subject too far, other than to be aware of its potential meaning/use, you may be well advised to staff your organization with intuitive talent—and then *pay attention* to the advice you get from these people. I am reminded of what Professor Jennings from Michigan State University once wrote, "Two minds are better than one as long as they are two different minds." Groupthink and the resulting disasters that will flow from it is your other alternative.[4]

There is another strong reason for you to pay attention to this subject. We have learned more in this last decade about how the brain functions than in the entire history of man up to that point.[5] What we are likely to learn in this remaining decade of the twentieth century is likely to grow still faster. Witness major breakthroughs in artificial intelligence, psychoimmunology, and related applications. The brain represents our last great frontier. It is the area in which enormous upside potential exists. Not investing in the proactive use of this resource would appear to be a grave mistake. After all, we know more about how to get to the moon than we do about how man's brain functions and grows—or dies. We have already substantially modified or corrected what we thought we knew about how the brain functions throughout this last decade. This process will continue. The executives and organizations that are on the cutting edge of this new knowledge as it emerges are likely to gain from it. Executives and organizations that are not are likely to pay a stiff price—even potential extinction.

Definitions—What Is Intuition?

If you can sense as I do that intuition may be an important brain skill that will become more important as this next decade unfolds, just what is it anyway? Any exploration you conduct of the existing literature on the subject will leave you more than frustrated. Scholars who have explored the topic *do not agree* on what it is really; you will find a wide array of methodological approaches—and sometimes no methodological approaches other than simple assertions—with which to approach it. Furthermore, as some writers perhaps sense, this topic will be "in vogue" soon, instant "experts" have suddenly emerged to offer their definition of what intuition *really* is! It should also be noted that there are almost no field studies on the applied use of intuition among practicing executives and no interdisciplinary studies of intuition that I have uncovered as yet.

We simply need more research on this topic. As Herbert A. Simon, Nobel Prizewinner in economics, writes in one of the selections that follows, "The description, in detail, of the use of judgmental and analytical processes in expert problem solving and decision making deserves a high priority on the agenda of management research."[6] Whatever assertions made at present about what intuition is probably should be classified as tentative theoretical or assertive comments often not backed up with empirical field research. What I have tried then to assemble in this book is some of the best theoretical and practical discourses presently available about what intuition is and how the skill might be practically used. I have also chosen an interdisciplinary array of articles, which include several scholars, several professional writers, and several observers and testers of executive decision-making behavior.

You will find the authors included here agree that intuition is an important skill for leaders and managers to have. But they really have widely different perspectives about what intuition is and how the process works. For example, Frances E. Vaughan is a Ph.D. graduate in psychology from Stanford University, who has written probably the best-known theoretical treatment of intuition to date.[7] Currently a practicing psychotherapist and adjunct professor, Dr. Vaughan believes that intuition functions on four distinct levels: physical, emotional, mental, and spiritual. At the physical level, intuitive awareness comes in the form of bodily sensations. Sometimes we have a strong bodily response to a person or situation when there is no apparent surface reason for doing so. We simply know something without knowing how or why. Put another way, our intuition is telling us what our body already knows to be true. If you are experiencing a very stressful environment daily, for example, your body is probably giving you numerous clues such as headaches or stomachaches. These clues may be practically translated into action in several ways: alter the environment, remove yourself from the environment, or learn through stress-reduction techniques how to handle the situation more effectively for your long-run well-being.

At the emotional level, Vaughan argues that intuitive signals are transmitted in the form of feelings. Surely many of us have had the experience sometime in our lives that we instantaneously liked or disliked someone we just met. Just feeling right or wrong about a situation or picking up visual clues about a person are good examples. Third, intuitive cues can come to you on a mental level, according to the author. This is when mentally you see a pattern or order to seemingly unrelated facts that may not be obvious to your colleagues just yet either. Charles Revson, the founder of Revlon, and Diane Von Furstenberg, designer and manufacturer of numerous cosmetic products, appear to be able to operate effectively on this level when predicting what the future consumers of their products would be likely to want.[8]

Finally, Vaughan asserts that intuition can function on a spiritual level. At this level, one becomes aware of the meaning of the old biblical saying, "As we sow so shall we reap." Emphasis is on the transpersonal and the underlying oneness of life. At this level, one would be conscious of how decisions today might come back to affect society in the future (e.g., dumping garbage at sea only to have it wash up again later on the shore).

Herbert A. Simon takes a somewhat less metaphysical view of the subject. Relying on recent research from the psychological laboratory, field observations, and efforts to model the human brain with modern digital computers (artificial intelligence and cognitive science studies), Dr. Simon believes that intuition is not a process that operates independently of analysis. Rather, he states, the "two processes are essentially complementary components of effective decision-making systems." By this he means that an executive can acquire by long experience an ability to seemingly instantly recognize patterns and consequences of alternative actions. This is what appears to give intuition the appearance of an "aha" quality. In fact, he posits, intuition is a rational process whereby the brain evokes past memories and experiences to address the problem at hand. Simon departs from many other authors on this subject then by stating that "it is a fallacy to contrast 'analytical' and 'intuitive' styles of management. Intuition and judgment—at least good judgment—are simply analyses frozen into habit and into the capacity for rapid response through recognition." Hence, in his view, every manager needs to cultivate his or her intuition in order to be able to respond to situations rapidly. But he believes this capacity is solely a product of many years of experience and training. I assume he also means by this that the experience and training mentioned is gained in this so-called lifetime, or real time, rather than over a process of generational development, but perhaps he does not.

Philip Goldberg is a professional writer as well as a scholar of industrial psychology and has been researching the subject of intuition for nearly a decade now. He sees intuition as being a consequential experience—a snapshot as opposed to a motion picture. For him, intuition is inexplicable. "The intuiter might be able to provide a plausible explanation for what led to his knowledge, but he would be reasoning retroactively." As you can see, Simon would probably take issue with this assertion, but Vaughan might well agree with it. On the other hand, Simon would most likely concur with Goldberg's view that intuition is part of rational thinking, although Simon appears to be inclined to say it is totally rational thinking.

Roy Rowan is another professional writer, but he has devoted much of his attention in recent years to the use of intuition by executives in their decision making. A former member of the board of editors at *Fortune* magazine, he has recently written a book based on extensive phone and field interviews with prominent executives in this country. He concludes that intuition is a "Eureka factor"— the sudden awareness that you have found the answer you are looking for. For Rowan, "intuition is knowledge gained without rational thought." Again, we have disagreement among our selected authors. Vaughan and Goldberg appear to agree with parts of this statement (although not all of it) while Simon clearly does not.

From a research perspective, we certainly have a dilemma. Every author agrees that intuition is an important skill in executive decision making, but they can hardly agree on an operational definition of exactly what it is. Other than personal interviews and related "expert" research that Simon alludes to (which has been conducted by others), no author has actually tested or worked with executives while they were making their decisions to test their own respective definitions of intuition. As I have engaged in a good bit of this type of research myself, let me muddy the definitional waters still further by offering one of my own here briefly. I will return to this subject again in the concluding chapter of this book.

My research among leaders and managers in a wide variety of organizational settings and management levels, which is included in Part III of this book, leads me to offer the following definition of intuition. In many ways, you will find that I lean towards Simon's definition of intuition, but I also include Vaughan's four levels of intuition in mine. I depart from Simon in that I am not convinced as yet than intuition is a product solely of "this lifetime." Rather, I think we start this lifetime with a genetic predisposition that has been passed on and developed over many previous generations or lifetimes. This predisposition can be altered and/or developed further by experiences we gain in this lifetime. I also believe that what Rowan calls "the Eureka factor" can and will be explained as a rational process, similar to Simon's description of the process, in the not too distant future.

Put another way, my operating definition for intuition at present is that it is a rational and logical brain skill than can be used to help guide decision making. It is not paranormal. Although hard science has not yet developed the ability to quantify step-by-step how this process in fact works, we will go a long way toward this end before the century is out. Intuition is a product of a series of input sources including both factual and feeling cues. Hence, it cannot be said to be a function localized in one side of the brain or the other. I believe that whether the potential array of input sources is *actually experienced* to help use and develop our intuitive ability will depend in part on how we process our life (or lives) through the filters of our own personal and cultural/societal egos.

Hence, your definition or my definition of "reality" may well depend not only on reality itself as it "truly exists" but at least in part on our own perceptions of reality and/or our willingness to accept what is in fact so—either about ourselves or about the organization in which we work. The more receptive and open we are to the potential cues that exist on all the levels (i.e., factual, feeling, preprogrammed), the greater our "consciousness" is of "reality." The greater this consciousness is, the greater is our potential intuitive ability. Whether we "actualize" this potential ability on any or all of the levels Vaughan mentions will also depend on whether we learn to "actualize" or bring it "on-line" on command. This takes practice. Some of the ways to achieve this facility can be through the techniques outlined later in this book—on both an individual and a group level. Other avenues are yet to be discovered.

What Is Leadership and Management?

When I picked the title for this book, I struggled for a while about whether to include both of the words *leadership* and *management*. Do they have the same meaning—or different meanings—or somewhere in between? Despite all that has been written on this (these) subject(s), it is amazing to find that we really do not have a clear operational definition of either word at the moment. For example, Tom Peters, the present guru of organizational excellence, states categorically that leadership and management are totally separate functions. "Leadership is growing and enhancing, creating a vision" where as managing is "arranging and telling."[9] Warren Bennis and Burt Namus draw a similar dichotomy in their recent book on leaders. "Managers do things right. Leaders do the right things."[10] On the other hand, John Gardner, who has served extensively in several top policy positions in every sector of our economy, offers another definition: "There is a considerable overlap between the functions of leadership and management, and it is one of the dependable characteristics of contemporary leadership that leaders must accomplish their purposes through large and complex organized systems."[11]

It seems to me that John Gardner's approach to these terms is more on the mark than either Peter's or Bennis and Namus's. I find it increasingly difficult in this age of flexible, rapidly changing, organizational structures characterized more and more by task force management, quality circles, and bottom-up communication structures to see much practical purpose to drawing "hard and fast" distinctions between the terms *leadership* and *management*. I think it is more productive to speak in terms of degree. A leader, for example, in an average day may do more "visioning" work than a manager, but it depends on the particular day. It depends on the particular leader and manager, the particular organizational setting, the personalities involved, and so on. It can actually be just the opposite. As John Gardner notes, in reality, aspects of leadership might also be described as managing. These include planning and priority-setting, organizing and institution building, keeping the system functioning, agenda-setting and decision making, and exercising political judgment.[12] Accordingly, it seems appropriate to include both the words *leadership* and *management* in this book title, or neither. My field research on executives, nationally and in several other countries, other scholarly research, and the testimony from executives themselves all indicate that intuition plays an important role in both "leadership" and "management" decision-making settings—whatever *you believe* these words to mean.[13]

Organization of the Book

The book is divided into six major parts to introduce you conveniently, step-by-step, to what intuition is, how it can be used in leadership and management decision making to increase productivity, and how you can strengthen your present level of intuitive skills still further for practical use. Each part of the book is introduced with a summary page outlining what the part contains and the major conclusions the authors selected have made thus far about the subject they explore there.

For example, Part I provides you with a variety of perspectives on what scholars/researchers believe intuition is. Part II outlines why many scholars and managers believe intuition is an important, practical, decision-making skill that can be used to increase productivity. Part III then provides you with a survey instrument that you can easily use to assess and compare your own scores with the national norms set by other executives thus far tested—controlling for management level, sex, ethnic background, and occupational specialty. Armed with these finding, Part IV discusses more precisely the many ways intuitive skills can be and have been used by executives in applied settings. For example, there you will find several actual case study illustrations from major private and public sector organizations, which demonstrate how intuitive skills can be/have been used to increase productivity—both on a personal and an organizational level. At this point, you are prepared and ready to explore ways you can strengthen your present level of intuitive ability for practical use. Part V outlines several alternative techniques and exercises that can be useful in applied settings such as meditation, hypnosis, keeping an "intuition journal," and establishing an "intuition network" in order to work on and exchange skill-building techniques with other executives for practical, day-to-day use. (The Appendix contains actual examples of forms that can be used for this purpose.) Finally, Part VI concludes the book with a call for interdisciplinary research on the use of intuition in leadership and management—a need identified by Nobel Prize winner Herbert Simon and many others. Here you will find a detailed outline of a proposed series of hypotheses about intuition that are offered for systematic study by researchers worldwide.

Methodological Note

The field research presented in this book on how executives score on intuitive ability and their actual use of this brain skill to help guide their most important decisions is based on national testing following accepted standards for academic research (e.g., random survey sampling techniques and statistical control procedures). It is the only such testing presently available anywhere in the world today so it is appropriate to discuss here how these studies have been conducted.

A detailed discussion of the methodology used in this field research and the reliability/validity of the survey instrument used in this research can be found elsewhere.[14] In summary, the research has been conducted over a period of eight years (1981-1988) in several stages. The first stage was a national survey sample of executives in both the private and public sectors controlling for such key variables as level of management, level of government, sex, occupational specialization, and ethnic background. The survey instrument used to assess intuitive ability was a series of questions selected from the Myers Briggs Type Indicator (MBTI), which has an established reputation for over 50 years of reliability and validity.

The second stage of my field research involved a follow-up study among those executives who were found in the first study to score in the top 10% on intuitive ability who also were in top management positions. They were asked a series of open-ended questions designed to determine how they *in fact used* their intuitive skills to help guide their most important decisions, to determine why they are not always successful when they use this brain skill, and to determine if a "technology" could be isolated that these executives use for helping to develop their intuitive ability still further for applied use.

The results of these studies are reported in Part III of this book. Based on continued, ongoing research and what has been learned from the field research noted above, I have totally modified the survey instrument in this part for you to take. Although you will still be able to benchmark your scores with those executives tested nationally, the survey instrument has been significantly improved for future use. As we learn more about intuition and how the process works, I anticipate further improvements in the survey instrument used.

Notes

1. For a critique of one recent such fad, see Terence Hines, "Left Brain/Right Brain Mythology and Implications for Management and Training," *Academy of Management Review* 12, no. 4 (1988), pp. 600-606.

2. See, for example, Micki McKisson, *Nurturing Creative and Independent Thought in Children* (Tucson, AZ: Jephyr Press Learning Materials, 1983).

3. Example articles that demonstrate the potential application of intuitive skills to several horizontally different fields can be found in the following: Prentice-Hall Information Service, *Public Personnel Administration Series*, January 23, 1989, pp. 521-23; *The School Administrator*, August, 1988, pp. 19-22; *Training & Development Journal*, March 1988, pp. 68-71; *Personnel Administrator*, October, 1987, pp. 54-61; *Personnel*, August 1986, pp. 42-46; *Organizational Dynamics*, Winter 1986, pp. 5-19; *Journal of Health and Human Resources Administration*, Winter 1985, pp. 386-95; and *Nursing Success Today*, November 1984, pp. 23-24.

4. Irving L. Janis, "Groupthink: The Desperate Drive for Consensus at Any Cost," in J. Steven Ott, *Classic Readings in Organizational Behavior* (Pacific Grove, CA: Brooks/Cole, 1989), pp. 223-32.

5. Geoffrey Montgomery, "The Mind in Motion," *Discover Magazine*, March 1989, p. 58 ff.

6. Herbert A. Simon, "Making Management Decisions: The Role of Intuition and Emotion," *Academy of Management Executive*, February 1987, p. 61.

7. Frances E. Vaughan, *Awakening Intuition* (Garden City, NY: Anchor, 1979).

8. Russel R. Taylor, *Exceptional Entrepreneurial Women: Strategies for Success* (Westport, CT: Praeger, 1988).

9. T. J. Peters and R. H. Waterman, Jr., *In Search of Excellence: Lessons from America's Best Run Companies* (New York: Harper & Row, 1982).

10. Warren Bennis and Burt Namus, *Leaders: The Strategies for Taking Charge* (New York: Harper & Row, 1985).

11. John W. Gardner, "Effective Sector Leadership," Speech Delivered Before the Independent Sector (Washington, DC, May 12, 1988).

12. John W. Gardner, *The Tasks of Leadership* (Washington, DC: Independent Sector, March 1986), p. 13.

13. Taylor, *Exceptional Entrepreneurial Women*; Gifford Pinchot, III, *Intrapreneuring* (New York: Harper & Row, 1985).

14. Weston H. Agor, *The Logic of Intuitive Decision Making: A Research-Based Approach for Top Management* (Westport, CT: Greenwood, 1986); and Weston H. Agor, *Intuitive Management: Integrating Left and Right Brain Management Skills* (Englewood Cliffs, NJ: Prentice-Hall, 1984).

PART I What Is Intuition?

Four chapters are contained in this part. You will find that these authors have a wide variety of perspectives on what intuition is and how it functions. This wide range and often conflicting set of perspectives is due in no small measure to the lack of applied field research on this topic and the disciplinary perspective each author brings with him or her.

Herbert Simon believes that intuition is a rational process whereby the brain evokes past memories and experiences to address the problem at hand. Simon also believes it is a fallacy to contrast "analytical" and "intuitive" styles of management. As far as he goes with this hypothesis, I agree with him based on my own field research. Frances Vaughan, on the other hand, believes intuition functions on four distinct levels: physical, emotional, mental, and spiritual. Her statements are totally theoretical, however, and are not empirically based, to date. Philip Goldberg argues that, although intuition is partially rationally based thinking, it is inexplicable. This statement is also not empirically based. Finally, we have Roy Rowan's contention that intuition is a "Eureka factor"—knowledge gained without rational thought. Rowan's basis for his position is a series of field interviews with executives nationally. However, he did not follow any structured interview protocol in conducting these interviews, and we have no way of knowing if the executives actually have/use the intuitive ability they discussed as no real assessment of their ability was carried out in an applied setting.

1

Making Management Decisions
The Role of Intuition and Emotion[†]

HERBERT A. SIMON

The work of a manager includes making decisions (participating in their making), communicating them to others, and monitoring how they are carried out. Managers must know a great deal about the industry and social environment in which they work and the decision-making process itself to make decisions well. Over the past 40 years, the technique of decision making has been greatly advanced by the development of a wide range of tools—in particular, the tools of operations research and management science, and the technology of expert systems.

But these advances have not applied to the entire domain of decision making. They have had their greatest impact on decision making that is well-structured, deliberative, and quantitative; they have had less impact on decision making that is loosely structured, intuitive, and qualitative; and they have had the least impact on face-to-face interactions between a manager and his or her co-workers—the give and take of everyday work.

In this article I will discuss these two relatively neglected types of decision making: "intuitive" decision making and decision making that involves interpersonal interaction. What, if anything, do we know about how judgmental and intuitive processes work and how they can be made to work better? Any why do managers often fail to do what they know they should do—even what they have decided to do? What can be done to bring action into closer accord with intention?

My article will therefore have the form of a diptych, with one half devoted to each of these topics. First, I will discuss judgmental

†SOURCE: Article by Herbert A. Simon, "Making Management Decisions: The Role of Intuition and Emotion," *Academy of Management Executive* (Vol. 1, No. 1), pp. 57-64; used by permission.

and intuitive decision making; then I will turn to the subject of the manager's behavior and the influence of emotions on that behavior.

Sometimes the term rational (or logical) is applied to decision making that is consciously analytic, the term nonrational to decision making that is intuitive and judgmental, and the term irrational to decision making and behavior that responds to the emotions or that deviates from action chosen "rationally." We will be concerned, then, with the nonrational and the irrational components of managerial decision making and behavior. Our task, you might say, is to discover the reason that underlies unreason.

Intuition and Judgment

As an appendix to the *Functions of the Executive* (Harvard University Press, 1938), Chester I. Barnard published an essay, based on a talk he had given in 1936 at Princeton, entitled "Mind in Everyday Affairs."[1] The central motive of that essay was a contrast between what Barnard called "logical" and "nonlogical" processes for making decisions. He speaks of "the wide divergence of opinion . . . as to what constitutes a proper intellectual basis for opinion or deliberate action." And he continues:

> By "logical processes" I mean conscious thinking which could be expressed in words or by other symbols, that is, reasoning. By "non-logical processes" I mean those not capable of being expressed in words or as reasoning, which are only made known by a judgment, decision or action.

Barnard's thesis was that executives, as contrasted, say, with scientists, do not often enjoy the luxury of making their decisions on the basis of orderly rational analysis, but depend largely on intuitive or judgmental responses to decision-demanding situations.

Although Barnard did not provide a set of formal criteria for distinguishing between logical and judgmental decision making, he did provide a phenomenological characterization of the two styles that make them easily recognizable, at least in their more extreme forms. In logical decision making, goals and alternatives are made explicit, the consequences of pursuing different alternatives are calculated, and these consequences are evaluated in terms of how close they are to the goals.

In judgmental decision making, the response to the need for a decision is usually rapid, too rapid to allow for an orderly sequential analysis of the situation, and the decision maker cannot usually give a veridical account of either the process by which the decision was reached or the grounds for judging it correct. Nevertheless, decision makers may have great confidence in the correctness of their intuitive decisions and are likely to attribute their ability to make them rapidly to their experience.

Most executives probably find Barnard's account of their decision processes persuasive; it captures their own feelings of how processes work. On the other hand, some students of management, especially those whose goal is to improve management-decision processes, have felt less comfortable with it. It appears to vindicate snap judgments and to cast doubt on the relevance of management-science tools, which almost all involve deliberation and calculation in decision making.

Barnard did not regard the nonlogical processes of decision as magical in any sense. On the contrary, he felt they were grounded in knowledge and experience:

> The sources of these non-logical processes lie in physiological conditions or factors, or in the physical and social environment, mostly impressed upon us unconsciously or without conscious effort on our part. They also consist of the mass of facts, patterns, concepts, techniques, abstractions, and generally what we call formal knowledge or beliefs, which are impressed upon our minds more or less by conscious effort and study. This second source of non-logical mental processes greatly increases with directed experience, study and education. (p. 302)

At the time I wrote _Administrative Behavior_ (1941-42), I was troubled by Barnard's account of intuitive judgment (see the footnote on p. 51 of AB), largely, I think, because he left no clues as to what subconscious processes go on while judgments are being made.[2] I was wholly persuaded, however, that a theory of decision making had to give an account of both conscious and subconscious processes (see the end of p. 75 to the top of p. 76). I finessed the issue by assuming that both the conscious and the unconscious parts of the process were the same, that they involve drawing on factual premises and value premises, and operating on them to form conclusions that became the decisions.

Because I used logic (drawing conclusions from premises) as a central metaphor to describe the decision-making process, many readers of _Administrative Behavior_ have concluded that the theory advanced there applies only to "logical" decision making, not to decisions that involve intuition and judgment. That was certainly not my intent. But now, after nearly 50 years, the ambiguity can be resolved because we have acquired a solid understanding of what the judgmental and intuitive processes are. I will take up the new evidence in a moment; but first, a word must be said about the "two brains" hypothesis, which argues that rational and intuitive processes are so different that they are carried out in different parts of the brain.

SPLIT BRAINS AND FORMS OF THOUGHT

Physiological research on "split brains"—brains in which the corpus callosum, which connects the two hemispheres of the cerebrum, has been severed—has provided encouragement to the idea of two qualitatively different kinds of decision making—the analytical, corresponding to Barnard's "logical," and the intuitive or creative, corresponding to his "non-logical." The primary evidence behind this dichotomy is that the two hemispheres exhibit a division of labor: in right-handed people, the right hemisphere plays a special role in the recognition of visual patterns, and the left hemisphere in analytical processes and the use of language.

Other evidence in addition to the split-brain research suggests some measure of hemispheric specialization. Electrical activity in the intact brain can be measured by EEG techniques. Activity in a brain hemisphere is generally associated with partial or total suppression in the hemisphere of the alpha system, a salient brain wave with a frequency of about ten vibrations per second. When a hemisphere is inactive, the alpha rhythm in that hemisphere becomes strong. For most right-handed subjects, when the brain is engaged in a task involving recognition of visual pattern, the alpha rhythm is relatively stronger in the left than in the right hemisphere; with more analytical tasks, the alpha rhythm is relatively stronger in the right hemisphere. (See Doktor and Hamilton, 1973, and Doktor, 1975, for some experiments and a review of the evidence.[3])

The more romantic versions of the split-brain doctrine extrapolate this evidence into the two polar forms of thought labeled above as analytical and creative. As an easy next step, evaluative nuances creep into the discussion. The opposite of "creative," after all, is "pedestrian." The analytical left hemisphere, so this story goes, carries on the humdrum, practical, everyday work of the brain, while the creative right hemisphere is responsible for those flights of imagination that produce great music, great literature, great art, great science, and great management. The evidence for this romantic extrapolation does not derive from the physiological research. As I indicated above, that research has provided evidence only for some measure of specialization between the hemispheres. It does not in any way imply that either hemisphere (especially the right hemisphere) is capable of problem solving, decision making, or discovery independent of the other. The real evidence for two different forms of thought is essentially that on which Barnard relied: the observation that, in everyday affairs, men and women often make competent judgments or reach reasonable decisions rapidly—without evidence indicating that they have engaged in systematic reasoning, and without their being able to report the thought processes that took them to their conclusion.

There is also some evidence for the very plausible hypothesis that some people, confronted with a particular problem, make more use of intuitive processes in solving it, while other people make relatively more use of analytical processes (Doktor, 1978)[3] [*sic*]

For our purposes, it is the differences in behavior, and not the differences in the hemispheres, that are important. Reference to the two hemispheres is a red herring that can only impede our understanding of intuitive, "non-logical" thought. The important questions for us are "What is intuition?" and "How is it accomplished?" not "In which cubic centimeters of the brain tissue does it take place?"

NEW EVIDENCE ON THE PROCESS OF INTUITION

In the past 50 years since Barnard talked about the mind in everyday affairs, we have learned a great deal about the processes human beings use to solve problems, to make decisions, and even to create works of art and science. Some of this new knowledge has been gained in the psychological laboratory; some has been gained through observation of the behavior of people who are demonstrably creative in some realm of human endeavor; and a great deal has been gained through the use of the modern digital computer to model human thought processes and perform problem-solving and decision-making functions at expert levels.

I should like to examine this body of research, which falls under the labels of "cognitive science" and "artificial intelligence," to see what light it casts on intuitive, judgmental decision making in management. We will see that a rather detailed account can be given of the processes that underlie judgment, even though most of these processes are not within the conscious awareness of the actor using them.

The Expert's Intuition

In recent years, the disciplines of cognitive science and artificial intelligence have devoted a great deal of attention to the nature of expert problem solving and decision making in professional-level tasks. The goal of the cognitive science research has been to gain an understanding of the differences between the behavior of experts and novices, and possibly to learn more about how novices can become experts. The goal of the artificial intelligence research has been to build computer systems that can perform professional tasks as competently as human experts can. Both lines of research have greatly deepened our understanding of expertise.[4]

INTUITION IN CHESSPLAYING

One much studied class of experts is the grandmasters in the game of chess. Chess is usually believed to require a high level of intellect, and grandmasters are normally full-time professionals who have devoted many years to acquiring their mastery of the game. From a research standpoint, the advantage of the game is that the level of skill of players can be calibrated accurately from their official ratings, based on their tournament success.

From the standpoint of studying intuitive thinking, chess might seem (at least to outsiders) an unpromising research domain. Chess playing is thought to involve a highly analytical approach, with players working out systematically the consequences of moves and countermoves, so that a single move may take as much as a half hour's thought, or more. On the other hand, chess professionals can play simultaneous games, sometimes against as many as 50 opponents, and exhibit only a moderately lower level of skill than in games playing under tournament conditions. In simultaneous play, the professional takes much less than a minute, often only a few seconds, for each move. There is no time for careful analysis.

When we ask the grandmaster or master how he or she is able to find good moves under these circumstances, we get the same answer that we get from other professionals who are questioned about rapid decisions: It is done by "intuition," by applying one's professional "judgment" to the situation. A few seconds' glance at the position suggests a good move, although the player has no awareness of how the judgment was evoked.

Even under tournament conditions, good moves usually come to a player's mind after only a few seconds' consideration of the board. The remainder of the analysis time is generally spent verifying that a move appearing plausible does not have a hidden weakness. We encounter this same kind of behavior in other professional domains where intuitive judgments are usually subjected to tests of various kinds before they are actually implemented. The main exceptions are situations where the decision has to be made before a deadline or almost instantly. Of course we know that under these circumstances (as in professional chess when the allowed time is nearly exhausted), mistakes are sometimes made.

How do we account for the judgment or intuition that allows the chess grandmaster usually to find good moves in a few seconds? A good deal of the answer can be derived from an experiment that is easily repeated. First, present a grandmaster and a novice with a position from an actual, but unfamiliar, chess game (with about 25 pieces on the board). After five or ten seconds, remove the board and pieces and ask the subjects to reproduce it. The grandmaster will usually reconstruct the whole position correctly, and on average will place 23 or 24 pieces on their correct squares. The novice will only be able to replace, on average, about 6 pieces.

It might seem that we are witnessing remarkable skill in visual imagery and visual memory, but we can easily dismiss that possibility by carrying out a second experiment. The conditions are exactly the same as in the first experiment, except that now the 25 pieces are placed on the board at random. The novice can still replace about 6 pieces and the grandmaster—about 6! The difference between them in the first experiment does not lie in the grandmaster's eyes or imagery, but in his knowledge, acquired by long experience, of the kinds of patterns and clusters of pieces that occur on chessboards in the course of games. For the expert, such a chess board is not an arrangement of 25 pieces but an arrangement of a half dozen familiar patterns, recognizable old friends. On the random board there are no such patterns, only the 25 individual pieces in an unfamiliar arrangement.

The grandmaster's memory holds more than a set of patterns. Associated with each pattern in his or her memory is information about the significance of that pattern—what dangers it holds, and what offensive or defensive moves it suggests. Recognizing the pattern brings to the grandmaster's mind at once moves that may be appropriate to the situation. It is this recognition that enables the professional to play very strong chess at a rapid rate. Previous learning that has stored the patterns and the information associated with them in memory makes this performance possible. This, then, is the secret of the grandmaster's intuition or judgment.

Estimates have been made, in a variety of ways, of the number of familiar patterns (which psychologists now call chunks) that the master or grandmaster must be able to recognize. These estimates fall in the neighborhood of 50,000, give or take a factor of two. Is this a large number? Perhaps not. The natural language vocabularies of college graduates have been estimated to be in the range of 50,000 to 200,000 words, nearly the same range as the chess expert's vocabularies of patterns of pieces. Moreover, when we recognize a word, we also get access to information in our memories about the meaning of the word and to other information associated with it as well. So our ability to speak and understand language has the same intuitive or judgmental flavor as the grandmaster's ability to play chess rapidly.

INTUITION IN COMPUTERIZED EXPERT SYSTEMS

A growing body of evidence from artificial intelligence research indicates that expert computer systems, capable of matching human performance in some limited domain, can be built by storing in computer memory tens of thousands of *productions*. Productions are computer instructions that take the form if "if-then" pairs. The "if" is a set of conditions or patterns to be recognized; the "then" is a body of information associated with the "if" and evoked from memory whenever the pattern is recognized in the current situation.

Some of our best data about this organization of expert knowledge come from the areas of medical diagnosis. Systems like CADUCEUS and MYCIN consist of a large number of such if-then pairs, together with an inference machine of modest powers. These systems are capable of medical diagnosis at a competent clinical level within their respective limited domains. Their recognition capabilities, the if-then pairs, represent their intuitive or judgmental ability; their inferencing powers represent their analytical ability.

Medical diagnosis is just one of a number of domains for which expert systems have been built. For many years, electric motors, generators, and transformers have been designed by expert systems developed by large electrical manufacturers. These computer programs have taken over from professional engineers many standards and relatively routine design tasks. They imitate fairly closely the rule-of-thumb procedures that human designers have used, the result of a large stock of theoretical and practical information about electrical machinery. Recognition also plays a large role in these systems. For example, examination of the customer's specifications "reminds" the program of a particular class of devices, which is then used as the basis for the design. Parameters for the design are then selected to meet the performance requirements of the device.

In chemistry, reaction paths for synthesizing organic molecules can be designed by expert systems. In these systems, the process appears relatively analytic, for it is guided by reasoning in the form of means-ends analyses, which work backward from the desired molecule, via a sequence of reactions, to available raw materials. But the reasoning scheme depends on a large store of knowledge of chemical reactions and the ability of the system to recognize rapidly that a particular substance can be obtained as the output of one or more familiar reactions. Thus, these chemical synthesis programs employ the same kind of mixture of intuition and analysis that is used in the other expert systems, and by human experts as well.

Other examples of expert systems can be cited, and all of them exhibit reasoning or analytic processes combined with processes for accessing knowledge banks with the help of recognition cues. This appears to be a universal scheme for the organization of expert systems—and of expert human problem solving as well.

Notice that there is nothing "irrational" about intuitive or judgmental reasoning based on productions. The conditions in a production constitute a set of premises. Whenever these conditions are satisfied, the production draws the appropriate conclusion—it evokes from memory information implied by these conditions or even initiates motor responses. A person learning to drive a car may notice a red light, be aware that a red light calls for a stop, and be aware that stopping requires applying the brakes. For an experienced driver, the sight of the red light simply evokes the application of brakes. How conscious the actor is of the process inversely, how automatic the response is, may differ, but there is no difference in the logic being applied.

INTUITION IN MANAGEMENT

Some direct evidence also suggests that the intuitive skills of managers depend on the same kinds of mechanisms as the intuitive skills of chessmasters or physicians. It would be surprising if it were otherwise. The experienced manager, too, has in his or her memory a large amount of knowledge, gained from training and experience and organized in terms of recognizable chunks and associated information.

Marius J. Bouwman has constructed a computer program capable of detecting company problems from an examination of accounting statements.[5] The program was modeled on detailed thinking-aloud protocols of experienced financial analysts interpreting such statements, and it captures the knowledge that enables analysts to spot problems intuitively, usually at a very rapid rate. When a comparison is made between the responses of the program and the responses of an expert human financial analyst, a close match is usually found.

In another study, R. Bhaskar gathered thinking-aloud protocols from business school students and experienced businessmen, who were all asked to analyze a business policy case.[6] The final analyses produced by the students and the businessmen were quite similar. What most sharply discriminated between the novices and the experts was the time required to identify the key features of the case. This was done very rapidly, with the usual appearances of intuition, by the experts; it was done slowly, with much conscious and explicit analysis, by the novices.

These two pieces of research are just drops of water in a large bucket that needs filling. The description, in detail, of the use of judgmental and analytical processes in expert problem solving and decision making deserves a high priority in the agenda of management research.

Can Judgment Be Improved?

From this and other research on expert problem solving and decision making, we can draw two main conclusions. First, experts often arrive at problem diagnoses and solutions rapidly and intuitively without being able to report how they attained the result. Second, this ability is best explained by postulating a recognition and retrieval process that employs a large number— generally tens of thousands or even hundreds of thousands—of chunks or patterns stored in long term memory.

When the problems to be solved are more than trivial, the recognition processes have to be organized in a coherent way and they must be supplied with reasoning capabilities that allow inferences to be drawn from the information retrieved, and numerous chunks of information to be combined. Hence intuition is not a process that operates independently of analysis; rather, the two processes are essential complementary components of effective decision-making systems. When the expert is solving a difficult problem or making a complex decision, much conscious deliberation may be involved. But each conscious step may itself constitute a considerable leap, with a whole sequence of automated productions building the bridge from the premises to the conclusions. Hence the expert appears to take giant intuitive steps in reasoning, as compared with the tiny steps of the novice.

It is doubtful that we will find two types of managers (at least, of good managers), one of whom relies almost exclusively on intuition, the other on analytic techniques. More likely, we will find a continuum of decision-making styles involving an intimate combination of the two kinds of skill. We will likely also find that the nature of the problem to be solved will be a principal determinant of the mix.

With our growing understanding of the organization of judgmental and intuitive processes, of the specific knowledge that is required to perform particular judgmental tasks, and of the cues that evoke such knowledge in situations in which it is relevant, we have a powerful new tool for improving expert judgment. We can specify the knowledge and the recognition capabilities that experts in a domain need to acquire as a basis for designing appropriate learning procedures.

We can also, in more and more situations, design expert systems capable of automating the expertise, or alternatively, of providing the human decision maker with an expert consultant. Increasingly, we will see decision aids for managers that will be highly interactive, with both knowledge and intelligence being shared between the human and the automated components of the system.

A vast research and development task of extracting and cataloging the knowledge and cues used by experts in different kinds of managerial tasks lies ahead. Much has been learned in the past few years about how to do this. More needs to be learned about how to update and improve the knowledge sources of expert systems as new knowledge becomes available.

Progress will be most rapid with expert systems that have a substantial technical component. It is no accident that the earliest expert systems were built for such tasks as designing motors, making medical diagnoses, playing chess, and finding chemical synthesis paths. In the area of management, the analysis of company financial statements is a domain where some progress has been made in constructing expert systems.

What about the aspects of executive work that involve the managing of people? What help can we expect in improving this crucial component of the management task?

Knowledge and Behavior

What managers know they should do—whether by analysis or intuitively—is very often different from what they actually do. A common failure of managers, which all of us have observed, is the postponement of difficult decisions. What is it that makes decisions difficult and hence tends to cause postponement? Often, the problem is that all of the alternatives have undesired consequences. When people have to choose the lesser of two evils, they do not simply behave like Bayesian statisticians, weighing the bad against the worse in the light of their respective possibilities. Instead, they avoid the decision, searching for alternatives that do not have negative outcomes. If such alternatives are not available, they are likely to continue to postpone making a choice. A choice between undesirables is a dilemma, something to be avoided or evaded.

Often, uncertainty is the source of the difficulty. Each choice may have a good outcome under one set of environmental contingencies, but a bad outcome under another. When this occurs, we also do not usually observe Bayesian behavior; the situation is again treated as a dilemma.

The bad consequences of a manager's decision are often bad for other people. Managers sometimes have to dismiss employees or, even more frequently, have to speak to them about unsatisfactory work. Dealing with such matters face to face is stressful to many, perhaps most, executives. The stress is magnified if the employee is a close associate or friend. If the unpleasant task cannot be delegated, it may be postponed.

The manager who has made a mistake (that is to say, all of us at one time or another) also finds himself or herself in a stressful situation. The matter must be dealt with sooner or later, but why not later instead of sooner? Moreover, when it is addressed, it can be approached in different ways. A manager may try to avoid blame—"It wasn't my fault!" A different way is to propose a remedy to the situation. I know of no systematic data on how often the one or the other course is taken, but most of us could probably agree that blame-avoiding behavior is far more common than problem-solving behavior after a serious error has been made.

THE CONSEQUENCES OF STRESS

What all of these decision-making situations have in common is stress, a powerful force that can divert behavior from the urgings of reason. They are examples of a much broader class of situations in which managers frequently behave in clearly nonproductive ways. Nonproductive responses are especially common when actions have to be made under time pressure. The need to allay feelings of guilt, anxiety, and embarrassment may lead to behavior that produces temporary personal comfort at the expense of bad long-run consequences for the organization.

Behavior of this kind is "intuitive" in the sense that it represents response without careful analysis and calculation. Lying, for example, is much more often the result of panic than of Machiavellian scheming. The intuition of the emotion-driven manager is very different from the intuition of the expert whom we discussed earlier. The latter's behavior is the product of learning and experience, and is largely adaptive; the former's behavior is a response to more primitive urges, and is more often than not inappropriate. We must not confuse the "nonrational" decisions of the experts—the decisions that derive from expert intuition and judgment—with the irrational decisions that stressful emotions may produce.

I have made no attempt here to produce a comprehensive taxonomy of the pathologies of organizational decision making, but simply have given some examples of the ways that stress interacts with cognition to elicit counterproductive behavior. Such responses can be come so habitual for individuals or even for organizations that they represent a recognizable managerial "style."

Organizational psychologists have a great deal to say about ways of motivating workers and executives to direct their efforts toward organizational goals. They have said less about ways of molding habits so that executives can handle situations in a goal-directed manner. When it comes to handling situations, two dimensions of behavior deserve particular attention: the response to problems that arise, and the initiation of activity that looks to the future.

RESPONDING TO PROBLEMS

The response of an organization to a problem or difficulty, whether it results from a mistake or some other cause, is generally one that looks both backward and forward. It looks backward to establish responsibility for the difficulty and to diagnose it, and forward to find a course of action to deal with it.

The backward look is an essential part of the organization's reward system. The actions that have led to difficulties, and the people responsible for those actions, need to be identified. But the backward look can also be a source of serious pathologies. Anticipation of it—particularly anticipation that it will be acted on in a punitive way—is a major cause for the concealment of problems until they can no longer be hidden. It can also be highly divisive, as individuals point fingers to transfer blame to others. Such outcomes can hardly be eliminated, but an organization's internal reputation for fairness and objectivity can mitigate them. So can a practice of subordinating the blame finding to a diagnosis of causes as a first step toward remedial action.

Most important of all, however, is the forward look: the process of defining the problem and identifying courses of action that may solve it. Here also the reward system is critically important. Readiness to search for problem situations and effectiveness in finding them need to be recognized and rewarded.

Perhaps the greatest influence a manager can have on the problem-solving style of the organization as a role model is making the best responses to problems. The style the manager should aim for rests on the following principles:

1. Solving the problem takes priority over looking backward to its causes. Initially, backward looks should be limited to diagnosing causes; fixing responsibility for mistakes should be postponed until a solution is being implemented.

2. The manager accepts personal responsibility for finding and proposing solutions instead of seeking to shift that responsibility either to superiors or to subordinates, although the search for solutions may, of course, be a collaborative effort involving many people.

3. The manager accepts personal responsibility for implementing action solutions, including securing the necessary authority from above is required.

4. When it is time to look backward, fixing blame may be an essential part of the process, but the primary focus of attention should be on what can be learned to prevent similar problems from arising in the future.

These principles are as obvious as the Ten Commandments and perhaps not quite as difficult to obey. Earlier, I indicated that stress might cause departures from them, but failure to respond effectively to problems probably derives more from a lack of attention and an earlier failure to cultivate the appropriate habits. The military makes much use of a procedure called "Estimate of the Situation." Its value is not that it teaches anything esoteric, but that through continual training in its use, commanders become habituated to approaching situations in orderly ways, using the checklists provided by the formal procedure.

Habits of response to problems are taught and learned both in the manager's one-on-one conversations with subordinates and in staff meetings. Is attention brought back repeatedly to defining the problems until everyone is agreed on just what the problem is? Is attention then directed toward generating possible solutions and evaluating their consequences? The least often challenged and most reliable base of managerial influence is the power to set the agenda, to focus attention. It is one of the most effective tools the manager has for training organization members to approach problems constructively by shaping their own habits of attention.

The perceptive reader will have discerned that "shaping habits of attention" is identical to "acquiring intuitions." The habit of responding to problems by looking for solutions can and must become intuitive—cued by the presence of the problem itself. A problem-solving style is a component of the set of intuitions that the manager acquires, one of the key components of effective managerial behavior.

LOOKING TO THE FUTURE

With respect to the initiation of activity, the organizational habit we would like to instil is responsiveness to cues that signal future difficulties as well as to those that call attention to the problems of the moment. Failure to give sufficient attention to the future most often stems from two causes. The first is interruption by current problems that have more proximate deadlines and hence seem more urgent; the second is the absence of sufficient "scanning" activity that can pick up cues from the environment that long-run forces not impinging immediately on the organization have importance for it in the future.

In neither case is the need for sensitivity to the future likely to be met simply by strengthening intuitions. Rather, what is called for is deliberate and systematic allocation of organizational resources to deal with long-range problems, access for these resources to appropriate input from the environment that will attract their attention to new prospects, and protection of these planning resources from absorption in current problems, however, urgent they may be. Attention to the future must be institutionalized; there is no simpler way to incorporate it into managerial "style" or habit.

It is a fallacy to contrast "analytic" and "intuitive" styles of management. Intuition and judgment—at least good judgment—are simply analyses frozen into habit and into the capacity for rapid response through recognition. Every manager needs to be able to analyze problems systematically (and with the aid of the modern arsenal of analytical tools provided by management science and operations research). Every manager needs also to be able to respond to situations rapidly, a skill that requires the cultivation of intuition and judgment over many years of experience and training. The effective manager does not have the luxury of choosing between "analytic" and "intuitive" approaches to problems. Behaving like a manager means having command of the whole range of management skills and applying them as they become appropriate.

Notes

1. Chester I. Barnard's (1938) *The Functions of the Executive* (Cambridge, Mass.: Harvard University Press), contains the essay on the contrast between logical and nonlogical processes as bases for decision making.

2. Simon, H. A. (1978) *Administrative Behavior*, 2nd ed. New York: Free Press.

For a review of the artificial intelligence research on expert systems, see A. Barr and E. A. Figenbaum's (eds.) The *Handbook of Artificial Intelligence*, Vol. 2, Los Alamos, Cal.: William Kaufmann, 1982, pp. 77-294.

3. Two works that examine the split brain theory and forms of thought are R. H. Doktor's "Problem Solving Styles of Executives and Management Scientists," in A. Charnes, W. W. Cooper, and R. J. Niehaus's (eds.) *Management Science Approaches to Manpower Planning and Organization Design* (Amsterdam: North-Holland, 1978); and R. H. Doktor and W. F. Hamilton's "Cognitive Style and the Acceptance of Management Science Recommendations" (*Management Science*, 19:884-894, 1973).

4. For a survey of cognitive science research on problem solving and decision making, see Simon, H. A. (1979) *The Sciences of the Artificial,* 2nd ed., Cambridge, Mass.: The MIT Press, Chapters 3 and 4.

5. Marius J. Bouwman's doctoral dissertation, *Financial Diagnosis* (Graduate School of Industrial Administration, Carnegie-Mellon University, 1978).

6. R. Bhaskar's doctoral dissertation, *Problem Solving in Semantically Rich Domains* (Graduate School of Industrial Administration, Carnegie-Mellon University, 1978).

2

Varieties of Intuitive Experience[†]

FRANCES E. VAUGHAN

*This term [intuition] does not denote something contrary to reason,
but something outside the province of reason.*

C. G. Jung: *Psychological Types*

Having defined intuition as a mode of knowing and a psychological function which is potentially available to everyone, let us turn our attention to examining the variety of human experiences which are commonly called intuitive. Intuitive experiences include, but are by no means limited to, mystical insights into the nature of reality. Experiences which are commonly called intuitive also include discovery and invention in science, inspiration in art, creative problem solving, perception of patterns and possibilities, extrasensory perception, clairvoyance, telepathy, precognition, retrocognition, feelings of attraction and aversion, picking up "vibes," knowing or perceiving through the body rather than the rational mind, hunches, and premonitions.

Intuition is often associated with having a hunch or a strong feeling of knowing what is going to happen. Often these hunches are vague, and since they are rarely recorded they are seldom verifiable. In conducting workshops and seminars on intuition I have often asked people to talk about whatever intuitive experiences they may have had, before defining or explaining the term. The most common response is of having experienced some instance of a hunch or premonition coming true. Do you remember a time in your own experience when you felt you knew something was going to happen, even though you had no reason for knowing it,

†SOURCE: From AWAKENING INTUITION by Frances Vaughan. Copyright © 1979 by Frances Vaughan. Reprinted by permission of Doubleday, a division of Bantam, Doubleday, Dell Publishing Group, Inc.

and it did? For example, many people say that they sometimes know who is calling on the telephone before they answer, although there is no logical way of determining who it is.

One example of inexplicable hunches which turned out to be accurate was the story of a young woman who had planned a honeymoon trip to Tahiti several years ago. Shortly before the date set for her wedding, she dreamed of an airplane crash. She had such a strong presentiment that the plane she expected to fly on would crash that she canceled the reservations and changed her plans. The airplane she would have taken did crash, and everyone on board was killed. Another woman in one of my groups told us that for years she had harbored an irrational fear that her youngest daughter would be run over. She had two older children, about whom she had never felt this worry. One day, when her daughter was thirteen years old, she was hit by a car and taken to the hospital for emergency treatment of head injuries. The girl was not seriously hurt, and recovered quickly. The mother said she felt a tremendous sense of relief, and has not been bothered by that anxiety since the accident. She felt as though she had been expecting it to happen, and had been dreading it, but now she did not have to worry about it any more.

Does having a strong hunch or presentiment allow one to do something to alter the course of events? The answer seems to be yes, as in the case of the young woman above, although it is not always clear what can be done. Some people are afraid of their hunches and would prefer not to notice them. Unfortunately, however, repression does not eliminate fear. If you are a person who is plagued by irrational fears and inclined to have pessimistic hunches which rarely come true, it would be advisable for you to examine your fears. Psychotherapy can help to overcome such fears, and by increasing self-knowledge it can also help in learning to distinguish fearful presentiments from intuition.

At times hunches may seem negative, such as the hunch that you will forget something when you go on a trip. At other times they may be positive, such as the hunch that you will get a job you applied for even though the competition is stiff, or the hunch that you will do well in an exam despite inadequate preparation. What is necessary in the beginning, regardless of whether the hunch is positive, negative, or neutral, is to learn to distinguish genuinely intuitive hunches from those which are simply a product of anxiety or wishful thinking.

The best way to do this is to keep a record of your hunches in a journal or a diary. In this way you can check up on yourself, to see how often your hunches turn out to be accurate. Subjectively you may begin to notice that intuitive hunches feel different from those which turn out to be accurate. Subjectively you may begin to notice that intuitive hunches feel different from those which turn out to be purely imaginary. The only way you can learn to make the distinction for yourself is to learn by trial and error. At first, when you begin to keep a record of your hunches, you may find a high percentage of errors. As our sensitivity to nonverbal cues, both internal and external is refined, your record may improve. Don't be discouraged by errors. Every time you make an error you have the opportunity to learn something about yourself. If you are willing to acknowledge yourself as the source of your error—that is, to take responsibility for it rather than blaming it on outside circumstances—you may quickly learn to see how your personal interests distort your perceptions and get in the way of clear intuition.

The conscious mind, or ego, frequently interferes with intuitive perception. The more you want something to happen, the less you are able to sense whether it will happen or not. For example, if you want someone you love to call you, you may think it is him or her every time the phone rings, only to be disappointed each time. On the other hand, someone you hardly know, or whom you have not thought about in weeks, may come into your mind inexplicably, and then, a few minutes later, that person may call. Fear and desire both interfere with intuitive perception. If you are anxious, angry, or emotionally upset, you are not likely to be receptive to the subtle messages which can come into consciousness via intuition.

At the same time, strong emotional ties between people often seem to facilitate telepathic communication. In the overwhelming majority of cases of spontaneous dream telepathy recorded by England's Society for Psychical Research, the sender and the receiver (i.e., the dreamer) were related to each other or were friends. The most common themes were death, danger, and distress. A mother, for example, dreamed of her son calling out to her when he was dying overseas, and later received the report that this actually happened.[1] During the Vietnam War, in the late 1960s, when I was leading dream groups in connection with my work as a psychotherapist, I personally heard of several instances of mothers dreaming of their sons being wounded or killed in battle either when it occurred or before they heard the news. A teen-ager in one of my groups recounted a vivid and disturbing dream of her father's death in an automobile accident, which she had the same night that it happened although he was in another state and she knew nothing about his life at the time.

The experimental research of Montague Ullman and Stanley Krippner at the Dream Laboratory of Maimonides Medical Center in New York provides convincing evidence of telepathy, clairvoyance, and precognition in dreams. Drs. Ullman and Krippner report that regardless of profession, walk of life, waking psychic ability, or knowledge of having ever before experienced ESP (extrasensory perception), the great majority of subjects described correspondences that were "suggestively telepathic." The authors attribute the success of their experiments in dream telepathy over waking telepathy, established by quantitative testing, to the use of potent, vivid, emotionally impressive human interest pictures to which both sender and receiver can relate. They also suggest that successful activation of ESP may be related to a relaxed, passive state of mind.[2]

Telepathic messages do not always come in dreams. A woman in one of my intuition workshops shared her experience of feeling a wave of strong emotion one afternoon while having coffee with a friend. Her strong feelings of apprehension seemed to be a mixture of fear and sadness related to her mother. After a short time, when the feelings did not subside, she called her mother, who was in a other city. She learned that her mother had suffered a heart attack at the moment when she and first been aware of the feelings, and was in a critical condition. Her apprehensive feelings had been so painful that she felt relief rather than shock when she heard the news.

Charles Tart, professor of psychology at the University of California at Davis, who has conducted extensive research on ESP, asserts that ESP is one of the most complex psychological processes. The information apparently flows in unknown quantities into the unconscious mind and is subject to all sorts of alterations and distortions because of the receiving subject's belief systems, psychological needs, and unconscious dynamics. One method for determining the effects of belief on performance in ESP described by Dr. Tart was to divide subjects into "believers" and "disbelievers" and analyze their ESP scores separately. For this purpose subjects were asked to indicate their degree of belief in whether they could exercise ESP in the testing situation, before being given the test. Dr. Tart reports that believers consistently tend to score above chance, whereas disbelievers score significantly below chance expectation.[3]

Lack of acceptance of intuition in the culture at large certainly contributes to its suppression in individuals who do not want to be "different." Many adults in my groups have said that they felt they were more intuitive as children, and that they learned to keep their intuitive perceptions to themselves after encountering skepticism or ridicule from adults. One woman who attended an intuition workshop recalled an incident in her life when she was about five years old. On a Friday she announced to her mother than Grandmother would not be coming to dinner on Sunday because she had hurt her foot. Her mother did not pay much attention to her remark, as she assumed she was making it up. To her amazement, the following day Grandmother called and said she would not come to dinner the next day because she had sprained her ankle the previous afternoon.

Such incidents may be frightening to adults who do not understand them or consider them paranormal. Parents who are afraid of what seems incomprehensible often respond angrily to intuitive observations by their children. They may attempt to explain them away, or to deny the child's experience, saying something like, "You couldn't possibly know that. Don't lie to me." At best, the child's remarks may be ignored.

Frances Wickes writes that a very intuitive child is often difficult for parents to handle. She describes the typically intuitive child as one whose rational thought processes are largely unconscious. "He frequently seems to grasp the situation by a sort of magic contact and so gives back the desired response, but how he arrived at his conclusions is a mystery even to himself. He just 'knows it is so.' Sometimes, because he cannot retrace his steps and supply the missing logic, he is accused of willful guessing in an attempt to assume knowledge which is not his, but this is as unfair an estimate of him as to accept his answer as a proof of his powers of logical thought."[4]

Young children learn very quickly that there are some things they are not supposed to talk about. For many this reticence persists into adulthood. Participants in intuition workshops often express appreciation for having the opportunity to talk about experiences which they would ordinarily not discuss for fear of being considered "weird" or "crazy." Children seldom share their inner world of fantasy and perception with adults, because sympathetic, understanding adults are rare. Although it is socially acceptable for a preschooler to indulge in fantasy play, when a child goes to school he or she is bombarded with external stimuli designed to teach him or her to live in the reality of the external world. Although children and adolescents often have a very active intuition, since it is unimpeded by other functions,[5] it is seldom dealt with in education. At school the inner world, where intuition is nourished, is usually closed. A child whose natural intuitive abilities are strong enough to survive social censure may develop into an exceptionally creative person, but what about all those whose talents simply remain repressed or undeveloped?

Most people fall into the second category. They are trained in school to use rational and intellectual abilities as well as they can. Individualized instruction attempts to allow each child to learn at his or her own rate, but even this learning is primarily geared to the acquisition of information from external sources. Little attention is given to the inner world. Even the advent of affective education, which takes into consideration a child's emotional development along with his or her cognitive development, does not include the development and training of intuition. Thus, as adults, many people feel a need to redress the balance, and learn to follow the promptings of their own psyche.

In general, intuition flourishes only when it is valued, and clearly certain lifestyles and experiences facilitate or nourish it. Inspiration needs space and attention if it is to take shape in a creative endeavor. Attention acts as psychic energy and enhances the process it values. The artist who is highly intuitive in his or her perceptions of reality knows that inspiration always seems to come of its own accord. Effort is invariably involved in the creative process, but flashes of inspiration tend to occur spontaneously. Seeking inspiration requires a receptive mode of consciousness, and is comparable to trying to remember something you know but have forgotten. Tarthang Tulku, a Tibetan Lama, writes: "If we wish to regain some memory or insight that is 'there,' but is temporarily elusive, it is often most effective to put aside any grasping or tight achievement-orientation and become passively receptive. By quietly opening the mind, the hidden element is allowed to present itself on its own. In a similar manner, artists seeking inspiration used to go to sleep, hoping for a visit from a muse, who would speak to them—and then through them—in their art. People courting divine intercession have long understood that they must *open* themselves to divine messages and purposes, as in the cases of prayer and oracles. According to all these various orientations, the importance of surrendering the self has been emphasized."[6]

In a sense, everyone is an artist in charge of designing his or her life. If the unexamined life is not worth living, what about the uninspired life? Certainly many, if not most, people in our society would not consider their lives to be particularly inspired. Yet the possibility is there for *everyone* to tap the creative source of inspiration which comes from well-developed intuition.

The kind of intuitive experience which leads most directly to a sense of well-being and harmony with oneself and the universe is the mystical or transpersonal experience. The mystical experience is characteristically described as one in which the individual transcends the subject/object dichotomy, feeling him- or herself to be at one with everything. In this experience there is no separation between inner and outer, knower and known. It is sometimes described as the experience of pure consciousness, with no specific content. Various levels of mystical experience are described in both Eastern and Western mystical traditions. Stanislav Grof has defined transpersonal experiences as those involving "an expansion or extension of consciousness beyond the usual ego boundaries and beyond the limitations of time and/or space."[7] What these experiences have in common, and what concerns us here, is a universal affirmation of the human capacity for transcending ego boundaries and the limitations of the rational mind, and the fact that the essential truth of reality can only be apprehended intuitively. It is this direct apprehension of truth which characterizes pure, spiritual intuition.

This type of intuitive experience is often fleeting, yet it can have a profound effect on a person's life, for an experience of cosmic consciousness dispels all doubts and answers all questions, and replaces them with feelings of bliss, awe, wonder and joy.[8] The individual who is open to this type of intuitive knowledge experiences a sense of unity or oneness with all things, and a sense of illumination or enlightenment. What was formerly hidden becomes clear, but not necessarily once and for all. Such an experience of enlightenment can continue to deepen and expand in the process of living, or it can be denied and repressed.

In contrast to the sudden, spontaneous flashes of pure intuition which occur with no particular preparation, the systematic development of intuition is one of the aims of yoga. In yoga true intuition is considered a stable reliable function of the higher levels of consciousness from which a wide range of information is accessible. Techniques of meditation provide the means through which one may discover and develop this type of awareness.[9]

Remember that intuition of spiritual truth is something you already have inside you. As you discover who you are and become more familiar with the transpersonal dimensions of your experience, you will become increasingly conscious of it. This kind of truth is recognized, not learned. For most people the process of learning to look within to find their truth requires spending some time clearing away the confusion that distorts clear awareness. But as this process is learned, personal benefit can result from the steps involved. The way itself is also the goal, as every step has intrinsic value and provides satisfaction.

Levels of Intuitive Awareness

The broad range of intuitive human experience falls into four distinct levels of awareness: physical, emotional, mental, and spiritual.[10] Although any given experience may have elements of more than one level, experiences are usually easy to categorize according to the level at which they are consciously perceived. For example, mystical experiences are intuitive experiences at the spiritual level, and as such they do not depend on sensory, emotional, or mental cues for their validity. Intuition at the physical level is associated with bodily sensations, at the emotional level with feelings, and at the mental level with images and ideas.

PHYSICAL LEVEL

The intuitive experiences defined as inspirational or psychic frequently depend on physical and emotional cues that bring them to conscious awareness. At the physical level a strong body response may be experienced in a situation where there is no reason to think that anything unusual is going on. The kind of jungle awareness which enables primitive people to sense danger when there are no sensory cues of its presence, is a highly developed form of intuition at the physical level. It differs from instinct in that instinct remains unconscious, while intuition becomes fully conscious, although a person may act on it without stopping to justify or rationalize it. The person simply know something he or she needs to know without knowing how he or she knows it.

For people living in an urban environment this type of awareness is no less useful. Though it may not always be particularly dramatic, it can also be a matter life and death. When you are in a situation that is uncomfortable for you, you may notice such bodily symptoms as tension, headaches, or stomachaches. If you stop to pay attention to these cues, you may find that you are indeed in a situation which is unhealthy and which is creating undue stress on the organism. If, for example, you always get a stomachache when you attend staff meetings at work, you should probably consider what needs to be changed in the situation to reduce the stress, even if this means a change in jobs. if you pay attention to physical symptoms which on the surface seem inexplicable, you may very well find out a lot about what your needs are. The cues of intuition on a physical level are not, however, always easy to perceive. Unfortunately, one often fails to acknowledge messages from the body until they become painful. If you are attuned to your body, you will notice your body responding differently to different people and different situations even without a stomachache or a headache. At times you may feel open, warm, and responsive, and at other times you may feel that you want to close up and withdraw. Learning to trust your bodily responses is part of learning to trust your intuition.

Bodily responses are a source of information about both yourself and your environment. Ann Dreyfuss, a Reichian therapist in San Francisco and professor of psychology at the California State College at Sonoma, reminds us that the body is one's access to the world. "It is possible," says Dr. Dreyfuss, "to be out of touch with oneself, unaware of one's body and in conflict with one's bodily process. Such disharmony distorts one's view of the world, one's perceptions and conceptions. A basic way of working toward personal enrichment involves increasing congruence between body and awareness . . . Whatever dimension of the outer world one considers, it is through the body that one experiences it, and it is through the body that one distorts it to make it comprehensible."[11]

Noticing physical symptoms of stress can often allow you to take care of your physical and emotional needs before they reach a painful or destructive level. Intuitive insight into your personal needs cannot only prevent serious disorders, but can also give you a direct indication of immediate needs. The desire to close up and withdraw, for example, may be an indication that the situation is not appropriate for you to open up in, or it may indicate an inner need for stillness and solitude. Or, if it is a habitual response, it may be related to some underlying fear which is preventing you from expanding your life and exploring new possibilities. If this is the case, you may want to change the pattern, and the first step is to become aware of what is happening to you. When you become aware of your body responses, you can choose whether or not you wish to act on them. Sometimes you may experience tension in response to a particular situation and choose to leave. Other times you may experience tension and choose to remain and confront the difficulty. Either way, being conscious of body responses is an essential part of a holistic intuitive awareness of yourself in relation to your environment.

Research indicates that one responds psychologically to events in the environment even when such responses remain below the threshold of consciousness. In an experiment carried out by Charles Tart at the University of California, a subject sitting in a darkened, soundproof chamber was asked to tap a telegraph key when he thought he received an "subliminal stimulus." He was not given any stimulus, but in another soundproof chamber several rooms away a "sender" received an electric shock at random intervals. The sender attempted to send a telepathic message to the subject each time he received a shock to make him react and tap the key. The attempt proved unsuccessful; the key taps were unrelated to the sender's messages. Bodily responses, however, *were* related. Brain-wave and heart-rate measurements indicated that the subject was responding physiologically to the telepathic stimulus, although he was not conscious of it.[12]

Dr. Tart's work suggests that one *can* be influenced by extrasensory stimuli even when one is not aware of it. The task of awakening intuition at the physical level, then, is inextricably linked to increasing awareness of what the body already "knows."

EMOTIONAL LEVEL

On the emotional level, as on the physical level, awakening intuition is inseparable from developing self-awareness. On this level intuition comes into consciousness through feelings. Sensitivity to other people's "vibes" or "vibrations of energy," instances of immediate liking or disliking with no apparent justification, or a vague sense that one is inexplicably supposed to do something, can be instances of intuition operating on this level.

When you learn to tune in to your feelings, they can become just as clear as bodily sensations in giving you information about a particular situation, be it a matter of changing jobs, finding a partner, or merely deciding what to do on a free weekend. How you feel about yourself, your relationships, and everything you do is related to how willing you are to take emotional intuitive cues into account when you are making choices. The better you know yourself, the more you can trust your intuition when it attracts you to someone you would like to know better, or warns you not to get involved. Occurrences of love at first sight, although they can be explained away as projection, may also be strongly intuitive. A woman in one of my classes described meeting her husband in a group five years ago. She said she knew the minute she saw him that he was *it* for her, despite the fact that "He didn't look like much," and she did not feel a strong physical attraction for him at first. Less romantic, but nonetheless meaningful instances of intuition at the emotional level occur every day.

What is commonly called "woman's intuition" is intuition on the emotional level. There is no evidence that men and women are inherently different in their intuitive capacities, but the popular belief that women are more intuitive than men is related to the fact that women in our society are not taught to repress feelings as much as men. Little boys are taught early not to cry and not to be emotional. Little girls may escape some of the rigorous training in rational intellectual development, which is stressed for boys wanting to be successful in a highly competitive society. Boys, however, are just as capable as girls when it comes to developing the intuitive functions of the right hemisphere of the brain.

Judith Hall, Assistant Professor of Psychology at Johns Hopkins University, Baltimore, reports that research in the area of sensitivity to nonverbal communication indicates that women tend to be more attentive to visual cues such as facial expression, body gestures, tone of voice, and the way people look at each other or touch each other. Females do score higher than males in tests designed to measure accuracy of interpretation of nonverbal communication. There is, however, no data to support the belief that these differences are inherent. On the contrary, one study cited by Dr. Hall showed that more traditional males scored lower at nonverbal judging than more liberal males, and more traditional females scored higher than more liberal females. The differences reported by Dr. Hall are not large, and she points out that these findings suggest that eliminating strong gender roles could make male and female scores converge.[13]

Although this type of perceptual awareness contributes to one's understanding of other people, it should not be confused with developing awareness of one's own internal feeling states. Intuition cannot be reduced to observation of behavior, body language, and other visual cues. It is a holistic awareness which includes both internal and external sensitivity, and which sometimes transcends sensory input altogether.

At the emotional level, women and men who are aware of their feelings and who follow them tend to be comfortable with their diffuse intuitive understanding, except when called upon to give a logical, rational justification for actions based on intuitive feelings.

Demands for explanations, either from oneself or from another, are usually met with inadequate rationalizations that fail to satisfy anybody. Rarely is someone willing to say simply that he or she chose to do something simply because it felt right. Nevertheless, people in all kinds of occupations and lifestyles do act on the basis of intuitive feelings, and feel that their decisions are better for it.

Expanding awareness of the emotional level of intuition is often associated with an increase in synchronicity and psychic experiences. For example, you might feel like calling someone with whom you have not spoken in some time for no particular reason. If you act on the feeling, you may discover that the person you called had been trying to get in touch with you, or that it was timely for you to call just then. You may discover later a reason for your intuitive feeling, or you may not. However, the more you act on your feelings and take the risk of checking out the validity of your intuition, the more reliable it can become.

Sometimes intuition on this level will tell you something about your interpersonal relations that you would rather not know, and in these instances it may seem easier to repress it than to act on it. You might, for instance, meet someone you think you would like to befriend, although you have a feeling that this will not happen. When I was in graduate school a friend of mine had told me how much he wanted to get to know one of our professors whom he greatly admired. One night he dreamed that he was talking to him, but the professor did not say much, and refused to take off his overcoat. As my friend reflected on what the dream was telling him, he realized that he had felt intuitively that this man had wanted to keep his distance ever since they met. Repeated attempts to get better acquainted were of no avail. He later regretted the time and effort expended, for he had "known" all along that it would be fruitless.

Recognizing and valuing what is true for you at a feeling level does not necessarily involve other people. A shift in mood, a change in perception, may also be experienced as an awakening of intuition. Elizabeth Herron, a contemporary poet, writes about her experience with this type of awakening, noting the difficulties of communicating verbally about this subjectively meaningful experience:

> I was depressed. The world had gone flat and colorless. I had withdrawn. I was a tiny kernel inside my body, adrift amid necessities and obligations, oppressed by my separateness, cut off from the wellsprings of my soul. I walked up to the pond, took off my clothes and

plunged into the water—a sudden shock, cold against my skin. Floating to the surface, I heard a bird call across the meadow. Suddenly, I
was at the stillpoint. The bird's call was my voice. We were separate
and yet one. I was out there and in here. . . . All things converged in me
and radiated from me. "The center of the circle is everywhere, the
circumference nowhere." I recognized this, knowing it had always
been so, though I had been cut off from my experience of it. My head
filled with poetic images. The dimension of the infinite was everywhere.

This was a repetition of similar experiences. It is a paradoxical awareness. In these moments I KNOW. But my knowledge is not enough. I
must struggle to comprehend what I know. My intuitive knowledge
must be expressed in order to be communicated. I cannot share my
experience merely by telling you about it. As a poet, I seek words for
my experience, but words alone are not enough. There are realities—
nuances of feeling and meaning, for which words are inadequate.[14]

Artistic endeavor in all its forms often provides a way of
expression for this type of intuitive awareness. But it is not
necessary to be an artist to benefit from conscious sensitivity to
feelings. Emotional states invariably color perceptions of reality as
well as provide information about one's relation to others and the
environment. Perceiving the world through feelings is like wearing
a pair of colored glasses which can increase acuity of vision yet
color everything with a particular hue. Recognizing that one is
wearing colored glasses (i.e., acknowledging that perceptions are
distorted by emotional states) is part of learning to distinguish
intuition from personal emotional reactions.

MENTAL LEVEL

Intuition on the mental level often comes into awareness through
images, or what is called "inner vision." Patterns of order may be
perceived where everything at first appears chaotic, or patterns of
change may be apprehended intuitively long before the verification process of careful observation is completed. In the West, the
intuitive flashes which follow the exhaustive use of logic and
reason tend to be more highly valued than other types of intuition,
since they are associated with the kind of discovery and invention
involved in technological progress.

Intuition on the mental level is operative in the formulation of
new theories and hypotheses in any field, for this type of intuition
implies an ability to reach accurate conclusions on the basis of

limited information. Although all intuition is mental in the sense that it is a function of the mind, intuition on the mental level refers particularly to those aspect of intuition related to thinking. Thus intuition on this level is often associated with problem solving, mathematics, and scientific inquiry.

Malcolm Westcott reviews the writing of mathematicians, with particular reference to Poincaré. Poincaré writes about the importance of intuition in his own work, and asserts that both intuitive and analytical activity are crucial to the advance of mathematics as well as the empirical sciences.[15] Jacques Hadamard confirms these views and adds the observations of other mathematicians. Hadamard quotes Einstein as follows: "The words or the language, as they are written or spoken, do not seem to play any role in my mechanism of thought. The psychical entities which seem to serve as elements in thought are certain signs and more or less clear images which can be 'voluntarily' reproduced and combined."[16] Einstein believed that objective physical reality can only be grasped by an intuitive leap, not directly empirically or logically.[17] He further asserts that the axiomatic basis of theoretical physics cannot be an inference from experience, but is a free invention of the human mind.[18] Writing on "The Structure of Creativity in Physics," Siegfried Muller-Markus supports this contention and concludes: "An idea like Planck's quantum of action was not logically entailed by experiment, nor could it be derived from previous theories. Planck conceived it out of his own self."[19]

The role of intuition in creativity and problem solving has also been recognized by individuals concerned with business management. Successful businessmen are typically intuitive on a mental level. Research indicates that successful executives tend to score far above average on ESP tests.[20] The ability to know intuitively what will succeed in any type of business certainly contributes to the success which is often attributed to luck. Henry Mintzberg suggests that managers should have well-developed right-hemispheric processes. It is important for managers to "see the big picture," says Mintzberg, and this implies a relational, holistic use of information (i.e., synthesis rather than analysis of data). He also points out the dearth of literature on this subject: ". . . despite an extensive literature on analytical decision making, virtually nothing is written about decision making under pressure. These activities remain outside the realm of management science, inside the realm of intuition and experience." Mintzberg supports the hypothesis that the important policy-level processes required to manage an organization rely to a considerable extent on the faculties identified with the brain's right hemisphere, and suggests that while policy makers conceive strategy in holistic terms, the rest of the bureaucratic hierarchy implements the policy in a linear sequence. Mintzberg points out that all intuitive thinking must be translated into linear order if it is to be articulated and put to use, and that truly outstanding managers are the ones who couple effective right-hemispheric processes with effective processes of the left.[21]

Although lateralization of brain functions may be overemphasized,[22] the basic point that intuitive thinking plays a vital part in decision making is supported by other authors in the field. Ostrander, Schroeder, Dean and Mihalasky maintain that people who have highly developed intuition are more successful. ESP seems to be particularly useful in decision making, economic forecasting, and personnel selection.[23]

Intuition in business is often referred to as a "gut feeling," yet a person whose intuition may be well-developed on a mental level is not necessarily one who is equally well-developed on an emotional level. Carson Jeffries, a physicist who attended one of my seminars at the University of California in Berkeley, told me that he valued his intuition and used it in his research, but felt out of touch with it in interpersonal relationships. For him intuition was working on the mental level, but not on the emotional level. After becoming aware of this he was able to expand the range of his intuitive ability to encompass more of his experience.

You do not have to be a scientist or a business executive to appreciate the value of intuition at the mental level. The sudden recognition of a pattern in your life, the "aha!" experience in psychotherapy when unconscious processes are suddenly illuminated, or the "eureka" of a new discovery, are ways in which anyone can experience this type of intuition. Such insights are often accompanied by mental imagery, but not necessarily. Pattern recognition is not always visual. It may be auditory to a musician, or simply a flash of understanding in which events or ideas seem to fall into place.

Melvin Calvin, Nobel Laureate in Chemistry in 1961, for example, describes his most exciting moment in research like this:

> One day I was waiting in my car while my wife was on an errand. I had had for some months some basic information from the laboratory which was incompatible with everything which, up until then, I knew about the photosynthetic process. I was waiting, sitting at the wheel,

most likely parked in the red zone, when the recognition of the missing compound occurred. It occurred just like that—quite suddenly—and suddenly, also, in a matter of seconds, the cyclic character of the path of carbon became apparent to me, not in the detail which ultimately was elucidated, but the original recognition of phosphoglyceric acid, and how it got there, and how the acceptor might be regenerated, all occurred in a matter of 30 seconds.[24]

Perhaps you have had the experience of struggling with a problem or a decision until you were sick of it, and then deciding to forget it for a while. Very often the solution pops into your head when you least expect it. The expression "sleep on it" refers to allowing this intuitive process to be completed during sleep. Many people report finding solutions to apparently insoluble dilemmas through their dreams and daydreams. When you stop trying to make something happen, intuition is allowed to operate.

In their biofeedback research at the Menninger Foundation in Kansas, Elmer and Alyce Green have used the term *passive volition* to describe the detached effortless volition required for the voluntary control of physiological functions regulated by the autonomic nervous system.[25] While active volition is necessary for the control of the voluntary nervous system, passive volition is necessary for the control of the so-called involuntary nervous system which regulates such physiological functions as heart rate, blood flow, and muscle tension. Subjects trained to increase or decrease the volume of blood flow in the hands at will, for example, learn to do so through visualization. As the subjects become aware of the subtle physiological changes taking place, they learn to let them happen. The Greens say: "Few people realize, however, that [the] feeling or intuition of freedom has unusual significance in respect to the autonomic nervous system."[26] In other words, knowing that you can do something to affect a process that you assumed was involuntary makes it easier to learn how to do it.

Intuition at all levels is often experienced as arising spontaneously, and any attempts at voluntary control may at first appear futile. Once you realize however, that there are some things that you can do to allow it to emerge, it can be expanded voluntarily, and the rate of expansion can be accelerated.

SPIRITUAL INTUITION

Spiritual intuition is associated with mystical experience, and at this level intuition is "pure." Pure, spiritual intuition is distinguished from other forms by its independence from sensations, feelings, and thoughts. In a discussion of intuition in spiritual psychosynthesis, Assagioli considers intuition as an independent psychological function which is "synthetic" in that it apprehends the totality of a given situation or psychological reality. Assagioli says: "Only intuition gives true psychological understanding both of oneself and others."[27] In its purest manifestations, Assagioli maintains, intuition is devoid of feeling, and as a normal function of the human psyche, it can be activated simply by eliminating the various obstacles to its unfolding. At this level intuition does not depend on sensing, feeling, or thinking. It is not associated with the body, the emotions, or pattern perception relating to specific problems or situations. Paradoxically, the cues on which intuition depends on other levels are regarded as interference on this level. However, an awareness of how intuition functions on other levels helps to dispel the misconception that intuition as a way of knowing is an all-or-nothing proposition. Degrees of intuitive awareness may also be affected by such factors as time, place, mood, attitude, state of consciousness, and many other variables.

In Spinoza's terms, spiritual intuition is knowledge of God. James Bugenthal equates this knowledge with man's experience of his own being and says: "Man knows God in his deepest intuitions about his own nature."[28] Dr. Bugenthal describes the inward vision through which man discovers his nature as a creative process that does more than observe what is already at hand, bringing into being fresh possibilities.

Among those fresh possibilities is the potential for transcending duality and personal separateness. The capacity for transcending duality is not particularly unusual. Abraham Maslow, in his study of self-actualizing persons in the 1960s, found that, "While this transcendence of dichotomy can be seen as a usual thing in self-actualizing persons, it can also be seen in most of the rest of us in our most acute moments of integration within the self and between self and the world. In the highest love between man and woman, or parent and child, as the person reaches the ultimates of strength, self-esteem, or individuality, so also does he simultaneously merge with the other, lose self-consciousness and more or less transcend the self and selfishness. The same can happen in the creative moment, in the profound aesthetic experience, in the insight experience . . . and others which I have generalized as peak experiences."[29]

Spiritual intuition as a holistic perception of reality transcends rational, dualistic ways of knowing and gives the individual a direct transpersonal experience of the underlying oneness of life. Describing the difference between dual (rational, conceptual) and non-dual (intuitive, holistic) modes of knowing, Ken Wilbur writes: "If we are to know Reality in it fullness and wholeness, if we are to stop eluding and escaping ourselves in the very act of trying to find ourselves, if we are to enter the concrete actuality of the territory and cease being confused by the maps that invariably own their owners, then we will have to relinquish the dualistic-symbolic mode of knowing that rends the fabric of Reality in the very attempt to grasp it. In a word, we will have to move from the dimness of twilight [dualistic] knowledge to the brilliance of daybreak [intuitive] knowledge—*if we are to know Reality, it is to the second mode of knowing that we must eventually turn.* Enough it is now to know that we possess this daybreak knowledge; more than enough it will be when at last we succeed in fully awakening it."[30]

In yoga spiritual intuition is called soul guidance,[31] and is said to emerge spontaneously when the mind is quiet. In writing about the teachings of Sri Aurobindo, Satprem describes the intuitive mind as follows: "The intuitive mind differs from the illumined mind by its clear transparency— . . . all is so rapid, flashing—terrible rapidities of the clearing of consciousness." Although intuitive knowledge may be translated or interpreted according to personal preoccupations, it is "always, essentially, a shock of identity, a meeting—one knows because one recognizes. Sri Aurobindo used to say that intuition is *a memory of the Truth.*"[32]

The practice of meditation prepares the mind for the experience of spiritual intuition, by clearing away the obstacles which ordinarily interfere with its becoming conscious. Learning to recognize pure awareness or consciousness as the context of all experience, distinct from the contents of consciousness, is one way of understanding this level of intuition.

In order to make a subjective distinction between your own consciousness and its contents you can try the following experiment: Write down everything you are conscious of at this moment. Do this for several minutes. When you have done this, notice what you left out. At any given moment you are conscious of only a fraction of what is going on in your mind. Consciousness is selective, and the normal range of awareness is extremely narrow in the ordinary waking state. When consciousness begins to observe itself, however, it begins to expand. You may notice that while you are reading this you are simultaneously aware of your surroundings, what time it is (approximately), whether you are feeling hungry or thirsty, and you may also be wondering when your friend will call and how you are going to make arrangements for what you want to do tomorrow. You may also be reviewing an unsatisfactory conversation you had with someone earlier in the day. Can you observe your own stream of consciousness in a manner that is satisfactory to you? Or are there so many streams running simultaneously in all directions that you cannot observe them all? Learning to empty the mind in order to experience consciousness devoid of contents is one of the objectives of meditation. By observing your thoughts, feelings, and sensations without interfering with them, you may begin to experience that quiet state in which spiritual intuition unfolds.

Activating spiritual intuition means focusing on the transpersonal rather than the personal realms of intuition. At this level it is consciousness as context, rather than the content of consciousness, which comes into awareness. Other forms of intuition focused on sensation, feeling, and thinking become obstacles to pure awareness, empty of content. If you become too engrossed with the powers that intuition can make available to you at other levels, you may fail to recognize your potential for developing spiritual intuition. Yet this dimension of intuition is the basic ground from which all other forms of intuition are derived.

Intuition in Your Life

Intuition at any level will lead you into what is new or unknown. No matter what level you are working on or which way you think you are going, intuition leads you past the boundaries of what you once knew into areas of new discovery. No matter how much you know, there is always more to be discovered. Intuitive experiences, regardless of whether they occur spontaneously or as a result of training, invariably expand consciousness to include more of reality, and more understanding of what is true.

If you reflect on your life and consider the turning points which led you into new experiences, you may recognize the role of intuition. You cannot know in advance what the outcome of a particular course of action will be. Decisions are based on what *is* known, *and* on what is intuitively felt to be the right course. Few people get married, move to a new place, or take up a new career without some doubts and uncertainties about whether they have made the right decision. Such decisions may even appear to be irrational or at least semirational. A person may leave a secure job in order to explore a new career in a completely different field. Or a person may impulsively inquire about attending a workshop or class which is of little interest, and end up enrolled in something that profoundly influences his or her personal growth. One couple attending a workshop on intuition said they had intuitively chosen the town in which they live as the place they wanted to be, without knowing why. Now, ten years later, they know they made the right decision.

How many times have you chosen one course of action over another on the basis of intuition? Make a list of the spontaneously occurring instances in your life when you were aware of acting on your intuition. Take time to reflect on whether you made the right choice, and what alternatives were open to you. Ask yourself whether you can trust your intuition, and notice how it works for you in your life. A good way to develop intuition further is to talk to a friend about intuition and discuss your intuitive experiences. Many people who are quite aware of their intuition do not talk about it because they are concerned about appearing strange or unusual. Yet when people are invited to discuss their intuitive experiences in my workshops they enjoy talking about them. They also seem pleased and relieved when they find others who share their interest and like to talk about their own experiences with a sympathetic listener. It is often reassuring, if you have not discussed how intuition works in your life, to know that it is operative in everybody's life, in one way or another.

Spontaneously occurring intuitive experiences can offer a renewed sense of vitality, excitement, and engagement with life. Mystical or transpersonal experiences which have no material goal or purpose can totally transform one's view of reality. Intuition is involved not only in the practical decisions which shape your life, but also in your choice of beliefs about the nature of the universe. Belief systems are often chosen unconsciously and they can shape one's perception in such a way as to vitiate alternative beliefs. The term "belief system" does not refer strictly to religious beliefs, but to all assumptions about reality. Today widespread exposure to a variety of religious doctrines makes it possible to choose beliefs that seem true rather than remain for a lifetime within the bounds of religious dogma, but unconscious assumptions may be hard to recognize.

Everyone makes assumptions about the nature of reality, and these assumptions form subjective belief systems rather than objective observations. These belief systems may be attributed to early conditioning, but as soon as one is willing to question them and consider alternative views, one opens up the possibility of choice. What you believe to be true shapes your experience, and beliefs are chosen intuitively, not rationally. Lawrence LeShan defines a metaphysical system as a set of assumptions about how the universe is put together and how it functions. He suggests that the metaphysical system you are using is the metaphysical system that is operating.[33] If this is so—and Dr. LeShan has done extensive research to support this view—it is worthwhile to examine the belief system you have chosen to run your life. The process of expanding intuitive awareness means exploring, questioning, and perhaps changing some of the assumptions you have taken for granted up to now.

Notes

1. M. Ullman and S. Krippner, *Dream Telepathy* (New York: Macmillan, 1973), pp. 13-14.

2. Ibid., p. 210.

3. "The Physical Universe, the Spiritual Universe, and the Paranormal," *Transpersonal Psychologies* (New York: Harper and Row, 1975), pp. 132-33.

4. *The Inner World of Childhood*, rev. ed. (New York: New American Library, 1966), p. 142.

5. R. Assagioli, *Psychosynthesis* (New York: Hobbs Dohrman, 1965), p. 221.

6. Tarthang Tulku, *Time, Space and Knowledge* (Emeryville, Ca.: Charma Publishing, 1977), p. 66.

7. *Realms of the Human Unconscious* (New York: Viking, 1975), p. 155.

8. M. Bucke, *Cosmic Consciousness* (New York: Dutton, 1969), p. 10.

9. Swami Rama, R. Ballantine, and Swami Ajaya, *Yoga and Psychotherapy* (Glenview, Ill.: Himalayan Institute, 1976), p. 265.

10. R. Gerard, Workshop notes. Professional training in psychosynthesis: Intuitive awareness. Berkeley, October, 1972.

11. A. Dreyfuss and D. Feinstein, "My Body Is Me: Body-based Approaches to Personal Enrichment," *Humanistic Perspectives: Current Trends in Psychology*, ed. B. McWaters (Monterey, Ca.: Brooks Cole, 1977), p. 43.

12. Tart, op. cit., p. 134.

13. "Female Intuition Measured at Last?" *New Society* (London; 1977).

14. Elizabeth Herron, Unpublished paper (1976).

15. *Toward a Contemporary Psychology of Intuition* (New York: Holt, Rinehart and Winston, 1968), pp. 49-51.

16. *An Essay on the Psychology of Invention in the Mathematical Field* (Princeton, 1945), p. 142, Appendix.

17. G. Holton, "Where Is Reality? The Answers of Einstein" *Science and Synthesis* (New York, Heidelberg, Berlin: Springer-Verlag, 1971), p. 69.

18. P. Schilpp (ed.), *Albert Einstein: Philosopher-Scientist*. The Library of Living Philosophers, Inc. (Evanston, Ill., 1949), p. 131.

19. "The Structure of Creativity in Physics," *Vistas in Physical Reality*, eds. E. Laszlo and E. Sellon (New York: Sellon Press, 1976), p. 154.

20. J. Mihalasky, "Extrasensory Perception in Management," *Advanced Management Journal* (July 1976).

21. "Planning on the Left Side and Managing on the Right," *Harvard Business Review* (July-August 1976): pp. 49-58.

22. D. Goleman, "Split-brain Psychology: Fad of the Year," *Psychology Today* (October 1977): p. 89.

23. *Executive ESP* (Englewood Cliffs, N.J.: Prentice Hall, 1974).

24. "Dialogue: Your Most Exciting Moment in Research?" *LBL Newsmagazine* (Fall, 1976): p. 2.

25. E. Green and A. Green, *Beyond Biofeedback* (New York: Delacorte, 1977).

26. E. Green, A. Green, and D. Walters, "Voluntary Control of Internal States: Psychological and Physiological," *Journal of Transpersonal Psychology* (1970): pp. 1-27.

27. Assagioli, op. cit., p. 220.

28. *The Search for Existential Identity* (San Francisco: Jossey Bass, 1976), p. 296.

29. *The Farther Reaches of Human Nature* (New York: Viking, 1971).

30. *The Spectrum of Consciousness* (Wheaton, Ill.: Theosophical Publishing House, 1977), p. 46.

31. P. Yogananda, *The Autobiography of a Yogi* (Los Angeles: Self-Realization Fellowship, 1969), p. 31.

32. *Sri Aurobindo, or The Adventure of Consciousness* (Pondicherry, India: Sri Aurobindo Society, 1970), p 192.

33. *The Medium, the Mystic and the Physicist* (New York: Viking, 1974), p. 154.

3

The Many Faces of Intuition[†]

PHILIP GOLDBERG

Following is one of a series of related incidents in a frequently quoted memoir by the French mathematician Henri Poincaré, a story that exemplifies the intuition of discovery: the sudden leap to understanding, the spark of insight, the precipitous penetration to the truth.

> The changes of travel made me forget my mathematical work. Having reached Coutances, we entered an omnibus to go some place or other. At the moment when I put my foot on the step the idea came to me, without anything in my former thoughts seeming to have paved the way for it, that the transformations I had used to define the Fuchsian functions were identical with those of non-Euclidean geometry. I did not verify the idea; I should not have had time, as, upon taking my seat in the omnibus, I went on with a conversation already commenced, but I felt a perfect certainty. On my return to Caen, for conscience's sake I verified the result at my leisure.

This kind of experience is what most people mean when they think of intuition, and it is one of six functional types we will discuss in this chapter. The first five categories interact with each other and occur in various combinations to comprise the full range of ordinary intuitive experience. The sixth type pertains to what is generally known as mystical experience and has intriguing implications for the other five.

Discovery

The history of thought contains innumerable examples of discovery intuition, or detection. Archimedes' fortuitous bath, in

†SOURCE: "The Many Faces of Intuition," Philip Goldberg, Jeremy P. Tarcher, Inc., Los Angeles, Copyright © 1983 by Philip Goldberg; used by permission.

which he discovered the principle of water displacement and gave us the term *Eureka!* ("I have found it"), is probably the most famous. A contemporary example is that of Nobel laureate **Melvin Calvin**, who was sitting in [his] car waiting for his wife to complete an errand when the answer to a perplexing inconsistency in his research on photosynthesis dawned. Calvin wrote of the discovery, "It occurred just like that—quite suddenly—and suddenly also, in a matter of seconds, the path of carbon became apparent to me."

While intuitive discovery often seems to occur when the mind is engaged in something other than the subject of the insight, that is not always the case. The key breakthrough in the search for the structure of the DNA molecule came when the discoverer was working on the problem itself. Like other researchers, James Watson and Francis Crick had labored arduously on the problem for some time. One day, after an interruption, Watson was shifting around components of a model molecule, trying different ways to fit them together. It had always been assumed that each segment had to be paired with its twin.

Then, in Watson's words, "Suddenly I became aware . . . that both pairs could be flip-flopped over and still have their . . . bonds facing in the same direction. It strongly suggested that the back-bones of the two chains run in opposite directions." Thus the famous double helix was discovered.

Intuitive discovery applies to the full range of knowable subject matter, including mundane questions, matters of personal or social importance, and abstract conceptual puzzles. What separates it from the other functions of intuition is its detective quality. It reveals verifiable facts. It might tell a businessman that his competitor has tried to interfere with a customer; it might reveal to a physician the real cause of a patient's pain; it might tell a parent exactly what is troubling a child who won't even admit he is troubled; it might signal a stymied inventor to put the gizmo in the widget instead of in its present location.

In short, this aspect of intuition can supply answers to a specific problem or to a more general need. We program our intuitive minds with our questions and desires. Sometimes the answer is not so much a solution as an insight into the real nature of the problem, as in the case of one boutique owner: "Sales were down and I just assumed it was because of the recession. But I kept getting this suspicious feeling inside about one of the sales staff. I though[t] I was nuts, but I investigated anyway, and sure enough she was ripping off the cash sales."

It should be noted that many students of scientific discovery object to assigning intuition a major role in the process. Howard Gruber, director of the Institute for Cognitive Studies at Rutgers University, says that, according to his research, breakthroughs emerge from a "lengthy complex pondering" and the growth of ideas over a long period of time, not a "magical moment." Similarly, Harvard's D. N. Perkins, author of *The Mind's Best Work*, contends that Poincaré-like experiences are rare and that discovery is the outcome of arduous, conscious, rational work. "I have never heard of a completely out-of-the-blue insight," writes Perkins.

This is true. Intuition doesn't come from nowhere. Dogged rational work in the preparation phase is of extreme importance, particularly in a specialized field. It supplies the intuitive mind with the incentive and raw material it needs. As already noted, intuition is not necessarily an all-at-once flash. The fireworks that are recorded for posterity are the dramatic prototypes. The key breakthrough may come either at once or in stages, as Perkins and Gruber point out, but part of that gradual process may be a series of incremental intuitions, perhaps with only candlelight intensity, that supply pieces of the total product.

Others who reject the notion of inspiration hold that the process of discovery is conscious and rational. Yale psychiatrist Albert Rothenberg, for example, contends that when James Watson made his DNA breakthrough he was "fully conscious, aware, and logical at that moment." But Rothenberg also calls Watson's discovery a "creative leap" that somehow was able to "transcend ordinary logic." I don't know how you can transcend logic and still be logical. It seems obvious that the leap was a function of intuition. Perhaps what Rothenberg meant is that such leaps would not ordinarily be made by formal logical thought, but they have a logic of their own that becomes obvious afterward. It is like one of those drawings in which you have to find the concealed face; once you find the face it is almost impossible *not* to see it. So it is with the illogical logic of many intuitions.

Rothenberg uses the term *Janusian thinking* to characterize a central element in creative breakthroughs—when seemingly opposite components are seen to be equally valid or complementary. He claims that Janusian thinking is fully intentional and fully conscious, thus disagreeing with Arthur Koestler, who, in *The Act of Creation*, used the term *bisociation* for essentially the same phenomenon and said the connections were made outside awareness. I think that the merging of opposites is characteristic of intuition, not the sort of thing that rational thought would readily accomplish. Rothenberg himself supports that conclusion by using the word *surprising* to describe the products of Janusian thinking. Watson used the term *suddenly*. To my mind, such terminology indicates that the event was spontaneous, unforeseen, and swift. The discoverer may have been conscious in the sense of being awake, but if he had been aware of the steps by which the crucial connection was made it would have been neither sudden nor surprising.

As for the word *intentional*, I don't doubt that some thinkers intend to find unusual connections. They certainly intend to find answers. Purposefulness and intensity of desire may well be important prerequisites for intuition, as is a certain open-minded attitude that expects the unexpected. But, again, the discoverers could not have *intended* to make the particular connections they did and then have been surprised when they did so. If you set out to pull a rabbit out of a hat, you will hardly be surprised when you perform the trick. For all these reasons, it seems safe to say that the sudden logic-transcending connections that typically accompany discoveries are a function of intuition.

Perhaps those who deny the importance of sudden intuition fear, with some justification, that accepting such a theory might downgrade the value of the conscious, rational preparation that precedes breakthroughs in formal work. Maybe they want to conteract the overly romantic view that discoveries are always flashy. But the danger is that by going too far in the other direction they erroneously negate the intuitive component.

Creativity

The poet A. E. Housman has given us a description of another function of intuition: "As I went along, thinking nothing in particular, only looking at things around me and following the progress of the seasons, there would flow into my mind, with sudden and unaccountable emotion, sometimes a line or two of verse, sometimes a whole stanza at once."

As Housman's remarks suggest, creative, or generative, intuition is quite similar to discovery intuition. The dynamics are more or less identical, the experience itself perhaps indistinguishable. I separate them because of one salient distinction: instead of singular truths, facts, or verifiable information, the creative function of intuition deals with alternatives, options, or possibilities. This function generates ideas that may not be right or wrong in the factual sense but are more or less appropriate to a situation. It might deliver alternatives in quantity, some of which will be more suitable than others.

Creative intuition can be compared to imagination. The distinction has to do with appropriateness. A merely imaginative person might not be intuitive but, rather, a fecund generator of lunatic fantasies or inane outpourings that are not satisfying on either the practical or esthetic level. The creatively intuitive person, on the other hand, would be imaginative in a relevant and apt manner. If he were a problem solver, he would generate a lot of unusual solutions, a high percentage of which would achieve the desired results. If he were an artist, his conceptions would "work" on canvas, on paper, or on stage, and the products would have the ring of "truth" that enables some art to endure. If he were a scientist or mathematician, he would generate hypotheses and theories, or unusual ways to test them, and a good proportion would contribute to the body of knowledge in his field.

Creative intuition works hand in hand with discovery intuition. You might, for example, detect the answer to a problem and then intuit alternative ways to prove it or execute it. Or you might intuitively apprehend what the problem itself is and then generate possible solutions. Sometimes the two functions overlap. In response to a perplexing question your intuition might generate a lot of hypotheses, one of which subsequently turns out true. Strictly speaking, when it is verified it would be termed a discovery.

The distinction is situation-dependent. Discovery intuition would apply when there is a single answer to such questions as, "What is the structure of the DNA molecule?" or "Who killed the victim?" Creative intuition would apply where there are a number of possible solutions, some better than others. Works of art would be an obvious example, although many artists will tell you there is one and only one way to finish this novel or paint that sunflower. Giacometti, for example, might have used the term *discovery* for this process: "In 1949 I saw the sculpture before me as if it were finished, and in 1950 it became impossible for me not to make it."

With great art, the distinction between creativity and discovery is often irrelevant. Art, wrote novelist Shirley Hazzard, is "an endless access to revelatory states of mind." That state of mind is what gives rise to creative intuition and makes great art an epiphany, not just entertainment. It is why we learn things about jealousy from Shakespeare or crime from Dostoevski that we can't learn from scientific studies. What psychologist Morris Parloff wrote of Lewis Carroll could have been said of any number of artists: "His contributions to the field of psychology, were we to enumerate them all, would undoubtedly qualify him for immediate fellowship status in at least two dozen of the 41 divisions of the American Psychological Association." You might also say the same of historical, sociological, and even physical-science associations.

The intuition of creativity is also important in solving practical problems and making decisions. The ability to generate alternative ways of viewing situations, or a variety of potential solutions, is an important component of innovation. Creative intuition will also seize opportunities to satisfy objectives. Always on the alert for new ways to generate business, liquor company executive Marshall Berkowitz was at a bar one day when he noticed that brandy Alexanders were extremely popular. He wondered why no one ever served them at home, and the answer came to him: they were too difficult to prepare. On the heels of that came the then-revolutionary idea of packaged cocktails.

There are probably personality differences between intuitive discoverers and intuitive creators. Some might be detective types; they come up with a small number of ideas, most of which are right on the mark. They are attracted to single-answer problems. Others might generate ideas in the same way that flowers produce pollen, and have a small percentage of healthy offspring. They are attracted to ill-defined, open-ended problems. Personally, I would like to have both types on my team.

Evaluation

"By the favour of the Gods, I have since my childhood been attended by a semi-divine being whose voice from time to time dissuades me from some undertaking, but never directs me what I am to do." Thus Socrates, in Plato's *Theagetes*, referred to a divine voice, and perhaps it was. In more secular terminology, I call it the evaluative function of intuition.

It is frequently said that intuition does not evaluate or decide; rational analysis does that, while intuition provides the possibilities. This division of labor short changes both intuition and rationality. Often the opposite of the customary description occurs. For example, financial planner Tom Duffy says, "I might make contingency plans on the basis of a formal analysis of technical data, but the actual decision—to commit or hold off or abandon—is a question of timing, and for that I look to my feelings."

What most people mean when they say that intuition does not evaluate is that it doesn't examine or investigate. Those functions are largely analytic, although intuition will help guide the process. But rational and quantitative evaluations often leave us with uncertainty or ambiguity, not with a single obvious decision. They might narrow down the alternatives and provide solid facts and figures to consider, but much of the time we turn to intuition for the ultimate choice.

Intuitive evaluation is a binary kind of function that tells us go or don't go, yes or no. Like other types of intuition, it can be clear or faint, resolute or hesitant, convincing or dubious. We have all had these promptings and urgings, although too often we ignore them. How many times have you run into trouble and afterward cursed yourself: "I *knew* I shouldn't have done that. Something told me not to. Next time I'll pay attention." Sometimes we feel strongly about something, but the inarticulate nature of intuition prevents us from convincing others. That happened to Socrates, as Plato's account suggests: "You know Charmides, the son of Glaucon. One day he told me that he intended to compete at the Nemean games. . . . I tried to turn Charmides from his design, telling him, 'While you were speaking, I heard the divine voice . . . "Go not to Nemea." ' He would not listen. Well, you know he has fallen."

Evaluative intuition might work directly on possibilities that present themselves from outside. Should you call that man you met on the train? Should you take that job offer? Much of the time we don't even have to ask the question; our intuition is programmed by our desires, needs, and goals. Here is an example from my own experience, when I was interviewing prospective literary agents. Usually I would leave such meetings feeling ambivalent, torn between rejecting and accepting the agent. In one case, however, I knew in the first minute that the person across the desk was not my future agent. I had not consciously evaluated her, and there were no remarkable traits that stood out as *the* reasons, but as she was describing one of her client's books, a strong by undeniable sensation came over me, wordlessly screaming "No!"

The evaluative function of intuition also works on the other products of intuition, adding the element of discrimination. Ideas feel more or less true; tentative solutions feel more or less right. Marshall Berkowitz, for example, had to decide whether or not his idea for packaging cocktails was worth pursuing, and later he had to decide whether to go ahead with production. Certainly, he gathered the facts and figures, consulted with colleagues, and thought it all through carefully. But at some point it was go or no-go, and he had to consult his inner barometer. Watson and Crick had to recognize that their Janusian connection was worth pursuing; something told them to go ahead and try to verify it.

Writers and artists have to evaluate intuitively all the time, for there is no objective, rational way they can evaluate their work beyond such technical considerations as syntax and grammar. Saul Bellow speaks of a commentator within that guides his work: "I think a writer is on track when the door of his native and deeper intuitions is open. You write a sentence that doesn't come from that source and you can't build around it—it makes the page seem somehow false. You have a gyroscope within that tells you whether what you're doing is right or wrong." And in his study of Beethoven's work, Roger Sessions writes that the composer's inspiration was an impulse that led him toward a goal: "When this perfect realization was attained, however, there could have been no hesitation—rather a flash of recognition that this was exactly what he wanted."

It is this discriminatory function of intuition that prompts a feeling of certitude or self-evidence about propositions, whether they come from within or from outside. It is important, however, and often difficult, not to confuse these feelings with ordinary emotions. We may like or dislike something, feel strongly attracted or repelled, but that may be hope or fear speaking, not intuition. There is a subtle distinction, and it can be discerned only by paying attention to our own experiences. The potential for confusion might be greater in some areas of life than others. As an advertising executive named Karen said, "When it comes to people, I often have urges to get involved with someone or stay away, whether it is a social or professional encounter. Those feelings often haunt me afterward; they get all tangled up in my own needs and desires. But when it comes to a slogan or a jingle or a storyboard, when I get a strong feeling it is almost always right."

Einstein must have had evaluative intuition working on his theory of general relativity, because he seemed to be unreasonably confident it would stand up to empirical testing. For two years the scientific world prepared for the solar eclipse of May 29, 1919, when conditions would allow them to see whether starlight would be affected by the sun's gravitational field as the theory predicted. According to Einstein's biographer, Jeremy Bernstein, the great man was in Princeton when the results were computed. A student reported that she was engaged in conversation with Einstein when he casually handed her a telegram that had been on a windowsill. It was from Sir Arthur Eddington, confirming the revolutionary theory. Overjoyed by the news, the student was somewhat surprised by the master's apparent indifference. "What if the theory had not been confirmed?" she asked. Einstein replied, "Then I would have been sorry for the dear Lord. The theory is correct."

I have never been able to determine whether Einstein was referring to Lord Eddington or the Almighty. Either way, he seemed awfully sure of his theory.

Operation

In the fall of 1941, when London was under siege, Winston Churchill regularly ventured out at night in a staff car to visit antiaircraft batteries. One evening as the prime minister prepared to leave a site, an aide opened the customary door, but Churchill walked around the car and let himself in the far door instead. Not long afterward, a bomb exploded, nearly turning the car over. "It must have been my beef on that side that pulled it down," laughed Churchill. When his wife, Lady Clementine, asked him why he had sat on the far side of the car, Churchill said, "Something said to me, 'Stop!' before I reached the car door held open for me. It then appeared to me that I was told I was meant to open the door on the other side and get in and sit there—and that's what I did."

Churchill had what I would call an operative intuition (he evidently had a lot of them). This most subtle, almost spooky form of intuition is what guides us this way and that, sometimes with declarative force, sometimes with gentle grace. It prompts us without telling us why, and sometimes without our knowing that we are being prompted at all. More like a sense of direction than a map, it can be ill defined or quite explicit. It might operate on minor, localized situations, nudging us toward this or tugging us away from that. Or it might manifest itself in larger issues, such as a sense of "calling," for example, that overpowering certainly that we are meant to follow a particular vocation or accept some mission. Such compelling attractions can often be justified logically, but they are never logically derived. Rather, we feel like an iron filing drawn quite irresistibly to a magnet.

In some ways operative intuition is similar to the evaluative function, since there might be a "do/don't do" or "go/don't go" quality to it. But with evaluative intuition there first has to be something to evaluate. For example, when Ray Kroc's consultants advised him not to buy McDonald's, he says, "I closed the office door, cussed up and down, threw things out of the window, called my lawyer back, and said, 'Take it!' I felt in my funny bone it was a sure thing." That was evaluative intuition working on a specific yes-or-no question. Not so with the toy manufacturer who, in June 1971, had an inexplicable urge to increase production of panda dolls. The next February Richard Nixon made his historic trip to China, where he was given two pandas, touching off a small fad.

Operative intuition might be responsible for what often seems like luck. Those persons who seem to be in the right place at the right time, to whom terrific accidents seem to happen, are perhaps gifted with a kind of radar system and the good sense to obey it. It might also account for the phenomenon that Carl Jung called "synchronicity," those uncanny coincidences of outer and inner events that have no apparent causal connection but have meaning or significant impact. One artist relates: "I had met someone at an opening who wanted to commission a painting. The next day, when I went to phone him, I could not find his business card. On a train ride to the suburbs to visit friends I thought I saw him, but it turned out to be a look-alike. When I arrived at the station, I felt irresistibly drawn to the flower shop, and I gave in to the urge despite the fact that I had brought a gift with me and had no intention of purchasing flowers. In the flower shop was the man I though I'd lost forever."

The role of accidents in scientific discoveries has often been noted. Perhaps it is operative intuition that tells the seemingly lucky discoverers that there is something worth looking into. Bacteriologist Alexander Fleming, for example, noticed that some of the plates on which he was growing colonies of bacteria had been contaminated by dust and that the bacteria on them had died. Most researchers would have thrown the plates out, since they were just nuisances in the context of the research. Fleming, however, sensed something significant and asked, "Why did the bacteria die?" The eventual result of that question was the discovery of penicillin.

Discoveries and creative ideas are often preceded by what Graham Wallas, in *The Art of Thought*, termed "intimations," those vague, fuzzy feelings that indicate something is about to happen. Jung also noticed a kind of emotional aura that accompanies synchronistic events. Perhaps it is a form of operative intuition, guiding the attention in the right direction, either alerting the mind to an impending thought of its own or to something about to occur in the environment. Wallas recalls a major shift in his own political attitude that was preceded by "a vague, almost physical, recurrent feeling as if my clothes did not quite fit me." Perhaps those intimations are like the early, barely perceptible glow that turns our attention toward the sunrise.

Operative intuition can be puzzling, since it might urge us to move in what seems to be a strange direction. If we follow it, we find ourselves doing things for no apparent reason, perhaps feeling somewhat foolish, wondering what on earth has possessed us. At times these whispers are easy to resist, since they might seem to go against our best interests.

Let's go back to that agent I discussed in the previous section. When it was time to depart her office, something told me to leave behind my outline for this book, which at the time had no publisher. There was no reason to do this, since I knew the agent was not going to represent me. Furthermore, there was every reason *not* to do it. I would have to go across the street to make a copy of the outline, and I was already late for my next appointment, which was quite important. Yet I did it. On the elevator, in the copy shop, in the cab, and all during the rest of the day I told myself what an idiot I had been for following this impulse.

The next day I got a call from an editor friend. She suggested that I contact Jeremy Tarcher, whom she had met the night before and who happened to mention an outline for a book on intuition that he had seen that afternoon on an agent's desk.

Coincidence? Who knows? I can only say that what I felt in that agent's office was as powerful and impelling as a strong wind. I have, of course, experienced other nonrational shoves and tugs; some led nowhere, or even to trouble—or at least they *seemed* to. Who can say what would have happened if I *had* followed the ones I battled against successfully? We usually resist those intuitive urges when they don't seem to make sense. Perhaps we ought not fight so stubbornly.

Prediction

"If you can look into the seeds of time," wrote Shakespeare in *Macbeth*, "And say which grain will grow and which will not, Speak then to me." In most intuitive experiences—indeed, in a large percentage of all mental activities—there is an element of prophecy. When a scientist intuits a hypothesis, he is, at least in part, predicting what will happen to certain phenomena under certain conditions. If your intuition tells you to accept a dinner invitation from a virtual stranger, you are predicting that the evening will be pleasurable. When you obey a feeling to hire someone, you are predicting that he or she will produce desirable results. When an artist is inspired to use a dab of red or an arpeggio suggests itself to a composer, they are predicting what the impact will be on the rest of the work and on the viewer or listener.

Decisions are by nature predictive—you are banking on a certain outcome. For this reason, the ability to forecast is a prized quality in executives and policy makers. Indeed, a study by John Mihalasky and Douglas Dean, authors of *Executive ESP*, found a significant correlation between the precognitive ability of company presidents and the profit ratings of their companies.

Certainly, predictions are routinely made by analyzing quantitative data, and specialized knowledge is often necessary. Without an understanding of probability theory, for example, an intuitive judgment might be way off the mark. To use a rather trivial illustration, suppose in five consecutive coin tosses heads were to come up each time. Would heads or tails be more likely to turn up on the sixth try? Most people choose tails. However, the actual odds are the same old 50/50.

But rational-analytic methods can seldom be used exclusively; by its very nature, prediction deals with the unknown, and we can calculate or measure only what is known. We can analyze past trends and determine probabilities, but we can never be sure the future will by anything like the past, particularly in human situations in a turbulent era like ours. At the very least, a forecaster has to use intuition in gathering and interpreting data and in deciding which unusual future events might influence the outcome. Hence in virtually every prediction there is always some intuitive component.

The predictive function can be either explicit or implicit. When I followed my urge to photocopy that outline and leave it with the agent, I had no idea why. But the intuition to which I give the credit must have had some implicit prophetic quality mixed in. The intuition would have been more predictive than operative if I'd had a strong feeling that something good would come of the behavior or if I'd had a premonition of what would actually take place.

This story, related by Harvard student Juliet Faithfull, is an example of predictive intuition at work. As a young girl, Juliet was on vacation in Barcelona with her parents. For days she implored them to take her to a particular nightclub, and on their last night in the city the parents relented. Juliet eagerly primped for the occasion. Shortly before they were to leave, however, a cloud of dread came over her, and she refused to go, despite the protests of her incredulous parents. The nightclub was destroyed by fire that evening. The difference between her story and Winston Churchill's fortuitous urge to switch seats in his car was the Juliet knew something bad would happen at the club, although she could not specify the nature of the danger.

As these rather dramatic incidents suggests, intuition is an excellent warning device. But not all predictive intuitions are warnings. You might have a strong feeling that the person you just met will have a positive influence on your life or you might have a hunch that you should wait a week before investing because the price is going to fall. The better your intuition can predict, the more your actions will resonate with your desires.

Whether a prediction deserves to be called intuitive hinges on its precision and on whether it is likely to have been made by most people. Let's look at an example. Henry Kissinger once said, "The dilemma of any statesman is that he can never be certain about the probable course of events. In reaching a decision, he must inevitably act on the basis of an intuition that is inherently unprovable. If he insists on certainty, he runs the danger of becoming a prisoner of events." Suppose you had been working in the State Department early in 1977. If you had said, "I have a hunch something big will happen in the Middle East this year," you would have been greeted with polite indulgence at best if you bragged about it at year's end. If you have said, "There is going to be a diplomatic breakthrough between Israel and an Arab nation, possibly Egypt," you might have been called intuitive, and your colleagues might subsequently have turned to you for predictions. But if you had said, "Anwar Sadat is going to make a plea for peace before the Israeli parliament in November," you might have been nominated for Mr. Kissinger's old job.

We play guessing games with life. Those who guess well are called intuitive; those who are intuitive, however, don't think they are guessing.

Illumination

"When all the senses are stilled," say the *Upanishads*, "when the mind is at rest, when the intellect wavers not—then, say the wise, is reached the highest state. He who attains it is freed from delusion." What I am calling illumination has been given other names in different places across time: *samadhi*, *satori*, nirvana, cosmic consciousness, Self-realization, union with God. Certain readers might wonder why it is included at all. Some might see it as too exalted and sublime to be spoken of in the same breath as intuiting what stock to buy; some might be solely interested in how to use their intuition in the "real world" and thus consider this classification irrelevant.

This category transcends the other five functions. In fact, it transcends categories. It transcends words, concepts, thoughts, perceptions, and everything we think of as experience. It is, in fact, *transcendence*, one of the terms used for it in this book. But it is very relevant indeed. Understanding it helps us understand all forms of intuition, and cultivating it simultaneously cultivates the others. Most important, illumination itself represents the highest form of knowing, the realization for which we all thirst whether we know it or not.

Illumination, or transcendence, is different from the ordinary experience of knowing, which always has two components: a subject (the experiencer), and the object of experience, which can be something we think. In the state we are describing, that subject/object duality is dissolved. There is no separation of knower and known. There is no object of experience—not a sensation or a perception or even a thought.

In transcendence, the experiencer is conscious, but not conscious *of* anything; awareness alone exists. The knower knows, but there is no object of knowledge; knowingness alone exists. It is as if the film in a movie projector has run out but the projector light remains on, illuminating the screen. Previously, the viewer's attention had been on the changing forms and colors that to him constituted reality. Now he is aware of the screen itself, the silent, formless background on which the variegated experiences depend. In transcendence, the silent backdrop to experience is illuminated. This is pure consciousness.

It is also the Self, capitalized to distinguish it from the individuated self—the ego or changing personality with which we normally identify. Thus in the state of transcendence what is illumined is one's ultimate identity. We come to know that which we are. "Soundless, formless, intangible, undying, tasteless, odorless, without beginning, without end, eternal, immutable, beyond nature is the Self," say the *Upanishads*.

There are degrees of illumination, and the traditional Eastern texts make clear the stages of development: from a fleeting, perhaps hazy glimpse of the transcendent, as might occur spontaneously or in meditation; to permanent Self-realization, in which the transcendent is a silent continuum behind all experience; to supreme enlightenment, in which the Self is known to be truly one with creation. Over time, the seeker comes to know that his true nature is the boundless Absolute, the ultimate constituent of all the changing objects and patterns we perceive around us. Admiral Richard Byrd, to use a contemporary, secular example, had a glimpse of this union: "In that instance I could feel no doubt of man's oneness with the universe. . . . It was a feeling that transcended reason; that went to the heart of man's despair and found it groundless. The universe as a cosmos, not Chaos; man was as rightfully a part of that cosmos as were the day and night."

Western science has not, as yet, reached this understanding, and it never will if it sticks to the constricting ideology of scientism. The pickax of rationality can't penetrate the Self, and the yardstick of empiricism can't measure it. "You ask how can we know the infinite?" asked the third-century A.D. Egyptian philosopher Plotinus. "I answer, not by reason. It is the office of reason to distinguish and define. The infinite, therefore, cannot be ranked among it objects. You can only apprehend the infinite by a faculty superior to reason, by entering into a state in which you are your finite self no longer— in which the divine essence is communicated to you. This is ecstasy. It is the liberation of your mind from its finite consciousness."

Rational thought uses symbols like words or numbers, and symbols have meaning only in relationship to particular entities. Since it has no attributes, the Absolute can't be compared to anything; since it is all-pervasive, it can't be separated from anything. Immanuel Kant did the world a service by demonstrating that all the arduous attempts of philosophers and theologians to prove or disprove the existence of God or an Absolute were pointless; with equal plausibility, we can construct an argument for either position. What Kant did not understand was that the Absolute was nevertheless knowable. It is knowable not through reason—although it can be expounded upon and elucidated with reason—but by direct experience. This is not the objective, sensory experience with which we are familiar, however, but a direct intuitive union.

As the empiricist philosopher David Hume found out, it is even more futile to try knowing the Self through objective experience as it is to deduce it. "When I enter most intimately into what I call *myself*," wrote Hume, "I always stumble on some particular perception or other, of heat or cold, light or shade, love or hatred, pain or pleasure. I never catch *myself* at any time without a perception, and never can observe anything but a perception."

And so Hume, like most of us, concluded that he was "nothing but a bundle or collection of different perceptions, which succeed each other with an inconceivable rapidity, and are in a perpetual flux and movement." The problem, of course, is that the Self is not an object, and so it can't be known the way we know objects. There is nothing to separate from the knower. Trying to know the Self objectively would be like the eye trying to see the eye.

Illumination can be considered the highest form of knowing because it tells us what we are and what the cosmos is, and establishes a genuine union between the two. It is also the most satisfying form of knowing; the state of consciousness itself has been called bliss, or *ananda*. For these reasons, supreme enlightenment has always been depicted as the end of ignorance, of alienation, of suffering. Even to the most pragmatic reader it should be clear that illumination has its own rewards. But it also has practical relevance in regard to our other categories. It is referred to throughout the book because it is a model for understanding the how and why of garden-variety intuition. Transcendence can be viewed as the exemplar to which all other forms of intuition can be related.

Furthermore, transcendence itself has a transformative impact on consciousness; those who experience it say that it upgrades all cognitive faculties. It is something like being on the roof of a building and then, once familiar with that vista, finding that the view from lower floors is somehow different. The expanded perspective becomes a reference point. And the actual process of going to the roof makes it easier to gain access to the other floors because of an overall familiarity with the terrain. In some way, illumination opens other intuitive channels, which is one reason why yoga and traditional consciousness disciplines made it their first order of business.

4

What It Is[†]

ROY ROWAN

"Hunch" is an odious word to the professional manager. It's a horseplayer's or stock market plunger's term, rife with imprecision and unpredictability. Yet, even in today's empirical world of business, where the fast track is paved over with MBAs who can figure the risk-reward ratio of any decision at the drop of a computer key, the old-fashioned hunch continues to be an important, though unappreciated, managerial tool. Logic and analysis can lead a person only part way down the path to a profitable decision. The last step to success frequently requires a daring intuitive leap, as many chief executives who control the destinies of America's biggest corporations will reluctantly concede.

Just as often the biggest roadblock to creative decision-making is not having the guts to follow a good hunch. And in no place is that roadblock more inhibiting than in the boardroom. "The chief executive officer is not supposed to say, 'I feel.' He's supposed to say, 'I know,'" says David Mahoney, former chairman of Norton Simon and now head of his own venture capital company in New York City. Mahoney is one of those executives who secretly prize their business intuition. But since management is an inexact science, frequently defined as the art of making decisions with insufficient information, even the most deliberate boss is sometimes forced to act prematurely on nebulous inner impressions.

Nevertheless, it's hard for a manager to heed those nagging voices from some mysterious echo chamber deep inside his brain without sounding very unprofessional. Like Mahoney, any self-respecting chief executive is loath to admit that an important decision is based on an ill-defined gut feeling. "So we deify the word 'instinct' by calling it 'judgment,'" he says.

†SOURCE: From THE INTUITIVE MANAGER by Roy Rowan, Copyright (c) 1986 by Roy Rowan. By permission of Little, Brown and Company, and the co-publisher, Gower, Hampshire, England.

Yet psychologists contend, feelings need no reasons. They know that a person doesn't pull answers out of a void, that intuition operates on subterranean levels where information is not consciously available. Although the realization may arrive at a seemingly magical moment, it comes usually after a long, hard pondering of a problem.

Archimedes, the ancient Greek physicist, was taking a bath, mulling over a question posed by King Hiero II of Syracuse—whether the king's crown was made of pure gold or alloyed with silver—when a way of finding the answer hit him. Observing the overflow from his tub, Archimedes realized that since gold is more dense than silver, a given weight of the yellow metal would displace less water. Excited by his discovery, he streaked out of his home without his clothes, shouting "Eureka" ("I have found it"). Archimedes then demonstrated to the king that his crown displaced more water than an equal weight of pure gold, proving that it was indeed fashioned from an alloy.

The Eureka factor, that sudden, illuminating, "I've found it" flash, has been referred to again and again by scientists attempting to describe the key element in their discovery process. Most are quick to admit that scientific breakthroughs do not seem to evolve slowly from a sequence of deductions. They spring finally from hunches that cannot be completely explained. "There are no logical paths to these [natural] laws," admitted Albert Einstein. "Only intuition resting on sympathetic understanding of experience can reach them." He called the theory of relativity "the happiest thought of my life."

Artists, certainly, have always assumed that creativity doesn't spring from a deductive assault on a problem. Yet there are instances where a melding of the intuitive and deductive helped produce magnificent results. From Leonardo da Vinci's pen flowed detailed drawings of the first flying machine, while much more recently from sculptor Ladislas Biro's imagination emerged the ballpoint pen. Both Robert Fulton, inventor of the steamboat, and Samuel Morse, inventor of the telegraph, started out life as artists. But intuition led them elsewhere.

Athletes, too, continue to demonstrate uncanny intuitive abilities. John Brodie, former quarterback of the San Francisco 49ers, refers to the "extraordinary state of mind" that performing sports stars sometimes get into, giving them a heightened focus and perception. Basketball star Larry Bird of the Boston Celtics says: "It's scary. When I'm at my best I can do just about anything I want and no one can stop me. I feel like I'm in total control of everything." Sometimes after shooting he'll turn tail and recoil down the court elated even before the ball has reached the basket. "I already know it's all net," he says.

Politics, we know, rewards its intuitive practitioners and demolishes those who can't sniff the winds correctly. Successful politicians have the ability to nudge public thinking positively or negatively, conservatively or innovatively, as long as they are within what John F. Kennedy called "the jaws of consent." The President told veteran pollster Lou Harris that most of the time he had confidence in his gut feelings. "But the time to scramble and take a poll," he warned, "is when you sense that you have made a decision that may be outside the jaws of consent."

A master of political timing, Ronald Reagan innately senses whenever those jaws are about to snap shut. That son of Eureka (Illinois) College has tried to beguile America into believing he is just an actor, while actually he is one of the most intuitive politicians ever to occupy the White House—and one of the Eureka factor's best salesmen. "The amazing thing," says Harris, "is how unerring his instinct is in knowing when to duck, when to go for the jugular, and how to go for broke communicating about it. He is the absolute opposite of Jimmy Carter, who immersed himself in detail and never sensed his political options."

John Sears, Reagan's former campaign adviser, pointed out right after the 1984 election: "Reagan has given us one thing the people will cling to regardless of our future problems. He has presided over the restoration of our confidence. Blindly optimistic, fiercely patriotic, and unbending in his loyalty, he is the embodiment of a peculiar American virtue that says that all things are possible if you will just make them so—that reality is an illusion that can be overcome."

It is the corporate leader, usually an appointee of the board of directors, who needs a little prompting on the powers of intuition. Once the modern manager understands how intuition works, he or she (after all, it is said to be "woman's intuition") may not be afraid to recognize that "a funny feeling" on the way to a decision can be crucial and worth paying attention to.

And it isn't just the big boss who needs this reassurance. Every employee makes decisions, if only what course of action to recommend to the bird one branch higher in the corporate pecking order. As a manager is promoted, the farther into the unpredictable future his decisions reach and the more he must rely on intuition. "Things keep changing too frequently, so planning may do more damage than good," says Howard Stein, who started out to be a concert violinist and is now chairman of the Dreyfus Corporation, which manages some forty mutual funds. "By the time you get a program approved, and people are committed to it, things change and it doesn't work." His prescription for using intuition is: "Make a decision, move forward, but don't feel wedded to what you're doing."

Male or female, top brass or lowly trainee, the decision-maker needs to understand how the brain constantly delves into the subconscious to retrieve buried fragments of knowledge and experience, which it then instantaneously fuses with new information. Appreciating the biological basis of this retrieval system may not make it easier to define a hunch or defend its reliability. But understanding how intuition works would make it seem less necessary to cover one's intuitive tracks or to offer some lame excuse to conceal the importance of intuition in arriving at a decision.

A Heritage of Profitable Hunches

The intuitive boss, after all, is a recurring figure in American business. Cornelius Vanderbilt consulted clairvoyants and believed in ghosts, J.P. Morgan was known to visit fortunetellers, while H. L. Hunt relied on a psychic to help pick oil properties. Traditionally, American entrepreneurs have taken enormous pride in their enormously profitable hunches, though usually without the counsel of mediums.

When Ray Kroc, the late hamburger king, was a boy his father took him to a phrenologist. "I was told that I would make my best living either in the food business or as a musician," he recalled. And he did both. After serving in the Red Cross Ambulance Corps in World War I, Kroc played piano in Chicago bars and restaurants and sold paper cups. His keyboard ability never earned him much of a living, but he sold enough cups to become midwest sales manager for Lily-Tulip. In 1937 he quit to buy exclusive sales rights to the "multimixer," a machine that could whip up six milkshakes at once.

In 1952 Richard and Maurice McDonald ordered eight multimixers for one restaurant in San Bernardino, California, pricking Kroc's curiosity about what kind of place could generate such a big order. So he flew out to deliver the multimixers himself. "When I got there," said Kroc, "I saw more people waiting in line than I had ever seen at any drive-in. I said to myself, 'Son of a bitch, these guys have got something.'"

Kroc talked the brothers into letting him franchise their outlets nationwide. During the next five years he organized a chain of 228 McDonald's. But he was collecting less than 2 percent of the gross and had to turn over more than a quarter of that to the brothers. Frustrated, he called the brothers in 1960 and asked them to quote a price for everything, including the name. They did—$2.7 million—and they also pulled the original San Bernardino restaurant out of the deal. Advised by his lawyer not to pay the exorbitant price, Kroc recalled: "I'm not a gambler and I didn't have that kind of money, but my funnybone instinct kept urging me on. So I closed my office door, cussed up and down, and threw things out the window. Then I called my lawyer back and said: 'Take it!'"

John Teets, chairman of the Greyhound Corporation, who is pictured in his company's dramatic two-page magazine ads peering perceptively over the Grand Canyon and other great American vistas, says, "What appears as a highly intuitive move at the time it is being made usually seems like common sense in the retrospect." Even the most daring business gambles, he claims, "look safe and sensible once they succeed." The investment banking community was extremely critical of his plans to restructure Greyhound. But the price of its stock doubled after he did.

In Teets's view, intuition is often augmented by adversity. At age thirty he was the father of two daughters and half-owner of a thriving restaurant, shopping center, and ice-skating complex in Meadowdale, Illinois. "Although I hadn't gone to college," he says, "I felt that I knew how to create things and make them work."

But that year a series of personal tragedies struck. His wife and brother died. Then the same week that President Kennedy was assassinated, the "fireproof" steel-and-concrete complex burned to the ground in the biggest fire Meadowdale ever had. "Those bitter experiences taught me that some occurrences are totally out of our control," says Teets. "I was severely depressed. But I never lost hope. My intuition told me that things would somehow work out." While deciding whether or not to rebuild the burned-out complex, he was offered a job running Greyhound's restaurants at the 1964 New York World's Fair. He calls intuition an "inexplicable interior force that resides in a halfway house between egotism and humility."

The feisty founder and chairman of Electronic Data Systems Corporation, H. Ross Perot, followed his gut feelings through a series of career changes from Texarkana (Texas) Junior College, to the U.S. Naval Academy, to IBM, from which he broke away to start up the Dallas-based computer services giant, EDS. In 1984 he became one of the biggest stockholders of General Motors, when it acquired his company for $2.5 billion.

Perot recalls a study done at Annapolis to find out what instinct made some midshipmen better leaders than others. The answer, he says, "was an intuitive feeling of being able to win, though in nearly every case it was not known how." When two of his EDS employees were taken prisoner in Iran in 1978, Perot personally mounted a commando force to free them. He didn't know how their escape would be worked out, but instinctively he felt it would succeed, and remarkably it did.

And how does Perot describe intuition? "It means *knowing your business*," he said, drawling out the three words for emphasis. "It means being able to bring to bear on a situation everything you've seen, felt, tasted, and experienced in an industry." Perot claims he operates a memo-less company. Like Napoleon, who reputedly tossed out all written reports from his generals, figuring he'd already heard the important news, Perot prefers to conduct all of his business by personal contact. "Written reports stifle creativity," he says. "They discourage the reader from responding intuitively."

Hardly had GM acquired EDS when the giant automaker's innovative chief, Roger Smith, announced at a staff meeting that Perot had a new mission. He was to transform GM's Saturn project—which was charged not only with turning out a revolutionary new car, but a whole new production system—into a paperless company. Both men knew what a hard job this would be in a bureaucracy like GM. "Smith," said Perot, "looked over at me and winked. He knew he dropped a boulder on my shoulder."

One Sunday morning Eleanor Friede, then an editor with Macmillan and now an independent book producer, was sitting on the deck of her beach house in East Hampton, Long Island, reading a dog-eared manuscript for a children's book that had made the rounds of two dozen publishing houses without a single taker. The sun was beating down warmly, and the sea gulls were swooping overhead. "I was totally captured by the images of the story," she says. "There was no suspension of belief. I went with it completely, and it made me feel wonderful." Suddenly, she saw the slim volume, encased in a jacket of soaring sea gulls, in bookstore windows across the entire country.

As she sensed then, *Jonathan Livingston Seagull* was a story for adults, not children. At Friede's urging, Macmillan published it in 1970, but with a meager first printing scaled down from ten

thousand to seventy-five hundred copies by the marketing department. Friede's Little Nothing Book, as it was called inside the
publishing house, appeared in September without any reviews.
Television talk show hosts, so important to book sales, declined to
invite author Richard Bach, scoffing, "What are we going to talk
about, sea gulls?" Nevertheless, the book sold out before Christ-
mas. Even so, Macmillan was not inclined to reprint.

Friede pressed for a second printing right away, intuitively
sensing that a *Jonathan Livingston Seagull* phenomenon could catch
the country by surprise. Then suddenly the talk show invitations
started to come, confirming her feeling. "As an editor, you're
supposed to know if what's in your head is going to transfer to
other people," she says. "I felt there were truths in this simple story
that would make it an international classic."

The book has since sold 3.2 million copies in hard cover and 7
million in paperback. It has also been published in twenty-seven
languages, including Eskimo. Adds Friede, "Too many forces came
together all at once in the publication of *Jonathan* not to believe in
the existence of some kind of a universal information matrix."

But a recitation of highly profitable hunches doesn't reveal the
intuitive process. It doesn't explain this perceptive power that
enables one individual to peer up into the night sky and see a faint
star twinkling while equally intelligent colleagues see only the
blackness.

The late business philosopher R. Buckminster Fuller, designer of
the geodesic dome, called intuition "cosmic fishing." But he
warned, "Once you feel a nibble, you've got to hook the fish." Too
many people, he said, "get a hunch, then light up a cigarette and
forget about it."

Defining Intuition

What is this mystical power, magical facility, this guardian angel
that is smarter than we are and can take care of us, provided it is
allowed to function? The athlete speaks of mind and movement
coalescing or, less poetically, of eye-hand coordination. The Zen
Buddhist describes the sound of one hand clapping. The businessman talks about his gut feeling. Their vocabularies differ, but their
inner messages have the same submerged origin.

Intuition is knowledge gained without rational thought. And
since it comes from some stratum of awareness just below the

conscious level, it is slippery and elusive, to say the least. Under hypnosis the unconscious can recall incredible things that we have no idea are being collected. These subconsciously perceived factors are sorted out and integrated into retained impressions that often can't even be verbalized though they guide our actions.

Not being able to articulate a hazy, indistinct, subliminal impression doesn't mean that it surfaced by accident. Or that it was pulled from a void. New ideas spring from a mind that organizes experiences, facts, and relationships to discern a path that has not been taken before. Somewhere along this uncharted path, intuition compresses years of learning and experience into an instantaneous flash.

There's no guarantee that it's going to be a positive flash, though that is usually the case. Some individuals instinctively invite negative feelings that become self-fulfilling prophecies ("Everything I eat turns to fat"). The way intuition operates, you tend to get what you ask yourself for. Or as Joseph McKinney, chairman of the Tyler Corporation says: "Intuition works in proportion to need." He also talks about "all that voltage down there in the subconscious." But that high power has to be invoked. It has to be coaxed into constructive use by desire. When confronted with what seems like an insurmountable business problem, John Fetzer, chairman of both the Detroit Tigers and the Fetzer Broadcasting Company, says: "I literally order my subconscious mind to do research and come up with some answers."

In thinking intuitively you may not realize you've asked for something. Dr. Benjamin Libet, a physiologist at the University of California in San Francisco who measures brain waves, claims that the brain begins to ask for something—and actually initiates the action—about four-tenths of a second before the brain's owner is aware of wanting it. So even the simplest voluntary actions may start deep in the subconscious, that dark, secret place where we harbor so many of our likes, dislikes, and desires.

So where does the first glimmer of a new concept, new product, new market, or new solution to a problem come from? Elusive as it is, we do know certain characteristics of this inner impression or hunch. It concerns relationships, involves simultaneous perception of a whole system, and can draw a conclusion—not necessarily correct—without proceeding through logical intermediary steps. That's why intuition comes with that queasy feeling of almost but not quite knowing.

Herman Kahn, a physicist turned futurist and director of the Hudson Institute until his death in 1983, said: "My research is a combination of intuition and judgment. I don't know where it comes from. The mind simply puts things together."

Testing Intuition

How the corporate chief's mind puts things together is being studied intensively by a handful of scientists and academicians. They have come up with measurable proof that subconscious elements play in important role in decision-making and have even discovered a correlation between the boss's precognitive power (the facility of deciphering telltale signs of the future) and the company's profitability. They point out that it isn't realistic for executives to rely solely on logic to cope with the complexities of modern business.

It is an explorer back from outer space, astronaut Edgar Mitchell, who has turned into one of intuition's most fervent evangelists. A doctor of science from MIT, a former navy captain, and the sixth man on the moon, Mitchell believes that man's potential knowledge is more than the product of his five senses.

Mitchell was obviously using two kinds of vision, seeing with both his physical eye and mind's eye, when he gazed back at our blue living planet from the dusty dead moon. From that distant vantage point he saw the earth's ills as curable only by intuition, and recalcitrantly incurable if mankind insists on sticking to a strictly analytical approach. He still speaks almost reverently of the "mysterious, creative process that works outside our conscious awareness," which he is convinced quietly remains available to help us solve our most difficult problems.

In preparing for a lunar flight, Mitchell explains, "we spent ten percent of our time studying plans for the mission and ninety percent learning how to react intuitively to all the 'what ifs.'" Reliance on the intuitive response, he claims, was the most important part of his astronaut's training.

Following his journey to the moon, Mitchell founded the Institute of Noetic Sciences ("noetic" is from a Greek word for intuitive knowing) in Sausalito, California. His aim is to help his fellow man—especially the businessman—develop intuitive decision-making powers to the point where, as Mitchell says, "we can control the scientific beast." Advocating use of a space-age spin-off called failure analysis,he believes that chief executives should interview managers, foremen, and workers to uncover their innate fears about all the things that can go wrong. Explains Mitchell: "With a computer printout of the resulting 'fault tree' in front of him, a boss can almost smell those failures before they occur." The disaster at Bhopal, India, might have been averted if Union Carbide had subjected itself to this kind of intuitive, "what if" failure analysis.

Intuition studies are already invading national defense. Clandestine experiments involving the Pentagon and the psychic community have been going on for a few years to discover if the movement of Soviet submarines can be determined extrasensorally. The Defense Department has spent several million dollars on ESP and mental telepathy research, or what it calls Novel Biological Information Transfer Systems. Also being explored by the Pentagon is the far-out possibility of weapons systems that might somehow be triggered by the power of the mind.

Doctors, of course, have already found ways of harnessing psychic power to trigger body changes. Biofeedback has certainly proved helpful in the healing process, though many executives may still consider it just short of sorcery. And while self-proclaimed psychics keep popping up all over the place, insisting that they can remove diseased organs—or for that matter, bend metal or project photographic images—by using nothing more than intense concentration, the business leader quite understandably shrinks from being associated with such kooks.

But society's current addiction to psychic advice is hardly what executives mean when they secretly admit to following hunches. To the businessman or woman, words like "precognitive" and "psychic" smack of the occult. But suggest to this same sophisticated leader—not only in business, but in sports, science, or the arts—that he or she might indeed possess certain intuitive powers that could be of real assistance in generating ideas, choosing alternative courses of action, and picking people, and you'll elicit a rapt response. At least that was true of the people interviewed for this book.

Such a response is not surprising. Today's decision-makers live intensely and have more obligations and money than they have time. For them the highest need is to cut through the complexities of the modern world and come to quick creative decisions intuitively. This book is designed to help identify, unlock, use, stimulate, and sometimes also temper business intuition, "that which is imprinted on the spirit of the man(ager)," to borrow from the farseeing seventeenth-century British philosopher Francis Bacon.

Merely recognizing the existence of intuition is a positive first step. This means having faith in the fact that answers to the toughest problems can leap fully conceived into our awareness—

and at the most unpropitious moment, as happened to Archimedes in the bath. But this amorphous, ill-defined instinct known as intuition has to be understood, nurtured, and trusted if is to be turned into a powerful management tool.

PART II The Importance of Intuition in Leadership and Management

Three articles are contained in this section that seek to establish the importance of intuition in leadership and management settings. Daniel J. Isenberg's field research indicates that "the higher you go in a company, the more important it is that you combine intuition and rationality." You will note, however, that he is making a distinction between intuition and rationality, which Herbert Simon and I would not make.

Stephen C. Harper seeks to establish the fact that top executives possess the intuitive skills that separate them from the average manager. He argues that this brain skill provides them with different perspectives and approaches to management that enable them to be more effective in these turbulent times.

My article outlines how intuitive skills can be critical in strategic board-level decision making. It is argued that board members who are highly intuitive should be minimally represented to help avoid "groupthink" and other major decision-making pitfalls.

5

How Senior Managers Think†

DANIEL J. ISENBERG

[*Harvard Business Review* editor's summary] *For the most part people view managers as rational, purposeful, and decisive. They see them as going through a series of stages of analysis before deciding what to do. The doing comes after the thinking. In his study of what senior managers think about and how they think, Daniel Isenberg found that this is only partly true. Most successful senior managers do not closely follow the classical rational model of first clarifying goals, assessing the situation, formulating options, estimating likelihoods of success, making their decision, and only then taking action to implement the decision. Nor do top managers select one problem at a time to solve, as the rational model implies.*

Instead of having precise goals and objectives, successful senior executives have general overriding concerns and think more often about how to do things than about what is being accomplished. In addition to depending on their ability to analyze, they also rely heavily on a mix of intuition and disciplined analysis in their decision making and incorporate their action on a problem into their diagnosis of it. The author discusses some of the implications of his findings on how managers can exercise and use the skills that senior management positions call for. . . .

> *It is not enough to have a good mind. The main thing is to use it well.*
>
> *René Descartes*

AUTHOR'S NOTE: Among the many people who have helped my research I want to single out Paul Lawrence and John Kotter. I also extend thanks to the corporate managers who have given freely of their time and ideas. Miriam Schustack made very helpful comments on a previous version of this article.

Jim LeBlanc phoned Steve Baum, who formerly worked in his division, to ask about the CEO's new corporate task force on quality control that wanted to meet with Jim. Jim, the head of the industrial equipment division of Tanner Corporation, thought that Steve, now director of technology, could help him figure out why the task force wanted to meet with him in two weeks.

"It's because you're doing so damn well down there, boss" Steve replied.

"Gee thanks. By the way, Steve, what's the agenda for Singer's staff meeting for next week?" (Singer was the president and Jim's boss.)

"Well, we're going to talk about the reorganization and look at the overhead reduction figures for each division. Then Singer's going to report on last week's executive committee meeting and his trip to Japan."

"How did it go?"

"His telex from Osaka sounded enthusiastic, but he just got in last night and I haven't seen him yet."

"Well," said Jim, "I guess we'll just have to see, but if you hear something, call me right away because if Osaka comes through I'm going to have to hustle to get ready, and you know how Bernie hates to shake it. Now, about the task force. . ."

In the space of three minutes, Jim LeBlanc got a lot done. In addition to collecting critical information about a task force that the CEO, with unusual fanfare, had personally commissioned one month ago, he also began to plan his approach to the upcoming staff meeting. He decided not to try to get a presentation by his marketing people on opportunities in the Far East on the agenda. Sensing that Singer was optimistic about the Osaka trip, Jim decided that he should get his people ready for the possibility that the deal would materialize, which meant pulling engineers off another project for a while.

What were the thinking processes that allowed Jim to get so much done so pointedly and so rapidly? What was going on in his mind during his conversation with Steve? How, given the incomplete and uncertain information that Steve gave him, did Jim conclude that the Japan deal was imminent?

For the past two years I have studied the thought processes used by more than a dozen very senior managers while on the job. (See the description of my research methodology, p. 107) The managers that I studied ranged in age from their lower 40s to their upper 50s, in managerial experience from 10 to 30 years, and in current job tenure from 4 months to 10 years. Their companies ranged from $1 billion divisions in *Fortune* "100" companies to $10 million entrepreneurial companies just beginning to take hold in the marketplace. Company products included low- and high-technology goods, and markets ranged from rapidly expanding to precipitately deteriorating. All but two of the executives were responsible for the overall performance of their business units. As all had been frequently promoted throughout their careers and were considered excellent performers across the board, they were a representative sample of today's successful business executives.

Two findings about how senior managers do *not* think stand out from this study. First, it is hard to pinpoint if or when they actually make decisions about major business or organizational issues on their own. And second, they seldom think in ways that one might simplistically view as "rational," i.e., they rarely systematically formulate goals, assess their worth, evaluate the probabilities of alternative ways of reaching them, and choose the path that maximizes expected return. Rather, managers frequently bypass rigorous, analytical planning altogether, particularly when they face difficult, novel, or extremely entangled problems. When they do use analysis for a prolonged time, it is always in conjunction with intuition.

Let me make myself clear. Obviously, decisions *do* get made in organizations and these *are* frequently justified by data and logic. In particular, when viewed retrospectively over a long time period, effective executives often appear quite rational. Yet when studying their concurrent thinking processes, being "rational" does not best describe what the manager presiding over the decision-making process thinks about nor *how* he or she thinks.

I have a fourfold purpose in this article. First, I want to present a more accurate and empirically grounded description of what goes on inside the minds of senior managers. (See the description of the good and bad news about cognition, p. 107) Second, I hope to offer a more accurate description of managerial thinking that should help provide a beginning language for talking about these elusive mental phenomena. Third, I hope that this language will also help to relieve some managers of the inconsistency between their view of how they are "supposed to" think and the thinking processes that, through experience, they have learned are actually quite effective. Fourth, I want to take advantage of successful senior managers' experiences to explore the managerial implications of their thinking processes.

What Senior Managers Think About

Senior managers tend to think about two kinds of problems: how to create effective organizational processes and how to deal with one or two overriding concerns, or very general goals. These two domains of thought underlie the two critical activities that John P. Kotter found general managers engaged in: developing and maintaining an extensive interpersonal network, and formulating an agenda.[1]

A FOCUS ON PROCESS

The primary focus of on-line managerial thinking is on organizational and interpersonal processes. By "process" I mean the ways managers bring people and groups together to handle problems and take action. Whether proposing a change in the executive compensation structure, establishing priorities for a diverse group of business units, consolidating redundant operations, or preparing for plant closings, a senior executive's conscious thoughts are foremost among the processes for accomplishing a change or implementing a decision: "Who are the key players here, and how can I get their support? Whom should I talk to first? Should I start by getting the production group's input? What kind of signal will that send to the marketing people? I can't afford to lose their commitment in the upcoming discussions on our market strategy."

During the first months of his tenure, one area general manager I studied asked all of his business unit management teams to evaluate their own units. Subsequently, the area manager and his staff spent a day or more with each team discussing the whole area, each business unit within it, and how the two interrelated. Although he was concerned with the substance of the business-unit priorities, uppermost in his mind was a series of process concerns: How could the review process help managers be increasingly committed to their goals? How could the process help managers to become increasingly aware of the interdependencies among business units? How did his business unit managers use their people in reviewing their business units? How much management depth existed in the units?

In addition to thinking about organizational processes, successful senior managers think a lot about interpersonal processes and the people they come in contact with. They try to understand the strengths and weaknesses of others, the relationships that are important to *them*, what *their* agendas and priorities are.

For example, the CEO of a small high-technology company spent over an hour with his personnel director, a woman he rated as having performed excellently so far and whom he saw as having great potential although still inexperienced. At the time of the discussion, the CEO was considering adopting a new top-management structure under which the personnel director would report to another staff member rather than directly to him.

The CEO explained the proposed change to the personnel director, pointing out that it was not definite and that he was soliciting her reactions. Managers' "maps" of people provide them with guides to action. In this case, because of his sense of the personnel director's needs, the CEO slowed the reorganizing process so that the people who reported to him could deal with the various issues that arose.

The CEO elaborately described to me his awareness of the personnel director's concern at being new and at being a woman, and her desire to be in direct contact with him. He also understood her worry that if she reported to someone lower than him, people would perceive that the new personnel function was not very important and she would lose power.

THE OVERRIDING CONCERN

The stereotypical senior executive pays a great deal of attention to the strategy of the business, carefully formulates goals, lays out quantified and clear objectives, and sets about to achieve these objectives in the most efficient way. Whereas senior executives certainly attend to specific strategies and objectives some of the time, in their day-to-day reality specific objectives lurk in the background, not in the forefront of their thoughts.

Approximately two-thirds of the senior managers I studied were preoccupied with a very limited number of quite general issues, each of which subsumed a large number of specific issues. This preoccupation persisted for anywhere from a month to several years and, when in effect, dominated the manager's attention and provided coherence to many of his or her chaotic and disorganized activities.

The general manager of one large division of an automotive company, for example, used the word "discipline" over a dozen times in the course of a two-hour interview. For him, this concept embodied his deep concern for creating order and predictability in a division that, in his view, had become too loose before he took it over. His concern for discipline appeared in a number of diverse actions—strongly discouraging his subordinates' fire-fighting mentality, criticizing their poor preparation for corporate reviews, introducing rigorous strategic planning, encouraging time management, putting out a yearly calendar with divisional and corporate meetings printed on it, publishing agendas for many of these meetings up to a year in advance, and, by keeping recent reports in the top drawer of his desk, forcing himself to review frequently the division's activities and performance.

Regardless of its substance, the overriding concern weaves its way in and out of all the manager's daily activities, at times achieving the dimensions of an all-consuming passion.

After his first 100 days in office, an area general manager described his experience turning around a subsidiary in these words:

"The personal cost of achieving our top priorities has been huge. I dropped all outside activities. Now I have a feeling of just having emerged, like a chap who's been taken by a surf wave and rolled. Suddenly he comes up and can look at daylight again. It has been like a single-minded rage or madness. At the end of the 100 days, somehow I have awakened. It was overwhelming."

Of course senior managers do think about the content of their businesses, particularly during crises and periodic business reviews. But this thinking is always in close conjunction with thinking about the process for getting *others* to think about the business. In other words,even very senior managers devote most of their attention to the tactics of implementation rather than the formulation of strategy.

How Senior Managers Think

In making their day-by-day and minute-by-minute tactical maneuvers, senior executives tend to rely on several general thought processes such as using intuition; managing a network of interrelated problems; dealing with ambiguity, inconsistency, novelty, and surprise; and integrating action into the process of thinking.

USING INTUITION

Generations of writers on the art of management have recognized that practicing managers rely heavily on intuition.[2] In general, however, people have a poor grasp of what intuition is. Some see it as the opposite of rationality, others use it as an excuse for capriciousness, and currently some view it as the exclusive property of a particular side of the brain.

Senior managers use intuition in at least five distinct ways. First, they intuitively sense when a problem exists. The chief financial officer of a leading technical products company, for example, forecast a difficult year ahead for the company and, based on a vague gut feel that something was wrong, decided to analyze one business group. "The data on the group were inconsistent and unfocused," he said after doing the analysis. "I had the sense that they were talking about a future that just was not going to happen, and I turned out to be right."

Second, managers rely on intuition to perform well-learned behavior patterns rapidly. Early on, managerial action needs to be thought through carefully. Once the manager is "fluent" at performance, however, and the behavior is programmed, executives can execute programs without conscious effort. In the words of one general manager:

"It was very instinctive, almost like you have been drilled in close combat for years and now the big battle is on, and you really don't have time to think. It's as if your arms, your feet, and your body just move instinctively. You have a preoccupation with working capital, a preoccupation with capital expenditure, a preoccupation with people, and one with productivity, and all this goes so fast that you don't even know whether it's completely rational, or it's part rational, part intuitive."

Intuition here refers to the smooth automatic performance of learned behavior sequences. This intuition is not arbitrary or irrational, but is based on years of painstaking practice and hands-on experience that build skills. After a while a manager can perform a sequence of actions in a seamless fabric of action and reaction without being aware of the effort.

A third function of intuition is to synthesize isolated bits of data and experience into an integrated picture, often in an "aha!" experience. In the words of one manager: "Synergy is always nonrational because it takes you beyond the mere sum of the parts. It is a nonrational, nonlogical thinking perspective."

Fourth, some managers use intuition as a check (a belt-and-suspenders approach) on the results of more rational analysis. Most senior executives are familiar with the formal decision analysis models and tools, and those that occasionally use such systematic methods for reaching decisions are leery of solutions that these methods suggest that run counter to their sense of the correct course of action.

Conversely, if managers completely trusted intuition, they'd have little need for rigorous and systematic analysis. In practice, executives work on an issue until they find a match between their "gut" and their "head." One manager explained to me, "Intuition leads me to seek out holes in the data. But I discount casual empiricism and don't act on it."

Fifth, managers can use intuition to bypass in-depth analysis and move rapidly to come up with a plausible solution. Used in this way, intuition is an almost instantaneous cognitive process in which a manager recognizes familiar patterns. In much the same way that people can immediately recognize faces that were familiar years ago, administrators have a repertoire of familiar problematic situations matched with the necessary responses. As one manager explained:

"My gut feel points me in a given direction. When I arrive there, then I can begin to sort out the issues. I do not do a deep analysis at first. I suppose the intuition comes from scar tissue, getting burned enough times. For example, while discussing the European budget with someone, suddenly I got the answer: it was hard for us to get the transfer prices. It rang a bell, then I ran some quick checks."

By now it should be clear that intuition is not the opposite of rationality, nor is it a random process of guessing. Rather, it is based on extensive experience both in analysis and problem solving and in implementation, and to the extent that the lessons of experience are logical and well-founded, then so is the intuition. Further, managers often combine gut feel with systematic analysis, quantified data, and thoughtfulness.

It should also be clear that executives use intuition during *all* phases of the problem-solving process: problem finding, problem defining, generating and choosing a solution, and implementing the solution. In fact, senior managers often ignore the implied linear progression of the rational decision-making model and jump opportunistically from phase to phase, allowing implementation concerns to affect the problem definition and perhaps even to limit the range of solutions generated.

PROBLEM MANAGEMENT

Managers at all levels work at understanding and solving the problems that arise in their jobs. One distinctive characteristic of top managers is that their thinking deals not with isolated and discrete items but with portfolios of problems, issues, and opportunities in which (1) many problems exist simultaneously, (2) these problems compete for some part of his or her immediate concern, and (3) the issues are interrelated.

The cognitive tasks in problem management are to find and define good problems, to "map" these into a network, and to manage their dynamically shifting priorities. For lack of a better term, I call this the process of problem management.

Defining the problem. After learning of a state health organization threat to exclude one of their major products from the list of drugs for which the state would reimburse buyers, top executives in a pharmaceutical company struggled to find a proper response. After some time, the managers discovered that the real problem was not the alleged drug abuse the availability of the drug on the street caused. Rather, the problem was budgetary: the health services department had to drastically reduce its budget and was doing so by trimming its list of reimbursable drugs. Once they redefined the problem, the pharmaceutical executives not only could work on a better, more real problem, but also had a chance to solve it—which they did.[3]

In another case, a division general manager discovered that, without his knowledge but with the approval of the division controller, one of his vice presidents had drawn a questionable personal loan from the company. The division manager told me how he defined the problem: "I could spend my time formulating rules to guide managers. But the real fundamental issue here was that I needed to expect and demand that my managers manage their resources effectively." Although he recognized the ethical components involved, he chose to define the problem as concerned with asset management rather than cheating. Because asset management was an issue the division frequently discussed, the manager felt that it was more legitimate and efficacious to define the problem in this way.

Making a network of problems. By forming problem categories, executives can see how individual problems interrelate. For instance, a bank CEO had a "network" of at least 19 related problems and issues that he was concerned about. Among these were: establishing credibility in international banking, strengthening the bank's role in corporate banking, increasing the range of financial services and products, being prepared to defensively introduce new products in response to competitors' innovations, developing systems to give product cost information, reducing operational costs, standardizing branch architecture, and utilizing space efficiently.

The bank CEO classified these problems in terms of broad issue categories. He found that many were related to the issue of expanding and broadening the banks' competence beyond consumer banking in which it was already firmly established. A second overarching issue was standardization of the bank's many branches with regard to architecture, physical layout, accounting systems, and so on.

Having an interrelated network of problems allows a manager to seize opportunities more flexibly and to use progress on one problem to achieve progress on another, related issue. The bank CEO likened himself to a frog on a lily pad waiting for the fly—the problem or issue—to buzz by. Having a mental network of problems helped him to realize the opportunities as they occurred.

Choosing which problem to work on. Although managers often decide to work on the problem that seems to offer the best opportunities for attack, determining which problems they ought to tackle can be hard. As one manager commented:

"I have to sort through so many issues at once. There are ten times too many. I use a number of defense mechanisms to deal with this overload—I use delaying actions, I deny the existence of problems, or I put problems in a mental queue of sorts. This is an uncomfortable process for me. My office and responsibility say I need to deal with all of these issues, so I create smoke or offer some grand theory as my only way to keep my own sanity. One of the frustrations is that I don't want to tell my people that their number one problems have lower priorities than they think they should get."

In my observations, how managers define and rank problems is heavily influenced by how easy the problems are to solve. Very shortly after perceiving that a problem exists, managers run a quick feasibility check to see if it is solvable. Only if they find it is solvable will they then invest further energy to understand its various ramifications and causes. In other words, managers tend not to think very much about a problem unless they sense that it is solvable. Contrary to some management doctrines, this finding suggests that a general concept of what is a possible solution often precedes and guides the process of conceptualizing a problem.

Thus, the two stages of problem analysis and problem solving are tightly linked and occur reiteratively rather than sequentially. By going back and forth between these two cognitive processes, managers define the array of problems facing them in terms that already incorporate key features of solutions and that thus make it easier for them to take action.

One outcome of this process is that managers have an organized mental map of all the problems and issues facing them. The map is neither static nor permanent; rather, managers continually test, correct, and revise it. In the words of one CEO, the executive "takes advantage of the best cartography at his command, but knows that that is not enough. He know that along the way he will find things that change his maps or alter his perceptions of the terrain. He trains himself the best he can in the detective skills. He is endlessly sending out patrols to learn greater detail, overflying targets to get some sense of the general battlefield."

Tolerating ambiguity. The senior managers that I observed showed an ability to tolerate and even thrive on high degrees of ambiguity and apparent inconsistency. As one top executive said:

"I think ambiguity can be destroying, but it can be very helpful to an operation. Ambiguities come from the things you can't spell out exactly. They yield a certain freedom you need as a chief executive officer not to be nailed down on everything. Also, certain people thrive on ambiguity, so I leave certain things ambiguous. The fact is we tie ourselves too much to linear plans, to clear time scales. I like to fuzz up time scales completely."

Because demands on a manager become both stronger and more divergent as responsibility increases, the need to tolerate apparent ambiguity and inconsistency also increases. For example, the top manager has to deal with stakeholders who may have adversarial roles. By responding positively to one set of demands, the manager automatically will create other conflicting sets of demands.

The reason I have called the inconsistency "apparent" is that senior managers tend to have ways of thinking that make issues seem less inconsistent. For example, the president of a leading high-technology company was considering whether to exercise or forgo an option to lease land on which to build expensive warehouse space for one of the divisions at the same time as the division was laying off workers for the first time in its history. "To spend a half million dollars on keeping the land and building warehouse space while the plant is laying off people looks terrible and makes no sense," he said, "but if next year is a good year, we'll need to be in a position to make the product."

Perceiving and understanding novelty. The managers I observed dealt frequently with novel situations that were unexpected and, in many cases, were impossible to plan for in advance. For example, one division general manager found himself with the task of selling his division, which was still developing a marketable product. In response to its shareholders, the corporation had shifted its strategy and thus decided to divest the fledgling division. How should the general manager look for buyers? If buyers were not forthcoming, would the corporation retain a stake to reduce the risk to potential new partners? How should he manage his people in the process of selling? Should he himself look for a new position or commit himself to a new owner? These were some of the unique questions the division head faced while selling his own division, and there was no industry experience to give him clear answers.

In general, the human mind is conservative. Long after an assumption is outmoded, people tend to apply it to novel situations. One way in which some of the senior managers I studied counteract this conservative bent is by paying attention to their feelings of *surprise* when a particular fact does not fit their prior understanding, and then by highlighting rather than denying the novelty. Although surprise made them feel uncomfortable, it made them take the cause seriously and inquire into it—"What is behind the personal loan by my vice president of sales that appears on the books? How extensive a problem is it?" "Why did the management committee of the corporation spend over an hour of its valuable time discussing a problem three levels down in my division?" "Now that we've shown the health services department beyond a reasonable doubt that this drug is not involved in drug abuse, why don't they reinstate it on the list?"

Rather than deny, downplay, or ignore disconfirmation, successful senior managers often treat it as friendly and in a way cherish the discomfort surprise creates. As a result, these managers often perceive novel situations early on and in a frame of mind relatively undistorted by hidebound notions.

What to Do About Thinking

Having looked at the inner workings of the managerial mind, what insights can we derive from our observations? Literally hundreds of laboratory and field studies demonstrate that the human mind is imperfectly rational, and dozens of additional articles, offering arguments based on every field of study from psychology to economics, explain why.[4] The evidence that we should curtail our impractical and overly ambitious expectations of managerial rationality is compelling.

Yet abandoning the rational ideal leaves us with two glaring problems. First, whether managers think in a linear and systematic fashion or not, companies still need to strive toward rational action in the attainment of corporate goals, particularly in their use of resources. Second, we still need to spell out what kinds of thinking processes are attainable and helpful to senior managers.

PROGRAM RATIONALITY INTO THE ORGANIZATION

Of course, rationality is desirable and should be manifest in the functioning of the company. One alternative to the vain task of trying to rationalize managers is to increase the rationality of organizational systems and processes. Although organizational behavior is never completely rational, managers can design and program processes and systems that will approach rationality in resource allocation and employment.

Decision support systems are one source of organization rationality. These generally computerized routines perform many functions ranging from providing a broad and quantitative data base, to presenting that data base in easily understandable form, to modeling the impact of decisions of various financial and other criteria, to mimicking expert judgment such as in the diagnosis and repair of malfunctioning equipment or in oil field exploration.

Another rational process that many businesses employ is strategic planning. Nonrational or partly rational managers can devise, implement, and use a plan that systematically assesses a company's strengths and weaknesses, logically extrapolates a set of its competencies, proposes a quantitative assessment of environmental constraints and resources, and performs all these tasks in a time-sequenced, linear fashion.

Of course, companies have used rational systems for information gathering, strategic planning, budgeting, human resource planning, environmental scanning and so forth for a long time. But I see these systems not only as useful but also as a necessary complement to a manager's apparent inability to be very systematic or rational in thought.

But is it possible for imperfectly rational managers to design even more perfectly rational systems? The answer is a qualified yes. There is evidence, for example, that with help people can design systems that are better than they are themselves at making judgments.[5] Creating organizational systems to improve on their own behavior is not new to managers. In order to still hear the beautiful sirens yet prevent himself being seduced by the music and throwing himself into the sea, Ulysses ordered his men to block their own ears with wax, bind him to the mast, and to tighten his bindings if he ordered them to let him go. Although Ulysses begged his sailors to release him, they obeyed his original orders and Ulysses succeeded in both hearing the sirens and surviving their perilous allure.[6]

Programming rationality into the organizational functioning is important for another reason: rational systems free senior executives to tackle the ambiguous, ill-defined tasks that the human mind is uniquely capable of addressing. Many senior managers today face problems—developing new products for embryonic markets, creating new forms of manufacturing operations, conceiving of innovative human resource systems—that are new to them and new to their companies and that they can deal with only extemporaneously and with a nonprogrammable artistic sense. In fact, it may even seem paradoxical that managers need to create rational systems in order to creatively and incrementally tackle the nonrecurrent problems that defy systematic approaches.

HONE INTELLECTUAL SKILLS

In the literature on managerial behavior there is disagreement as to how much or how often senior managers engage in thoughtful reflection. Many executives that I studied do make time for in-depth thinking, sometimes while they are alone, sometimes with their peers or subordinates, and sometimes in active experimentation.

Furthermore, most senior managers I studied constantly maintain and sharpen their intellectual abilities in order to better analyze their current or past experiences. Rigorous thinking is a way of life for them, not a task they try to avoid or to expedite superficially.

These senior managers read books outside their fields, engage in enthusiastic discussions of political and economic affairs, attend academic lectures and management seminars, and tackle brain teasers such as word problems, chess, and crossword puzzles. One company president I studied is a regular theatergoer who can discuss Shakespearian and contemporary plays at great length, while another often immerses himself in classical music and allows ideas about different work-related issues to float around in his consciousness. These activities are valuable not only for their content but also for the thinking processes that they establish, develop, and refine. Whether managers indulge in such "blue sky" irrelevant activities at work or outside, they are developing critical mental resources that they can then apply to problems that arise in their jobs.

THINK WHILE DOING

One of the implications of the intuitive nature of executive action is that "thinking" is inseparable from acting. Since managers often "know" what is right before they can analyze and explain it, they frequently act first and think later. Thinking is inextricably tied to action in what I call thinking/acting cycles, in which managers develop thoughts about their companies and organizations not by analyzing a problematic situation and then acting, but by thinking and acting in close concert. Many of the managers I studied were quite facile at using thinking to inform action and vice versa.

Given the great uncertainty of many of the management or business issues that they face, senior managers often instigate a course of action simply to learn more about an issue: "We bought that company because we wanted to learn about that business." They then use the results of the action to develop a more complete understanding of the issue. What may appear as action for action's sake is really the result of an intuitive understanding that analysis is only possible in the light of experience gained while attempting to solve the problem. Analysis is not a passive process but a dynamic, interactive series of activity and reflection.

One implication of acting/thinking cycles is that action is often part of defining the problem, not just of implementing the solution. Frequently, once they had begun to perceive the symptoms, but before they could articulate a problem, the managers I studied talked to a few people to collect more information and confirm what they already knew. The act of collecting more data more often than not changed the nature of the problem, in part because subordinates then realized that the problem was serious enough to warrant the boss's attention. Managers also often acted in the absence of clearly specified goals, allowing these to emerge from the process of clarifying the nature of the problem.

Yet how often do managers push their subordinates to spell out *their* goals clearly and specify *their* objectives? A creative subordinate will always be able to present a plausible and achievable goal when pressed, but in the early stages of a tough problem it is more helpful for managers to provide a receptive forum in which their people can play around with an issue, "noodle" it through, and experiment. Sometimes it will be necessary for managers to allow subordinates to act in the absence of goals to achieve a clearer comprehension of what is going on, and even at times to *discover* rather than achieve the organization's true goals.

MANAGE TIME BY MANAGING PROBLEMS

All managers would like to accomplish more in less time. One of the implications of the process of mapping problems and issues is that when a manager addresses any particular problem, he or she calls a number of related problems or issues to mind at the same time. One by-product is that a manager can attain economies of effort.

For example, when working on a problem of poor product quality, a division manager might see a connection between poor quality and an inadequate production control system and tackle both problems together. To address the issues, she could form a cross-functional task force involving her marketing manager, who understands customers' tolerance for defects. (One reason for bringing him in might be to prepare him for promotion in two or three years.) She might intend the task force to reduce interdepartmental conflicts as well as prepare a report that she could present to corporate headquarters.

Managers can facilitate the process of creating a problem network in many ways. They can ask their staff to list short- and long-term issues that they think need to be addressed, consolidate these lists, and spend some time together mapping the interrelationships. Or they can ask themselves how an issue fits into other nonproblematic aspects of the company or business unit. How does product quality relate to marketing strategy? To capital expenditure guidelines? To the company's R&D center with a budget surplus? To the new performance appraisal system? To the company's recent efforts in affirmative action? To their own career plans? Managers should never deal with problems in isolation. They should always ask themselves what additional related issues they should be aware of while dealing with the problem at hand.[7]

SOME SUGGESTIONS

A number of suggestions on how managers can improve their thinking emerge from my study of senior managers' thought processes:

- Bolster intuition with rational thinking. Recognize that good intuition requires hard work, study, periods of concentrated thought, and rehearsal.
- Offset tendencies to be rational by stressing the importance of values and preferences, of using imagination, and of acting with an incomplete picture of the situation.
- Develop skills at mapping an unfamiliar territory by, for example, generalizing from facts and testing generalities by collecting more data.
- Pay attention to the simple rules of thumb—heuristics—that you have developed over the years. These can help you bypass many levels of painstaking analysis.
- Don't be afraid to act in the absence of complete understanding, but then cherish the feelings of surprise that you will necessarily experience.
- Spend time understanding what the problem or issue is.
- Look for the connections among the many diverse problems and issues facing you to see their underlying relationships with each other. By working on one problem you can make progress on others.
- Finally, recognize that your abilities to think are critical assets that you need to manage and develop in the same way that you manage other business assets.

Research Methodology

In studying these dozen executives, I conducted intensive interviews, observed them on the job, read documents, talked with their colleagues and, in some cases, subordinates, and engaged them in various exercises in which they recounted their thoughts as they did their work. I also reported my observations and inferences back to the managers to get feedback. I spent anywhere from 1 to 25 days studying each manager (the mode was two and a half days in field interviews and observation).

Some Good and Bad News
About Cognition

Although the study of cognition is not new, in the past 30 years the popularity and practical importance of the "cognitive sciences" have increased dramatically, adding to our knowledge of the capabilities and limitations of the human mind. The news is both "good" and "bad" in terms of our accuracy as judges and decision makers.

SOME GOOD NEWS

The good news is that each of us possesses a wide range of cognitive capabilities, including many that even the most powerful computers cannot match. For all intents and purposes the long-term storage capacity of the human memory is unlimited, capable of storing perhaps trillions of bits of information. Furthermore, much of this memory is almost immediately accessible.

The human mind is also capable of performing very complicated simulations such as giving directions to someone on how to get to an office from an airport or rehearsing an upcoming meeting. We are also capable of making huge inferential leaps with rarely a hitch. Try interpreting the following sentences: "The manager prepared the forecast using an accepted inflation estimate. He knew that it was imprecise but figured that it was better than no projection at all." Who is "he"? What is "it"? What does "projection" refer to? We know what these sentences mean, yet to interpret them correctly required the reader to make a number of inferences, which he or she usually makes with unhesitating accuracy.

Finally, we are capable of using our unlimited memory, our rapid retrieval system, and our unconscious rules of inference to attain extremely high levels of skill, such as playing chess, analyzing stocks, conducting performance appraisals, or speaking a language. These skills do not come easily, requiring years of experience and many thousands of hours of practice. Nevertheless, when we use them we compress years of experience and learning into split seconds. This compression is one of the bases of what we call intuition as well as of the art of management.

SOME BAD NEWS

The same cognitive processes that underlie our greatest mental accomplishments also account for incorrigible flaws in our thinking. For instance, we easily believe that salient events occur more frequently than they really do: for example, despite the fact that dozens of examples exist where missed budgets did not lead to termination, managers interpret Sam's being fired for not making a budget as "There is a good chance that division heads who do not meet budgeted profit objectives will get axed."

A second family of flaws arises from our overconfidence in our own expertise at making complex judgments. Various cognitive biases such as the "hindsight bias," our retrospective confidence in judgments that we hesitated about making at the time ("I *knew* it wouldn't work when she first proposed it"), and our tendency to search for confirming but not for disconfirming evidence of our judgments, conspire to exaggerate that belief.

And finally, research has shown that when presented with data, we are not very good at assessing the degree of relationship among variables—even though this skill is critical for successful management. Unless the relationships are very obvious, we tend to rely on preconceptions and perceive illusory correlations.

A number of excellent books on human cognition are in print. For a nontechnical discussion of the good news, Morton Hunt's *The Universe Within* (Simon & Schuster, 1982), is a good starting place. A more technical discussion of human cognition is Stephen K. Reed's *Cognition: Theory and Applications* (Brooks/Cole, 1982). A somewhat technical but very comprehensive presentation of the bad news can be found in Daniel Kahneman, Paul Slovic, and Amos Tversky's edited volume, *Judgment Under Uncertainty: Heuristics and Biases* (Cambridge University Press, 1982).

Notes

1. John P. Kotter, *The General Managers* (New York: Free Press, 1982).

2. See, for example, Chester I. Barnard, *The Functions of the Executive* (Cambridge: Harvard University Press, 1938), also Henry Mintzberg, "Planning on the Left Side and Managing on the Right", *HRB*, July-August, 1976, p. 49.

3. See my study, "Drugs and Drama: The Effects of Two Dramatic Events in a Pharmaceutical Company on Managers' Cognitions," Working Paper #83-55 (Boston: Harvard Business School, 1983).

4. Some of Herbert K. Simon's classic work on bounded rationality and "satisficing" is collected in *Models of Thought* (New Haven: Yale University Press, 1979). More recently, Amos Tversky, Daniel Kahneman, and other psychologists have described the mechanisms producing imperfect judgment and normative choice. See, for example, Daniel Kahneman, Paul Slovic, and Amos Tversky, ed., *Judgment Under Uncertainty: Heuristics and Biases* (Cambridge, UK: Cambridge University Press, 1982).

5. Louis R. Goldberg, "Man vs Model of Man: A Rationale, Plus Some Evidence for a Method of Improving on Clinical Inferences," *Psychological Bulletin*, 1970, 73, p. 422.

6. Jon Elster, *Ulysses and the Sirens: Studies in Rationality and Irrationality* (Cambridge, Mass.: Cambridge University Press, 1979).

7. For an interesting application of these ideas to a different leadership setting, see my chapter, "Some Hows and Whats of Managerial Thinking: Implications for Future Army Leaders" in *Military Leadership on the Future Battlefield* (New York: Pergamon Press, 1984).

6

Intuition
What Separates Executives from Managers[†]

STEPHEN C. HARPER

Each year, business magazines report the salaries and benefit pack-
ages of many of the top executives in corporate America. Each year,
the same question is raised: "How can any company justify paying
one person so much money?" In this era of sophisticated software
programs designed to model corporate strategies, how can a CEO's
annual pay package be more than what many of the high-powered
computers on the market today cost? Most people will agree that
the salaries for top professional athletes are beyond reason. Has the
same ridiculous trend now begun in our corporate suites?

The question can be stated in simple terms: What qualities do
these people have that justify a salary four to five times that of most
vice presidents and ten to fifteen times that of middle managers?
Can one CEO really be worth more than 25 freshly minted MBAs?

Why did it take ITT nearly three years to find a replacement for
Harold Geneen? Is the right stuff so rare that firms have been
forced to try offices of the president, with three or four people
sharing the duties, because the board of directors was unable to
groom or steal a new chief executive?

Has our environment become too complicated and have our
firms grown too large for any one person to be able to comprehend
and manage? Or is it just that there are so few people who are truly
able to meet the challenges facing today's firms that the ones who
are capable can command at least $1 million a year?

It is ironic that in the midst of the computer age, human talent
may still be a scarce commodity. Herein may lie the answer to the
perennial question. These top executives seem to possess skills

†SOURCE: Reprinted from *Business Horizons* September - October, 1988. Copyright 1988 by the
Foundation for the School of Business at Indiana University. Used with permission.

other managers lack. In addition to the usual managerial skills, they possess intuitive skills that provide them with different perspectives and different approaches for managing in these turbulent times. Whether called insight, judgment, intuition, executive ESP, wisdom, or a sixth sense, these skills help executives see things that other people don't see and incorporate factors computers still cannot handle. This quality, more than any other, may be what separates the true executive from the hundreds of thousands of managers.

In a world moving toward quantification, most important business decisions include qualitative and relatively intangible factors that continue to elude even the most sophisticated mathematical models. Some person still has to make the decisions that will have a definite impact on whether the firm will be around in the next century, even the next decade. This situation is captured in a recent advertisement for Columbia University's Executive Program that shows a picture of an executive alone looking out a window, with the caption, "You've surrounded yourself with people who are paid to give you good advice. And they do. . . . Then the ball's in your court." This is where the top executive earns his or her salary. Like the brain surgeon, the top executive may not have to use intuition very often. But when the data do not provide a clear answer, these executives have the uncanny ability to sense what should be done and the courage of their convictions to act decisively.

Executives vs. Managers

The higher the position in the organization, the more the job involves conceptual rather than technical matters, a long-term rather than a short-term time horizon, and issues of what type of business the firm should be rather than issues of how the firm should do business. Thus, top executives need to be concerned with the big picture. In research by Daniel Isenberg, Jr., two-thirds of the senior managers studied were preoccupied with a very limited number of quite general issues, each of which subsumed a large number of specific issues.[1] According to Leonard Sayles, "True intuitives are rare. They . . . appear in top management as a source of brilliant new strategies that are not slight modifications or extensions of what has been done before. They are great synthesizers — taking a large quantity of current information about tastes, trends, and demographics and sensing what the real implications will be that others can't see because they are too close to the present."[2] Irving Shapiro, as chairman of the board for DuPont, was noted for his intuitive skills. One of his associates said, "One of Shapiro's greatest gifts was his ability to put complex and often emotional issues into simple, practical terms."[3]

The ability to distill tangible and intangible factors and to see the forest without getting lost in the trees is a mark of the true executive. This is not to say that the trees are not important; they are. Top executives, however, must delegate the job of looking at the trees, also known as running the numbers, to their staff specialists and middle managers. Only then are top executives able to concentrate on the forest — what the numbers mean and don't mean. According to John Rockart, "These executives are, and must be, dependent on future-oriented, rapidly assembled, most often subjective, and informal information delivered by word of mouth from trusted advisers."[4]

The ability to see the big picture and the opportunities other, less intuitive executives cannot see may explain why Steve Jobs believed that people would buy personal computers and why Fred Smith was so sure the concept of Federal Express would succeed. They capitalized on their intuitive skills and changed the way people live and work today. As entrepreneurs, they were gamblers. But they knew the opportunities were there. They also know that if they studied every factor many times, someone else would harvest the opportunities. Today's truly great leaders, in both the public and private sectors, are visionaries and pathfinders. They stand out because of their ability to size up the situation and their sense of timing. In a recent study of 90 leaders, Warren Bennis and Burt Namus found they all seemed to know intuitively, to paraphrase Kenny Rogers, when to hold and when to fold.[5]

The Value of Intuition

Top executives seem to blend their visions of the future with their intuitive skills when they venture forth into new industries, products, and processes. Research conducted by Charles Ford indicated that "in their approach to decisions, perhaps the most profound characteristic that distinguished (intuitive) decision makers from other executives is their propensity for making high-risk decisions.[6] These executive follow the preface to Star Trek: they are not afraid to "boldly go where no one has gone before."

Because of their experience in making judgment calls, intuitive executives have the courage to sail into uncharted waters. Most managers are reluctant to make a decision—even though one must be made—because they do not have enough data or prior precedent. The intuitive executive, however, will not hesitate; he will tap his knowledge for direction and action. David Mahoney, former chairman of Norton Simon, credits his judgment with helping him make his most difficult business decisions.[7] It was also for this reason that NASA selected pilots who had flown in all sorts of conditions to be Mercury astronauts. NASA executives knew that situations could arise that may not have preformulated answers or when time would be short, and the astronauts would have to make decisions without the benefit of computer simulations or additional studies. In these situations their intuitive skills would have a significant influence on the mission's success and their personal safety. NASA officials knew intuition is like a parachute. You hope it will not be used, but when all the sophisticated systems cannot help you, it's nice to have around!

Intuitive executives are characterized not just by having different perspectives; they also tend to be more perceptive of organizational situations. They come up with dramatically different, usually revolutionary ways to address the problems and opportunities that exist in times of change. Yet intuition is not merely coming up with answers to pressing questions. Intuition is also evident in the types of questions asked. As a manager ascends the organization, his or her job becomes one of identifying the questions that will need to be answered, not answering those questions. As Peter Drucker noted, "When approaching a business problem, don't try to come up with the answers. . . . Focus on what the problems are. . . . If you get the wrong answer to the right question, you usually have a chance to fix it. . . . But if you get the right answer to the wrong question, you're sunk. . . . And business does altogether too much of that."[8]

Top executives frequently go one step further by coupling anticipatory management with intuition. The true function of the executive is to create an environment in which the firm comes up with the answers before any one else is even aware of the questions. For this to happen executives must have foresight, the perceptiveness to identify the real questions, and the ability to flexibly allocate resources to cultivate and capitalize on emerging opportunities. This last point, however, raises an interesting question: Are top executives really more intuitive, or do they merely occupy positions where they do not have to get approval to implement their ideas? It may be true that lower-level managers have to present their ideas to top management for approval before they are allowed to run with them, but on the whole middle managers and staff specialists appear reluctant to act in the absence of thorough analysis.

Weston Agor's study of 2,000 managers indicated that top executives rated significantly higher in intuition than middle or low-level managers.[9] Whether these top executives developed and refined their intuitive skills while at the top, or were promoted to the top because they possessed and utilized more intuitive skills than fellow middle managers, is not certain.

Intuition vs. Quantitative Analysis

In the last few years terms have been coined to characterize the reluctance of managers and staff specialists to make decisions. In the early 1970s *Business Week* used the term "MBA Syndrome" to describe the flocking of business-school graduates to staff positions that serve as sanctuaries for people who want to avoid being on the firing line. To update Teddy Roosevelt, if you can't take the heat, get an MBA and find a nice secure staff job running the numbers in a *Fortune* 500 firm! Thomas J. Watson, Jr., while chairman of IBM, expressed serious concern about the cautious attitudes of so many young men in middle management. According to Watson, "They seemed reluctant to stick their necks out or to bet on a hunch . . . I wish we could stir them up a bit and encourage a little more recklessness among this group of decision makers.[10]

Middle managers today need to be willing and able to handle the intangible side of the firm if they are to show they can successfully meet the challenges they would face as executives. Even with IBM's state-of-the-art technology, Watson was quick to note that "every time IBM moved ahead, it was because someone was willing to take a chance, put his head on the block, and try something new."[11] Peters and Waterman provided a 1980s version of this phenomenon with their "paralysis by analysis." When you try to eliminate risk, you are probably eliminating action. In describing the qualities of the excellent companies, they found that "tools didn't substitute for thinking. Intellect didn't overpower wisdom. Analysis didn't impede action."[12] The purpose of planning is not merely to develop plans: it is to formulate plans that will be implemented and improve performance.

Intuition is not to be confused with flying by the seat of one's pants or relying solely on gut feelings. If a decision continuum was formed, using none of the data available would be at one end and using 100 percent of the information available would be at the other end. Intuition would be found in the gray area in between, toward the "use of data" side (we hope).

Intuition is not the opposite of quantitative analysis, nor is it an attempt to eliminate quantitative analysis. The need to understand and use intuition exists because few strategic business decisions have the benefit of complete, accurate, and timely information. It would be easier to manage if we lived in a world that was totally quantifiable and predictable. As long as corporations exist in a world of rapid and unprecedented change, however, intuition will play a significant role in decision-making processes. And although many top executives may like the excitement of making judgment calls, many actually welcome efforts to find ways to make management more scientific. By having fewer decisions to make, executives will be able to concentrate more of their time on areas that require their intuitive skills.

Executives need to recognize the value of quantitative analysis and use their intuition to help size up the situation and come up with solutions when quantitative information is not available. Executives who do not incorporate relevant data and utilize proven mathematical models are destined to fail. Operating from the "I've already made up my mind, don't confuse me with the facts" mode is not management by intuition; it is management by ignorance. As Drucker noted, "I believe in intuition only if you discipline it. The 'hunch' artists, the ones who make a diagnosis but don't check it out with the facts, with what they observe, are the ones who, in medicine, kill people and, in management, kill businesses."[13]

The development of intuitive skills may in fact be more closely related to running the numbers than most intuitives would like to accept. Of all the executives to manage in recent years, Harold Geneen had the reputation for running the numbers more than anyone else at the top. Geneen, however, made the following statement:

At ITT, we always used the numbers. However, the numbers will not tell you what to do. The key issue in business is to find out what is happening behind those numbers. Numbers serve as a thermometer that measures the health of an enterprise. Once you start digging into those areas that the numbers represent, then you get into the guts of the business. You don't want your managers to manage by the numbers . . . this is like treating the thermometer, rather than the patient. Comprehension seeps into your brain by a process of osmosis and gradually you find yourself at ease with the numbers and what they really represent.[14]

Management can be viewed as a five-step process: awareness, understanding, making decisions, initiating change, and achieving desired results. The awareness stage is important because it includes identification of where the firm should be in the future as well as where it is now. Accordingly, this step is an attempt to identify all the factors that will need to be considered in the decision-making step. The awareness stage includes the collection of quantitative data as well as the use of intuitive skills to define present and future states of affairs.

The understanding stage focuses on mapping the relationships between various factors. Mathematical modeling is also useful here, at least for depicting relationships. But identification of the multitude of factors at play is difficult enough. Depicting the relationships between the factors in most policy-level decisions is nearly impossible, even with the most advanced computer software. This is particularly evident in econometric modeling and forecasting. Even with all the coefficients, exponents, and functions, too many factors remain that are continuously changing for any model to represent reality. Making policy-level decisions is similar to investing in the stock market. You have to gather and analyze all the information available. But you ultimately have to rely on what you feel the future holds and what the numbers mean. Intuition therefore plays a key role in the development of an understanding of the situation (a prerequisite to decision making).

One of the most interesting dilemmas faced by executives involves the role information plays in the decision-making process. Either there is too little information or too much. It has already been noted that intuition plays a key role by filling in the blanks when there is not enough information. Intuition may also be important when there is too much information. As the president of Heinz, Anthony J. F. O'Reilly, indicated, "The information explosion crosses and criss-crosses executive desks with a great deal of data. Much of this is only partly digested and much of it irrelevant."[15] According to Harold Geneen, "The highest art of professional management requires the ability to 'smell' a real fact from all the others."[16] Theodore Roznak made an interesting point about the relative limitations of computers. He noted that "computer boosters confuse data with ideas and mistake information with knowledge."[17] It is an interesting paradox that in the middle of the computer revolution, the intuitive skill to sift through all the information—to see the forest through the trees—may be as important as the information itself.

Left Hemisphere vs. Right Hemisphere

It is widely recognized that the left side of the brain is the base of analytical activities, whereas the right side is geared to more intuitive processes. In the last few decades, management theory and education have been far more concerned with the left side of the brain. American managers have prided themselves on how professional, systematic, and rational they are when conducting corporate affairs. Academicians and practitioners have made diligent efforts to make management a science. They have tried to develop models and formulas so people will not have to make judgment calls. The situation is not that different from the effort to establish bureaucratic organizations a few decades ago. At that time few people in the work force had much education, so organizational processes were established to minimize individual decision making and insure the consistency of operations. We call the newer version of bureaucracy "management science." The effort to develop formulas to help managers make decisions is to be commended, but we must recognize that management will also be an art as long as there are situational factors that cannot be quantified.

The formal study of management is still in its infancy. The study of economics has been around a lot longer, but economics still remains more of an art than a science. As someone once said, "Economics is as close to being a science as astrology is to astronomy!" Those in the field of management must recognize that models and rules are not the whole picture. Formulas exist to improve management; they are not substitutes for managers.

One of the reasons the "science" side of management has received far more attention than the "art" side is that it is easier to teach the formulas than the way to find the uniqueness in a situation. The philosophy adopted by many business schools today is if that you can't teach students the art of management, then teach them the tools of management. Unfortunately, students graduate believing that knowing the formulas is all it takes to manage. After graduation they have the rude awakening that organizational life also includes human behavior that continues to elude formulas and an environment that won't stay still long enough to be measured. It is because of these realities that the right side—the more intuitive side—of the brain needs to receive a commensurate share of attention in management education.

But increasing the amount of time devoted to increasing intuitive skills is not enough. It is not a question of which side of the brain is most important, or even a question of which is easier to teach. The most important point is that to meet the challenges ahead, managers at all levels must not only strengthen their skills in both areas; they must learn to use them together. For years people have argued about which side of the brain is the most important. This argument is not too different from the seemingly endless debate in businesses and business schools over whether finance is more important than marketing. These debates are not just exercises in futility; they continue to separate factions that should be working together. Our educational and occupational programs may have gone too far in promoting specialization. Business may have the same problem as medicine—too many specialists and too few generalists.

Because today's environment is becoming increasingly complex, businesses need people who can both develop models and formulas for dealing with the complexity, and handle the turbulence and ambiguity that come with change. Our educational and corporate training programs have come a long way in the last few years. Intuitive education however, remains in the dark ages. The true mission of intuitive education should not be to train a new breed of intuitives but to enhance the intuitive skills of people who are also developing their left-side, analytical skills. According to Louis Pondy, "The rational and the intuitive are equal partners, each providing the context within which the other can operate; neither makes sense alone."[18] The answer to the question, which side of the brain is more important, is that both sides are equally important.

Certain situations may lend themselves better to quantitative analysis. Other situations may necessitate intuitive interpretation. Few situations, however, are likely to be exclusively right or left-brain problems. Executives and managers will need to develop and utilize a combined-hemispheres mental framework if they are to successfully meet the challenges ahead.

Developing the Right Side While Utilizing the Left

Intuition is like a muscle. To work well, it needs to be strengthened and exercised. Although certain aspects of intuition can be taught, most people develop their intuitive skills through experience. As Geneen noted, being able to understand and go beyond the numbers comes from extensive experience running the numbers. Weston Agor's study of intuition reported, "Many top executives stressed that good intuitive decisions were, in part, based on input from facts and experience gained over the years, combined and integrated with a well-honed sensitivity or openness to other, more unconscious processes."[19]

Intuition draws on our subconscious mental processes and incorporates previous experiences to foster new insights. The development and deliberate use of one's subconscious powers appears to strengthen intuitive skills. The subconscious is not only faster than conscious thought, it is also more flexible. Conscious thought is linear in nature and prone to tunnel vision. The subconscious is capable of lateral thinking, when the mind runs freely through the infinite amount of information stored in the brain. With lateral thinking the mind may combine seemingly unrelated facts and come up with innovative approaches for addressing problems that conscious thought had not solved. The conscious mind is regimented; it tends to go through the front door. The subconscious is not inhibited; it will come through the back door, the windows, or even down the chimney in its pursuit of a better way to do things and better things to do.

One of the best ways to tap the power of the subconscious is to incorporate the idea of mental incubation. Incubation is the process of giving the subconscious time to run free after all the relevant facts of a situation have been gathered and analyzed. Whether it is called letting one sleep on it or giving the ideas a chance to jell before making a decision, intuitive executives have learned the value of utilizing their subconscious.

Most top executives believe that being on the firing line may be the best place for young, rising managers to develop their intuitive skills. If these people are given the opportunity to make frequent decisions, they also develop confidence in their ability to make judgment calls. One of the classic examples of giving people lots of rope but not enough to hang themselves took place when Thomas Watson, Jr., was running IBM. A young executive had been given the responsibility to oversee a major project, which turned out to be a disaster. Watson called the nervous executive into his office and asked him if he knew why he had been summoned. The young executive exclaimed, "To be fired!" Watson, in the true IBM tradition, responded, "Fired? We can't afford to let you go. We just gave you a $10 million dollar education. We want you to stay around and show what you learned!" Top management at IBM realized long ago that experience may be one of the best teachers. Their management-development philosophy reflects the immortal words of General Bolivar Buckner: "Judgment comes from experience and experience comes from bad judgment." The value of learning from one's experiences is reinforced by the following statement by an executive interviewed by Daniel Isenberg: "I suppose intuition comes from scar tissue, getting burned enough times."[20] The time will come when managers will have to make decisions without the benefit of complete information. The best way to prepare them for those times is to put them today in situations where they are given the opportunity to stand on their own two feet.

The Behavioral Side of Intuition

A person's level of self-confidence can determine whether he or she will utilize intuitive skills. Some people feel very comfortable using their intuition, while others will use it only as a last resort. As stated earlier, intuition is most often used when there is not enough information. The very nature of decision making under uncertainty implies risk. Three types of risk are associated with intuition. The first type is associated with drawing on one's intuitive skills. If your decision proves unsuccessful, then the question may be posed, "Whose hare-brained idea was that one?" Some executives have been known to make up their minds and then seek out tangible data to reinforce the decision so other, less intuitive people will find the idea more acceptable.

The second type of risk involves going against the numbers. Corporate annals are full of times when executives deliberately chose a plan of action other than the one that received the most quantitative support. If the course of action is successful, then the executive may be heralded as a genius. Even Harold Geneen went in the opposite direction from the numbers on a few occasions. Geneen acquired the Sheraton hotel chain even though all the numbers indicated that the hospitality industry was not a good investment at that time. When Geneen recommended that ITT acquire coal-mining properties, he used his success with the Sheraton acquisition as ammunition to support the coal acquisition—which was not supported by the numbers either. Spectators to this process, however, may postulate that it is more luck than genius at play. To them it is just a matter of time before executives who deliberately go against numbers fall flat on their faces. Geneen's intuition was right about Sheraton, but his decision to invest in high-sulfur coal was certainly not one of his finer moments.

Skeptics will make every effort to dissociate themselves from executives who take the second type of risk. By keeping their distance, they will not be found guilty by association when the eventual failure comes. The second type of risk is the most personal type of risk. Going against the numbers means you are opening yourself up to, "You have a lot of gall to deliberately ignore all the data. Who do you think you are?" If an executive makes the first type of mistake, he uses poor judgment. But when an executive makes the second type of mistake, he may be on the street looking for another job.

The third type of risk does not tend to be visible. For some people it may actually be a way to avoid risk. This type of risk associated with covering your hide with data is similar to paralysis by analysis. If an individual is reluctant to make a decision, he may blame his hesitancy on a lack of data. Unlike the executive who has learned to use his or her intuitive skills to supplement the data, the insecure person will try to throw as much data as possible at the decision. In this situation, the quantity of data serves as a security blanket. The person avoids risk by saying, "We don't have enough information to make a decision at this point." If the decision proves unsuccessful, he will quickly cover his hide by stating, "I can't be blamed for this mistake, the data clearly indicated . . ." or "I told them all along that we didn't have enough data to go ahead." Of the three types of risks, this one may be the most dangerous to the organization in the long run. Organizations will need to be more entrepreneurial in the years ahead. The "cover your hide with data" approach to decision making can be a cancer that saps the firm's ability to go where no firm has gone before.

Two other behavioral aspects of intuition should be noted. Many people who possess intuitive skills have difficulty communicating their thoughts to others in the firm. Intuition by its very nature is relatively intangible. Feelings are more difficult to communicate than data. The intuitive executive may be operating from a clear mental map, but other people may be lost and less willing to follow.

The other behavioral characteristic worth noting about intuitive executives is that they like operating in environments where change is commonplace. They like the challenge of thinking on their feet. The worst thing that can be done to them is to put them in a bureaucratic position. It is similar to having an emergency room physician filing insurance forms. In a world full of challenges and opportunities, the ultimate sin in human resources would be to not cultivate and capitalize on intuitive talents. Strategically placing people with intuitive skills in areas that will make them utilize their skills is essential. Some of the best places for intuitive people are new product development, project management, management consulting, and policy-level positions.

Intuition can play a valuable part in corporate decision making. The question is not whether it should be used. It can be developed under supportive conditions. And it is not a matter of whether the right side of the brain is superior to the left side. Decision making should incorporate a combined-brain mental framework.

The renewed interest in intuition is a reflection of our times. Managers are recognizing that not everything can be quantified and that times of change require approaches that have never been tried before. According to Peters and Waterman, "It is probably only the intuitive leap that will let us solve problems in the complex world."[21] The ability to size up the situation, integrate and synthesize large amounts of data or deal with incomplete information, and have the courage to find better ways to do things and better things to do, will be of immeasurable value in the years ahead. Executives will need to be explorers. They may have the latest technology, but they will also need to rely on their feel for the situation to guide them as they steer their firms through uncharted waters.

Notes

1. Daniel J. Isenberg, "How Senior Managers Think," *Harvard Business Review*, November-December 1984, p. 84.

2. Leonard Sayles, *Leadership* (New York: McGraw-Hill, 1979), p. 222.

3. Don Hellriegel and John W. Slocum, Jr., *Organizational Behavior* (New York: West Publishing Company, 1976), p. 235.

4. John F. Rockart, "Chief Executives Define Their Own Data Needs," *Harvard Business Review*, March-April 1979, p. 81.

5. Warren Bennis and Burt Namus, *Leaders* (New York: Harper and Row, 1985), p. 61.

6. Charles H. Ford, "The Elite Decision Makers: What Makes Them Different?" *Human Resource Management*, Winter 1977, p. 17.

7. John Naisbett and Patricia Aburdene, *Re-inventing the Corporation* (New York: Warner Books, 1985), p. 70.

8. Ron Nelson, "How To Be a Manager," *Success*, July-August 1985, p. 69.

9. Weston H. Agor, "The Logic of Intuition: How Executives Make Important Decisions," *Organizational Dynamics*, Winter 1986, p. 9.

10. Thomas J. Watson, Jr., *A Business and Its Beliefs* (New York: McGraw-Hill, 1963), p. 60.

11. Watson (note 10), p. 60.

12. Thomas J. Peters and Robert H. Waterman, *In Search of Excellence* (New York: Harper and Row, 1982), p. 13.

13. Nelson (note 8), p. 68.

14. "The Case for Managing by the Numbers," *Fortune*, October 1, 1984, p. 80.

15. Interview with Anthony J. F. O'Reilly *M.I.S. Quarterly*, March 1977, p. 7.

16. Patricia O'Toole, "No Patience for Genius," *Success*, October 1984, p. 79.

17. "Throwing Cold Water on All That Computer Hype," *Business Week*, April 28, 1986, p. 10.

18. Louis R. Pondy, "The Union of Rationality and Intuition in Management Action," in S. Srivasta, ed., *The Executive Mind* (San Francisco: Jossey-Bass, 1984), p. 181.

19. Agor (note 9), p. 8.

20. Isenberg (note 1), p. 86.

21. Peters and Waterman (note 12), p. 63.

7

Wanted: The Intuitive Director
How to Enhance the Board's Intuitive Decision-Making Powers[†]

WESTON H. AGOR

Intuition is an important brain skill for boards and directors to learn in order to meet the global competitive challenges unprecedented in modern times. How a board *thinks* when it approaches the problems it faces will determine the possible critical solutions perceived and implemented. Intuitive brain skills need to be adequately represented on corporate boards today and integrated with more traditional styles of decision-making. I will outline several specific ways boards can systematically use intuitive brain skills to perform more effectively their strategic role as a board.

Every board has one strategic role to perform. Simply stated, this role is to determine the best way to survive at a profit level that meets both the short-term and long-term interests of its stockholders without losing sight of the corporation's place in the community at large. Performing this strategic role is no easy task in a business environment increasingly characterized by crisis, rapid change, globalization of the marketplace, and demands for corporate responsibility.

There have been a number of classic suggestions made about how a board can enhance its ability to meet this challenge. Examples that quickly come to mind range from greater professionalism of a board's activities to the establishment of "truly" independent boards *vis à vis* corporate management by insuring that outsiders are well represented on a board. There has also been a trend to place women on boards in the belief that they are more

†Source: Weston H. Agor, "Wanted: The Intuitive Director: How to Enhance the Board's Intuitive Decision Making Powers," *Directors & Boards* Vol. II, No. 3, Spring, 1987, pp. 13-15; used by permission.

sensitive to such issues as how a corporation can profitably be responsive to community and emerging consumer demands.

How a Board Thinks

It seems to me that these and numerous other proposals for enhancing board effectiveness have one common underlying theme. They all are designed to impact *how a board thinks*. By this, I mean such issues as:

—Is the board really open to and in touch with the reality in which strategic corporate decisions need to be made, or is a board comfortably isolated from it?

—How does a board gather and process information? Are both "factual" and "feeling" cues taken into account freely and openly?

—How are committee and full meetings of the board conducted? Can it be said honestly that good hard objective questions are facilitated and encouraged, or is a "board think" at work which suppresses hard questions and other dissent?

When one focuses on this central question of "How do boards think?", several recent trends appear to present a mixed picture. This should be cause for some concern and careful assessment. For example, on the one hand, the trend of appointing more women to boards might be viewed positively as long as the women selected really do think differently than the males already on the board. But are the women actually selected different in this respect? Or are boards tending to select women who are safely like their male counterparts? If the women selected are truly innovative and different in the way they think, are they well received by the full board?

Productive Additions

In this same vein, one should not take lightly the recent trend reported by a leading director-search firm that shows through mid-1986 a lower percentage of board appointees are from outside the corporation. Again, however, an outside board appointee is more likely to be a truly productive addition to the way the board thinks if the person thinks somewhat differently than the inside members do and/or has additional information and other important linkages to bring to the party. This needs to be objectively assessed. And then let's not ignore the impact on how a board thinks of the trend to make greater use of professionals such as lawyers and financial advisers for input to the decision-making process, which some observers say results in less intuitive decision making now by boards.

A number of wise and experienced directors across the country are arguing that a board today must function as a force for innovation and as an agent for change if it is to perform its strategic role effectively. Boards increasingly are being called upon for major decisions in times of crisis, which are occurring more frequently in corporate life. What steps can a board take to help ensure that it functions effectively as a force for innovation and change in times of crisis?

It is my contention that boards will think more productively and thereby perform their strategic mission more effectively if they take the following steps:

- Design and implement a process for recruiting and selecting their own membership that ensures the presence of intuitive brain skills of high quality to complement the more traditional "left brain" analytical skills that are usually dominant on most boards today.
- Implement board management practices (both at the committee and full-board level) to ensure that intuitive input is *systematically solicited and integrated* with more traditional approaches throughout the board's decision-making process. This should include input both from individual board members and support staff who are highly skilled in the use of intuitive techniques.

Why is it so important to have intuitive brain skills well represented on a board's membership and systematically integrated into its decision-making process? The reason is simple. Just as more traditional "left brain" board members are particularly skilled in performing certain functions (e.g., reading a financial statement of the company), highly intuitive board members have special skills. They are highly creative thinkers—the "change masters" and entrepreneurs—who are particularly adept at:

—Seeing totally new opportunities in the marketplace which others do not see;

—Asking penetrating questions of corporate management that are provocative yet also supportive in tone and direction;

—Supplying new ingenious solutions to seemingly intractable corporate problems;

—Dealing with and resolving complex issues where data are incomplete or unavailable in a timely manner; and

—Selecting and motivating CEOs to perform at peak levels.

Reaching Crucial Decisions

Directors who have these brain skills also function best in the "megatrend" environment that corporations increasingly face—characterized by rapid change, crisis, and where time is limited for making crucial decisions. They are particularly adept at reaching productive decisions where:

—There is a high level of uncertainty;

—There is little previous precedent for action in the face of new emerging trends;

—"Facts" are limited or of little use;

—There are several plausible alternative solutions to choose from with good factual support for each option; and

—Time is limited and there is pressure to be right.

There are a number of specific ways a board can acquire and make use of intuitive skills in board decision making. The first step is to ensure that some board members *themselves* possess these brain skills. I recommend that a minimum of two members on every board be selected primarily for their intuitive ability. This "critical mass" will help to ensure that the board both considers and actually sees the full range of options available to it during deliberations. It will also help ensure that these board members are not easily shut out by a majority that may think in a more traditional fashion. Finally, by having each other to consult with throughout the decision-making process, a minimum support system will be present to help avoid feeling isolated from the full board, which could eventually lead to their resignation.

High Intangible Factor

Depending on the nature of the business in question, it can be productive to increase the representation of intuitive brain skills on a board beyond the minimum of two members. This will be particularly so when major business activity is characterized by such factors as a highly cyclical marketplace, highly intangible consumer preferences, and various other uncontrollable events—e.g., in the entertainment industry, oil business, and the field of fashion/cosmetics.

One of the reasons that boards seek outside membership and other types of representation, e.g., women, is for their thinking style—what they may see and take into account before making a decision. Whether the recruitment process is handled internally or through an outside search firm, I recommend that boards take steps to ensure that new members being considered for this role *actually in fact think differently* than the present board majority. One of the ways to ensure this is to assess the thinking styles of the present board membership and recruit new members to complement the dominant pattern. For most boards, this will usually mean filling more vacant seats with persons who are highly skilled at making sound decisions employing an intuitive style.

If it is found that this is the case for your particular board, and you have decided to actively search for new members who possess intuitive decision-making skills, how can the person(s) be found? There are two basic methods.

As a rule, such individuals already have a well-established reputation for creativity and ingenuity in their particular industry. You and your recruiting firm can pursue them in earnest.

Short of this, there are a number of other more formal assessment tools and techniques presently available which can be used to verify a person's reputed skill or for identifying individuals who are not yet so well known but who possess the intuitive skills you are searching for. One tool I have designed for this purpose is called the AIM Survey, which not only assesses how intuitive a person is, but also how the individual actually goes about using this skill when making decisions.

Once you are satisfied that you have the intuitive brain skills you need on the board, the next step is to establish board practices which facilitate their use. Broadly speaking, this means a willingness to organize and operate board deliberations in a somewhat less traditional manner than has been the case in the past. For example, one technique to use is to hold some full board and committee meetings where the agenda is not formally outlined in great detail. Instead, a common general purpose for the meeting is clearly stated in one sentence, but the board is allowed to deal with the problem as the discussion naturally emerges and flows.

Open Times and Deliberations

Another useful technique is to segment meetings into creative open times to complement structured times. Highly intuitive board members I have worked with function best in such settings where deliberations—and even seating arrangements—are open and informal and where they are given a problem to solve but not given too much direction and guidance as to how to solve it.

Finally, a third approach is having formal presentations made to the full board that are designed to outline and demonstrate how intuition can be used by each board member to make strategic decisions. I often find that even the most traditional board members are both amazed and pleased to find that they possess intuitive skills that can be unlocked and developed for use in solving the corporate problems they face.

Failure to take steps to develop a board's intuitive thinking patterns and powers and integrate these brain skills with more traditional styles of decision making raises the high probability that boards will not think as productively as they need to for America's very survival and future prosperity.

PART III Test Your Intuitive Ability and Compare Yourself to National Norms

One of the first steps to take in using and developing your intuitive skills is to identify the level and type(s) of skills you may already possess and compare your findings with the normative scores for executives across the country. This section gives you an opportunity to do this.

The *AIM Survey* instrument contained here enables you to identify your *present* overall level of intuitive ability and to determine whether you are *using* this skill on the job to guide management decisions. After you have scored and interpreted your results, the other articles in this part provide you with data to compare your scores to norms established through extensive testing of executives across the country in a wide variety of management settings. You will be able to compare your score by sex, ethnic background, and occupational specialty.

The research findings presented here show that the use of intuition appears to be a skill that is more prevalent as one moves up the management ladder. Top managers in *every* sample group tested scored higher than their subordinates in their underlying ability to use intuition to make decisions. Within this top management group, only 10% nationally can be classified as highly intuitive executives. If your intuition scores fall in this range, your ability ranks among the top 10% in the country.

Women consistently score higher on their ability to use intuition than men in *every group* sampled. Available data also indicate that managers from Asian ethnic backgrounds appear to have a higher level of intuitive ability than the average manager, followed by Caucasian, black, and finally Hispanic American managers. You are cautioned, however, not to conclude that this is due to any inherent or physiological reasons. At the moment, this range in intuition scores appears to be more a product of cultural conditioning and upbringing than any other single factor.

The national test scores also indicate that brain skills vary significantly between occupational specializations and by management level within occupations. These findings have obvious potential use for job recruitment, placement, and training, which are discussed in detail in Part IV.

8

Test Your Intuitive Powers
AIM Survey[†]

WESTON H. AGOR

The results of the AIM Survey will indicate the underlying *potential* intuitive ability that you have and also whether you are in fact *using* this ability on the job to guide your management decisions. After you have scored and interpreted your results, you may compare your scores to the national norms for highly intuitive managers for your sex, ethnic background, and occupational specialty.

Directions:

Complete the Survey *as quickly as you can* (10 to 15 minutes should be sufficient). *Be honest with yourself.* In Part I, questions 1-12, select the response that first appeals to you most. Circle the letter of that response. In Part II, respond to each question as indicated.

†SOURCE: *AIM Survey* (El Paso, TX: ENFP Enterprises, 1989). Copyright © 1989 by Weston H. Agor. Used by permission.

AIM Survey

PART I: YOUR INTUITIVE ABILITY

1. When working on a project, do you prefer to:
   a. be told what the problem is, but left free to decide how to solve it?
   b. get very clear instructions about how to go about solving the problem before you start?

2. When working on a project, do you prefer to work with colleagues who are:
   a. realistic?
   b. imaginative?

3. Do you admire people most who are:
   a. creative?
   b. careful?

4. Do the friends you choose tend to be:
   a. serious and hard working?
   b. exciting and often emotional?

5. When you ask a colleague for advice on a problem you have, do you:
   a. seldom or never get upset if he/she questions your basic assumptions?
   b. often get upset if he/she questions your basic assumptions?

6. When you start your day, do you usually:
   a. seldom make or follow a specific plan to follow?
   b. make a plan first to follow?

7. When working with numbers, do you find that you:
   a. seldom or never make factual errors?
   b. often make factual errors?

8. Do you find that you:
   a. seldom daydream during the day and really don't enjoy doing so when you do it?
   b. frequently daydream during the day and enjoy doing so?

AIM Survey

9. When working on a problem do you:
   a. prefer to follow the instructions or rules when they are given to you?
   b. often enjoy circumventing the instructions or rules when they are given to you?

10. When you are trying to put something together, do you prefer to have:
    a. step-by-step written instructions on how to assemble the item?
    b. a picture of how the item is supposed to look once assembled?

11. Do you find that the person who irritates you *the most* is the one who appears to be:
    a. disorganized?
    b. organized?

12. When an unexpected crisis comes up that you have to deal with, do you:
    a. feel anxious about the situation?
    b. feel excited by the challenge of the situation?

PART II: DO YOU USE YOUR INTUITIVE ABILITY TO MAKE IMPORTANT DECISIONS?

13. Do you believe that you use intuition frequently to guide your most important decisions? (Check one.)
    Yes _____ No _____

14. If yes, in which circumstances or situations do you use your intuition to make your most important decisions? (Circle the letter(s) of all choices that apply.)
    a. where there is a high degree of certainty
    b. where there is little previous precedent
    c. where variables are less scientifically predictable or where "facts" are limited
    d. where there are several plausible alternative solutions to choose form with good arguments for each
    e. where time is limited and there is pressure to be right
    f. other (specify) _____
       _____

AIM Survey

15. What kinds of feelings or signals do you get when you "know" that a particular decision is "right"? What do you rely on for cues? (Circle the letter(s) of all choices that apply.)
    a. excitement
    b. warmth
    c. peaceful/calm
    d. high energy
    e. sudden flash of insight
    f. other (specify) _____

16. Give an example (or two) of a very important decision where you followed your intuition and it proved to be the "right" decision.

    _____
    _____
    _____
    _____

17. What feelings or signals do you get when you "know" you are heading in the wrong direction or should delay your decision for awhile? (Circle the letter(s) of all choices that apply.)
    a. anxious
    b. upset stomach
    c. mixed or conflicting signals
    d. other (specify)_____

    _____

18. What kinds of conditions have obstructed the use of your intuition in important decision-making situations? (Circle the letter(s) of all choices that apply.)
    a. when angry
    b. under stress
    c. too ego involved in the decision
    d. rushed my decision
    e. lack of confidence
    f. other (specify) _____

    _____

AIM Survey

---

19. Do you tend to "keep it a secret" that you use intuition to make decisions, or do you feel comfortable sharing this fact with others? (Check one.)

    Keep it a secret. _____   Share with others. _____

    Please explain. _____

    _____

    _____

20. When using your intuition to make a decision, where have you found it functions best? (Circle the letter of the choice that applies.)

    a. at the very beginning when I am trying to assess the future or the options available to me

    b. at the very end when I am trying to sift through and digest all the cues and information available to me

    c. it really varies depending on the problem or issue at hand (specify) _____

21. When making a major decision, do you use any particular technique or method(s) to help draw on your intuitive ability more effectively? (Check one.)

    Yes _____ No _____

    If *Yes*, please describe. _____

    _____

    _____

    _____

22. Do you use or regularly practice any particular technique or method(s) to help develop further your intuitive ability? (Check one.)

    Yes _____ No _____

    If *Yes*, please describe _____

    _____

    _____

AIM Survey

23. Depending on whether you are a business or government executive, answer the appropriate section of this item. If you are a student, select the answer that best indicates your expected occupational specialty and goal for management level.

Business Executive: Select *one* Occupational Specialty and *one* Management Level in which you are currently functioning. Circle *one* letter for each category.

Occupational Specialty
a. General Administration
b. Financial/Budget
c. Planning
d. Personnel/Organization Development
e. Production
f. Other (specify) _____

Management Level
a. Top
b. Middle
c. Lower

Government Executive: Select *one* Occupational Specialty, *one* Government Level and *one* Management Level in which you are currently functioning. Circle *one* letter for *each* category.

Occupational Specialty
a. General Administration
b. Policy Program Planning
c. Urban and Regional Planning
d. Fiscal and Budget
e. Management Analysis
f. Personnel Administration
g. Law Enforcement
h. Health and Hospital Administration
i. Other (specify) _____

Government Level
a. Federal
b. State
c. Local
d. County

Management Level
a. Top
b. Middle
c. Lower

AIM Survey

24. I like my occupation and feel it is right for me. (Check one.)
    Yes _____ No _____

25. Is your sex . . .
    a. female?
    b. male?

26. Ethnic background. (Circle the *one* with which you identify
    most closely.)
    a. American Indian, Alaskan Native
    b. Asian American, Asian Indian, Oriental, Southeast Asian
    c. Filipino
    d. Pacific Islander
    e. Black Non-Hispanic
    f. Mexican American, Chicano
    g. Latin American, Puerto Rican, Cuban, other Hispanic
    h. White Non-Hispanic, Caucasian, European, Middle Eastern,
       North African
    i. Other

Scoring and Interpreting Your AIM Survey Results

WHAT THE AIM SURVEY MEASURES

Part I of the AIM Survey (the first twelve questions) measures your *underlying* or *potential intuitive ability,* of which you may or may not be aware. The second part of the Survey (the next ten questions) indicates whether you actually *use* this intuitive ability on the job to make important decisions; how and under what circumstances you use this brain skill; and whether you practice any particular techniques or methods right now that have the potential of helping you to develop further your intuitive ability.

SCORING PART I OF THE SURVEY

To score *Part I of the Survey,* return to page two and complete the following steps.

1. Total the number of "a" responses you have circled for questions 1,
   3, 5, 6 and 11. Enter that total in the space provided in the Scoring
   Chart below.

2. Total the number of "b" responses circled for questions 2, 4, 7, 8, 9, 10, and 12. Enter that total in the space provided in the Scoring Chart.

3. Add the "a" and "b" totals. This represents your *Intuitive Score*. Enter that score in the space provided in the Scoring Chart.

4. Because there is a total of twelve questions in this part of the Survey, take the number 12 and subtract your Intuitive Score. The result equals your *Thinking Score*. Enter this score below.

5. To plot your Survey results on the diagram below, look at your *Intuitive Score* and your *Thinking Score*. Take the *highest of these two scores* and put a checkmark on the corresponding scale at the point representing your score. If your scores are tied, record the numbers on both scales.

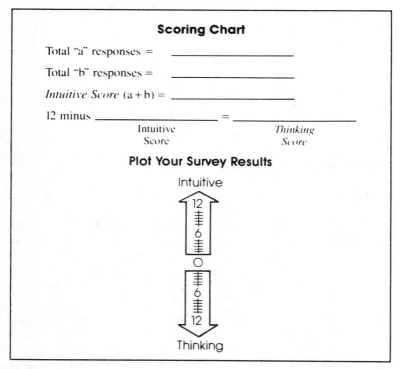

INTERPRETING PART I OF THE SURVEY

If your highest score is *Intuitive*, you have the ability to base your decisions on unknowns or possibilities. You have the potential ability to apply ingenuity to problems, to see how best to prepare for the future and can tackle difficulties with zest. You are more likely to prefer management situations that are unstructured, fluid and spontaneous.

With a high score for intuition, you have the potential ability to function best in occupations that are characterized by crisis or rapid change and where you are asked to chart new, emerging trends from data including many unknowns. You also prefer to solve new and different problems versus the same or similar problems time after time.

On the other hand, if your highest score is *Thinking*, you have the ability to apply experience to problems, to bring up pertinent facts, to keep track of essential details and face difficulties with realism.

With a high score for thinking, you have the potential to function best in occupations which demand ability to work logically, where attention to detail, procedures and precision is valued highly and where you are asked to implement existing policy usually made elsewhere.

If your Intuitive and Thinking scores are tied, you have the potential to rely on both feeling cues and factual cues to guide your decisions. However, there is the danger that you will have a difficult time making up your mind about the set of cues to which you should listen. Therefore, it is quite possible that you will be either slow in making critical decisions, or will have difficulty making a decision at all, without experiencing considerable stress.

Refer to the following chart for an overview of the use of Thinking and Intuition in an organization setting.

Brain Skill Overview

Brain Skill Emphasized	Type of Organization Where Predominant	Task Preference	Problem Solving/ Decision-Making Style	Example Applications	Sample Occupational Specialty
Thinking	Traditional Pyramid	Routine Precision Detail Implementation Repetitive	Deductive Objective Prefers solving problems by breaking down into parts, then approaching the problem sequentially using logic.	Model building Projection	Planning Management Science Financial Management Engineering Law Enforcement Military
Intuitive	Open Temporary Rapidly changing	Non-routine Broad issues General policy options Constant new assignments	Inductive Subjective Prefers solving problems by looking at the whole, then approaching the problem through patterns using hunches.	Brainstorming Challenging traditional assumptions	Personnel Marketing Organization Development Intelligence

INTERPRETING PART II OF THE SURVEY

If you obtain a high score on the Intuition scale, it does not necessarily follow that you *actually use* this skill on the job to make decisions. People often select careers or occupations that have little to do with their underlying abilities. It is possible for a person to reach middle age without having a clear grasp of what his or her dominant underlying brain skill really is—although he or she may well have been receiving cues over the years in the form of relatively high stress levels and poor health.

Part II of this Survey provides a detailed indicator as to *whether* you are using your present intuitive powers to help guide your decision making. It also gives you information as to *how* you are using your ability; for example, secretly versus openly or under special conditions and circumstances. Finally, this information, along with our scores from Part I, can be used to begin a program of networking with others to further develop your intuitive skills.

Using the AIM Survey Results

COMPARISON TO NATIONAL NORMS

More than 3000 managers have been tested nationally in both private and public sector organizations representing a wide variety of situations and settings. The test group included private sector executives at all levels including CEO's, emergency preparedness military personnel, college presidents, state health and rehabilitative services managers, city managers, and legislators and staff.

Clearly, the brain skills that are predominant in organizations vary by management level, by sex, by occupational specialty and to some degree by ethnic background.

Top Manager's Scores

The use of intuition appears to be a skill that is more prevalent as one moves up the management ladder. Top managers, in *every* sample group tested, scored higher than their subordinates in their *underlying ability* to use intuition to make decisions (6.5 mean score nationally). Bearing this fact in mind, note that John Naisbitt, the author of the best selling book, *Megatrends*, predicts in his latest, coauthored book, *Reinventing the Corporation*, that intuition "will gain new respectability" in the organizations of the immediate future.

Within this top management group, only ten percent nationally can be classified as *highly intuitive executives*—their scores fall in the 10 to 12 range on the intuition scale. If your intuition score falls in this range, your ability ranks among the *top ten percent* in the country.

Scores by Sex, Ethnic Background and Occupational Specialty

Women consistently scored higher on their ability to use intuition than men in every group sampled nationally. Available data also indicate that managers from Asian ethnic backgrounds appear to have a higher level of intuitive ability than the average manager, followed by Caucasian and finally by black managers.

The national sample also indicates that brain skills vary significantly between occupational specializations and by management level within occupations. Managers specializing in financial management, engineering, law and law enforcement have higher test scores on thinking vs. intuitive ability because these professions tend to place greater emphasis on facts and figures for decision-making, value hierarchical models of management and stress quantitative techniques of analysis. On the other hand, managers specializing in such fields as general administration, policy, marketing and sales, and organizational development score higher on intuitive ability. This occurs because these fields tend to be characterized by elements of uncertainty and rapid change. Decisions often involve choices between shades of grey vs. black or white options. Intuitive skills in this context would appear to be particularly useful.

Use the chart below to compare your intuitive scores to the national norms based on management level, sex, ethnic background and occupational specialty.

National Norms on Intuition: Mean Scores

Management Level		Sex		Ethnic Background		Occupational Specialty	
Top	6.5	Female	6.9	Asian	6.5	General Adminis-	
High		Male	6.3	Caucasian	6.2	tration, Policy	7.9
Intuitive				Black	5.2	Marketing, Sales,	
Top	10-12					Organizational	
Middle/				Hispanic		Development	6.7
Lower	5.8			American	4.6	Finance, Military	
						Engineering	5.1-6.3
Total National Sample Mean Score: 6.4						Law Enforcement	6.4

Now that you have one measure of your *potential* intuitive ability and also an indication as to how (or whether) you *actually use* this skill to help guide your most important decisions, turn to the next two articles in this book. You will find here a detailed explanation of how executives tested nationally scored on an earlier version of the AIM Survey which is very similar to the one you just took. This will enable you to compare your overall scores and your intuitive decision-making style with theirs. After that, we will then turn in the book to the question of how intuitive skills can and are actually being used to increase productivity in pioneering organizations today. Later in the book, we will discuss how you can develop your present level of intuitive skills still further, and we will tell you about some of the new emerging global efforts to research this subject further for applied use in decision making.

9

The Intuitive Ability of Executives
Findings from Field Research[†]

WESTON H. AGOR

Several criteria were used to select the managers to be tested nationally. First, an effort was made to select managers from a wide horizontal range of different organizations and settings. This was done so that whatever the findings turned out to be, statements could be made more precisely about conditions under which the results appeared or did not appear to be valid in organizational life (e.g., for only certain organizations and settings vs. all). Second, in each of the groups selected, an effort was made to obtain a representative sample of the total management structure so that meaningful statements (statistically significant) could be made from the findings about what the intuitive management style and ability were really like in each organization. Third, access also played a part in the organizations actually selected. In each management group tested, a major peer leader or top manager provided the necessary access to ensure that the questionnaire instrument was distributed and returned at a high rate.

For the first stage of my study, which involved the measurement of intuitive ability, 6,757 questionnaires were distributed between 1981 and 1988. From this group, actual responses received totaled 3,157 (48 percent). The response rate for all the groups tested was so high because peer leaders either wrote cover letters explaining the test instrument and encouraged each manager to return the questionnaire or they provided direct access to the management groups tested. Table 9.1 summarizes that range of management groups actually tested along with response rates. For the private sector, eighty-eight CEOs were included as well as management

†SOURCE: "The Intuitive Ability of Executives: Findings from Field Research" from Weston H. Agor, *The Logic of Intuitive Decision Making: A Research Based Approach for Top Management* (Westport, CT: Greenwood Press, Inc., 1986), pp. 13-26; used by permission.

TABLE 9.1
Range of Groups Sampled

Group	Number Sampled	Response Rate Number	(%)
Private Sector			
• South Florida CEOs of major corporations	88	54	(61)
• Managers from other sample sets	763	763	(100)
Total	851	817	(96)
Public Sector			
• National survey sample of ASPA members	5,000	1,679	(34)
• Four State Sample			
• Civil servants	313	289	(92)
• Educators	100	43	(43)
• Military	50	44	(88)
• Politicians	110	47	(44)
• City managers	157	63	(40)
Subtotal	730	486	(67)
• Managers from workshops	175	175	(100)
Total Private and Public Sector Samples	6,757	3,157	(47)

groups from such major organizations as Dow Chemical Company, Walt Disney Enterprises, Tenneco Oil, and several of the companies in the Bell telephone system. For the public sector, a large random sample of the public administration profession was included (membership of the American Society for Public Administration [ASPA] minus academics), five large sample groups representing four of the largest states in the nation (California, Florida, and Michigan, and Texas),and samples from workshop groups tested at the Federal Executive Institute, the National Security Agency, and the City of Phoenix.[1]

The second stage of my study, which was completed in 1984-88, involved the actual use of intuitive ability. For this stage of my study, I selected as my sample group for follow-up study only those executives who scored in the top 10 percent on the intuition scale from the national sample population previously tested. The reasoning for selecting this group was that if intuition were actually being used as a decision making skill, it should be most apparent to and among those executives who had the highest ability to use it. One hundred top executives have been tested in depth here, including major executives at the corporate headquarters of General Motors and Dow Chemical Company and board members of such major organizations as Chrysler, Burroughs, and the Ford Foundation.

Responses were stratified by such key variables as level of management, level of government, sex, occupational specialization, and ethnic background. All the responses were analyzed by computer, and all the findings were subject to statistical significance tests. That is, are the differences found in scale scores between management levels, sex, occupational specialty, and ethnic background likely to occur by chance—or are they a measure of the actual differences that exist between these groups?[2]

Test Findings

The findings from this national testing were dramatic! Clearly, intuitive management ability appears to vary by management level, by level of government service, by sex, by occupational specialty, and, to some degree, by ethnic background.[3]

TOP MANAGERS

Intuition appears to be a skill that is more prevalent as one moves up the management ladder. Top managers in every sample group tested scored higher than middle/lower level managers in their underlying ability to use intuition to make decisions (see Table 9.2). It also appears that the higher one goes in the level of government service (from county to national), the greater the ability to use intuition becomes (see Table 9.3). As outlined in the first section of this book, it appears plausible that one of the skills that top managers rely on most frequently is their intuitive ability to make the right decisions.

For example, as Donald A. Schon points out in a recent book entitled *The Reflective Practitioner: How Professionals Think in Action*, they have had to constantly make choices in turbulent environments where problems do not lend themselves to the techniques of benefit-cost analysis or to probabilistic reasoning.[4] Similarly, Martin Lasden in a recent article in *Computer Decisions* reports that top executives he interviewed in the computer industry assert time and again that intuition is a critical factor in their success at making the right decision.[5]

When executives in top management positions who also score in the top 10 percent in intuitive ability are tested, the results overwhelmingly indicate that these executives do use their brain skill to guide their most important decisions. Not only do the vast majority of these top executives admit that they use intuition to

TABLE 9.2

Score on Intuition Scale by Level of Management

Intuition Scale	Group Sampled			
	Private Sector		Public Sector	
	Level of Management		Level of Management	
	Top	Middle/ Lower	Top	Middle/ Lower
Maximum Score (12) ↓ High (8-12) ↓ Average (4-6) ↓ Low (1-3) ↓ No Score	6.5	5.8	6.2	5.6

TABLE 9.3

Score on Intuition Scale by Level of Government

Intuition Scale	Group Sampled				
	National	State	Local	County	Total Sample
Maximum Score (12) ↓ High (8-12) ↓ Average (4-6) ↓ Low (1-3) ↓ No Score	6.7	6.4	6.1	5.9	6.2

help guide their most important decisions, but they go on to specify the situations and settings in which they find their intuition is *most helpful* in making key management decisions:

- There is a high level of uncertainty.
- There is little previous precedent.
- Variables are often not scientifically predictable.
- "Facts" are limited.
- Facts do not clearly point the way to go.
- Time is limited and there is pressure to be right.
- There are several plausible alternative solutions to choose from, with good arguments for each.

It is also significant to note that when these top managers intuitively "know" they have reached the correct decision, they share a "consensus set" of feelings that tell them so: a sense of excitement—almost euphoria; a total sense of commitment; a feeling of total harmony; warmth and confidence; a burst of enthusiasm and energy like a bolt of lightning or sudden flash that "this is the solution." Alternatively, when they sense an impending decision may be an incorrect one or that they need to take more time to adequately process the cues they are receiving, these managers speak of feelings of anxiety, mixed signals, discomfort, or an upset stomach [see the next selection for more details on how managers use their intuitive ability to make important decisions].[6]

SEX DIFFERENCES

Another extremely important finding is that there are statistically significant differences between the sexes regarding intuitive ability for both private and public sector executives. Women consistently scored higher on the intuition scale than men in every group sampled (see Table 9.4). This fact is supported by other research that has recently appeared. For example, one group of research findings suggests that there may be different patterns of physiological growth of the brain for men and women, which could help to account for some of the score difference.[7] Another possible explanation is that women have learned culturally to use and develop their native intuitive ability. In contrast, men historically have learned through societal and cultural pressure to suppress feelings and to rely on deductive processes vs. inductive ones.[8]

TABLE 9.4
Score on Intuition Scale by Sex

Intuition Scale	Group Sampled	
	Men	Women
Maximum Score (12) ↓ High (8-12) ↓		6.9
	6.3	
↓ Average (4-6) ↓ Low (1-3) ↓ No Score		

DIFFERENCES BY OCCUPATIONAL SPECIALTY

It would not be surprising to find differences in intuitive scores for managers by occupational specialty in organizations across the country. Historically, certain professions such as engineering, financial management, and law enforcement, e.g., have emphasized analytical, quantitative, and deductive techniques for decision making in preference to management skills normally associated with the use of intuition. Presumably, executives would also self-select themselves to that profession that emphasized the brain skills they excelled in.[9]

At the same time, one might expect that as one moved from lower/middle levels of management to top management in any professional specialty, the skills required for successful decision making would change in character. Top management positions would appear to be more likely to require a greater capacity to solve complex problems, deal with uncertainty, motivate subordinates to act, and integrate factual information along with personal needs, wants, and preferences into an effective management program that could be implemented. This job description would seem to place a greater premium on the ability to use intuitive brain skills to help guide management choices.[10]

Available test scores indicate that intuitive ability does vary significantly by occupational specialization and by management level within occupations. Take, e.g., the occupational specializations of general administration and policy as compared with the specializations of financial management and law enforcement. We might expect managers specializing in financial management and law enforcement to have higher test scores on thinking vs. intuitive ability since these professions tend to place greater emphasis on facts and figures for decision making, value hierarchical models of management, and stress quantitative techniques of analysis. On the other hand, we would probably expect that the brain skill used most in the other two occupational specialties might be intuition. This is so because general administration and policy tend to be broader in scope. The issues a manager would be more likely to face would probably be significantly more complex. Elements of uncertainty and rapid change might be more common problems that would have to be dealt with along with a complex array of clientele groups demanding conflicting services. Intuitive skills in this context would appear to be particularly useful.

Table 9.5 compares the intuitive scale scores by occupational specialties. You will note that managers in general administration and policy clearly have higher intuition scores than managers specializing in financial management or law enforcement. However, as we move up the management ladder within each occupational specialty, it is important to note that top managers tend to score higher in intuitive ability across the board (see Table 9.6).

Now this does not suggest that top managers in these occupations necessarily have an inherently higher intuitive ability at the outset than middle/lower level managers. This may indeed be true in part. But as we shall see in the next selection, my field research suggests it is also probably due to the fact that these top managers have learned through practice to develop their inherent ability to the point that they can use this brain skill effectively on-the-job to make decisions. In fact, it could well be that managers aspiring to top levels of responsibility in their respective organizations need to learn to make this transition before their career goals can be successfully achieved.

TABLE 9.5
Score on Intuition Scale by Occupational Specialty

Intuition Scale	Thinking ←		Range of Scores		→ Intuitive
	Financial Management/ Law Enforcement	Military	Health	General Administration/ Policy	Personnel
Maximum Score (12) ↓ High (8-12) ↓ Average (4-6) ↓ Low (1-3) ↓ No Score	4.9	5.1	6.3	6.7	7.9

TABLE 9.6
Score on Intuition Scale Within Occupational Specialty
by Management Level

Selected Occupational Specialties	Level of Management		
	Top	Middle/Lower	Total
General administration/policy	6.9	6.4	6.6
Health	6.8	6.5	6.5
Financial management	6.1	5.7	5.9
Engineering	6.0	5.6	5.8
Law enforcement	6.5	5.9	6.0
Total	6.5	5.8	6.4

ETHNIC BACKGROUND

Managers tested were also asked to identify their ethnic background. The purpose was to determine if there were any discernible differences in intuitive ability. Since the vast majority of the

TABLE 9.7
Score on Intuition Scale by Ethnic Background

Intuition Scale	Thinking ←——— Range of ———→ Intuition Scores			
	Hispanic American	Black	White	Asian
Maximum Score (12) ↓				
High (8-12) ↓				6.5
			6.2	
Average (4-6) ↓		5.2		
	4.6			
Low (1-3) ↓				
No Score				

respondents classified themselves as white, only three other groups (Asians, blacks, and Hispanics) had large enough numbers represented to statistically measure whether significant differences were apparent.

The available data indicate that managers from Asian ethnic backgrounds appear to have a higher level of intuitive ability than the average manager who responded (see Table 9.7). As has been suggested by Richard Pascale and Anthony Athos in *The Art of Japanese Management*, this could well mean that managers who were brought up in Asian family background settings were socialized from birth to emphasize and practice the Eastern world's approach to life, which encourages the development of intuitive brain skills.[11] One of the practical implications of these findings is that executives with Asian ethnic backgrounds could potentially be highly effective in management settings where intuitive skills are a premium (e.g., crisis management, brainstorming).

Black and Hispanic managers, on the other hand, appeared to score somewhat lower than the mean respondent on intuitive ability. Taken at face value, it would appear that black and Hispanic managers, on the average at present, would function best in situations where thinking vs. intuitive brain skills are emphasized. Examples would be management situations where authority patterns are clear and where the management task requires detail and precision. Managers from these ethnic groups aspiring to top management positions or occupational specialties requiring an emphasis on intuitive brain skills could also probably benefit from workshop and training programs that would develop their ability to use these skills more effectively than they presently appear able to do.

It should be emphasized that the findings reported here in no way suggest that a particular ethnic group is inherently "superior" or inherently "more intuitive" than another. It is quite possible that the differences found are more a product of cultural conditioning and upbringing than any other single factor. Accordingly, if a manager wishes to develop his or her present level of intuitive ability further (no matter what his or her ethnic background), it is probable that workshops and training programs designed for this purpose would be beneficial.

JOB SATISFACTION

One of the questions that was asked managers was whether they liked their present position or occupation. Nearly 6 percent of the respondents indicated that they did not. When their scores on the intuition test were examined alongside the occupations in which they were specializing, the findings were striking. The common thread throughout the data appeared to be that the vast majority of these managers had selected an occupational specialization that did not comfortably match their brain style preferences. These findings suggest that there is considerable opportunity within organizations for increasing not only job satisfaction but also productivity if these individuals could be more appropriately placed where their brain skills fit more comfortably.

Summary

So far, we have reported on how the intuitive ability of managers varies in the national sample group tested. One of the most significant findings is that top managers on average score higher than their subordinates in every sample group tested. We have also found that women score higher than men on average, that there are significant differences by occupational specialty, and that Asian managers score the highest among all ethnic groups for which data are available. The next selection will now outline in detail how these highly intuitive executives (those who score in the top 10 percent nationally) actually use this brain skill to guide their most important decisions.

Notes

1. Private sector CEOs were made up of a sample of 88 top executives who were members of the Greater Miami Chamber of Commerce in Florida. Ray Goode, president of the Babcock Company in Coral Gables, Florida, and former Dade County manager, wrote a letter endorsing the questionnaire and mailed the test out of his office over his letterhead. Other private sector executives tested were from a wide variety of sample groups. Access to some groups was gained through the Alden B. Dow Creativity Center in Midland, Michigan, which helped support some of my research on this study. Other samples came from executives who had taken my workshops across the country for such organizations as Tenneco Oil, several Bell system companies, and Walt Disney Enterprises.

Public sector samples were gathered as follows. All the community college presidents in California were mailed the test over Dan Angel's signature, then president of Citrus Community College in Azusa, California, and former state legislator in Michigan. Neil E. Allgood, brigadier general and director of the California Specialized Training Institute in San Luis Obispo, California, administered the test personally to his 40th Infantry Division emergency management staff. David Pingree, secretary of the Florida State Department of Health and Rehabilitative Services in Tallahassee, Florida, mailed the test out of his office with a cover letter of support to 110 of his managers statewide. Robert Donly, president of the Florida League of Cities in 1982, also wrote a cover letter explaining the test that was mailed to city managers in Florida statewide. State legislators and staff were tested in Michigan with the assistance of Senator Robert Vander Laan, former State Senate majority leader, whom I served as executive assistant in 1973-74. In addition, the ASPA meeting attendees of Orange and Los Angeles counties were tested in the spring of 1982. Together, nearly 800 executives were mailed questionnaires besides the national random sample of the ASPA profession. The national ASPA mailing was endorsed with a joint cover letter by three national council members at the time—Gus Turnbull III (who was also a member of the board of editors of *Public Administration Review*), Jerry O'Neil, and Carolyn B. Lawrence.

Finally, the public sector sample was completed with executives who had taken my workshops across the country, representing such organizations as the National Security Agency, the Federal Executive Institute, the city of Phoenix, and by a 1987 sample drawn from executives in the states of New Mexico and Texas.

2. The statistical test, one-way analysis of variance, was used to measure significance. The standard of 0.05 or better was established for rejecting the null hypothesis; i.e., the chances of obtaining the differences in scores noted was five times in one hundred or less. For a discussion of how this procedure is conducted, see Lyman Ott and David K. Hildebrand, *Statistical Thinking for Managers* (Boston: Duxbury Press, 1983).

3. For a much more detailed discussion of the findings reported in this chapter, see Weston H. Agor, *Intuitive Management Integrating Left and Right Brain Management Skills* (Englewood Cliffs, NJ: Prentice-Hall, 1984).

4. Donald A. Schon, *The Reflective Practitioner—How Professionals Think in Action* (New York: Basic Books, 1983).

5. Martin Lasden, "Intuition: The voice of success?" *Computer Decisions* (February 26, 1985), p. 98.

6. For further details, see the next selection in this book.

7. Pamela Weintraub, "The Brain: His and Hers," *Discover* (April 1981), pp. 15-20.

8. Alice G. Sargent. *The Androgynous Manager* (New York: AMACOM 1981). It should also be noted that recent brain research at UCLA conducted by Eran Zaidel also suggests that women possess a better corpus callosum, the hard, fibrous band in the center of the brain that bridges the two hemispheres. This helps enable women to better switch information from one side of the brain to the other—hence a capacity to integrate intuitive cues into applied settings. Zaidel also notes the right hemisphere of the brain is especially important in processing new information and in putting things together from individual parts, which is one intuitive process.

9. Available research thus far does seem to indicate that personality types vary significantly by occupational specialization. See Isabel Briggs Myers and Peter B. Myers, *Gifts Differing* (Palo Alto, CA: Consulting Psychologists Press, 1980), particularly Chapter 14 on occupations and types.

10. For a discussion of this possibility, see Al Siebert, "The Survivor Personality," *Portland Oregonian—Northwest Magazine* (January 27, 1980).

11. Richard Tanner Pascale and Anthony G. Athos, *The Art of Japanese Management: Applications for American Executives* (New York: Warner Books, 1981), especially Chapter 4 on Zen and the art of management.

10

The Logic of Intuition
How Top Executives Make Important Decisions[†]

WESTON H. AGOR

You have already seen how executives score nationally on their potential ability to use intuition in management decision making. During 1984, I completed a major follow-up study to answer the question: How do executives who score highly intuitive *actually use* their skill to guide their decisions—particularly their most important ones? Only those executives who scored in the top 10% on the intuition scale from the national sample population previously tested were included in the follow-up. They numbered 200. The reason for selecting this group was that if intuition were actually being used in decision making, it should be most apparent to and among those executives who had the highest ability to use it.

The questionnaire consisted of 11 open-ended questions that could be administered either by mail or in a personal interview. These questions let me probe more deeply into how managers actually use their intuitive ability. It was my hope that the answers to these questions would give me a more complete picture of the total intuitive process in a managerial context. Topics covered were whether these top executives *believed they used their intuition* to guide their most important decisions; *how they actually used their intuition* to guide their most important decisions; *specific examples of key decisions; which particular technique (s) they used* (if any) to help draw on their intuitive ability more effectively and *develop it*

AUTHOR'S NOTE: I would like to thank the Alden B. Dow Creativity Center in Midland, Michigan, which provided financial and staff support for conducting this study as well as a 1984 Summer Residence Fellowship to complete this research.

†SOURCE: Reprinted, by permission of publisher, from ORGANIZATIONAL DYNAMICS, Winter 1986, © 1986. American Management Association, New York. All rights reserved.

further; and *whether they kept it a secret that they used intuition* to make key decisions or shared this information with their colleagues.

Most of the questionnaires were administered both by mail and in personal interviews in the summer of 1984. Seventy detailed responses were received from top executives in such major organizations as General Motors, Chrysler Corporation, Burroughs, the Ford Foundation, the National Security Agency, and the Department of the Army. The excellent response rate to a lengthy questionnaire (three typed pages of open-ended questions) suggests that top executives value intuition as a tool for managing organizations.

The Study Findings

All but one executive acknowledged that they actually used their intuitive ability to guide their most important decisions. One experienced executive volunteered, "I do believe in using my intuitive powers on most of my decisions, large or small." Another respondent described the process this way: "I don't think intuition is some magical thing. I think it is a subconscious drawing from innumerable experiences that are stored. You draw from this reserve without conscious thought."

These descriptions of how the intuitive process works are much like Frances E. Vaughan's, psychologist and author of *Awakening Intuition.* She states:

> At any given moment one is conscious of only a small portion of what one knows. Intuition allows one to draw on that vast storehouse of unconscious knowledge that includes not only everything that one has experienced or learned, either consciously or subliminally, but also the infinite reservoir of the collective or universal unconscious, in which individual separateness and ego boundaries are transcended.

As a group, however, the executives were quick to point out that they considered intuition to be *only one* tool of many to use in guiding their decisions. They did not advocate relying exclusively on intuition or abandoning traditional "left brain" management practices. On the other hand, respondents emphasized that intuition is also a key management resource that should be used to help guide strategic decisions. Many top executives stressed that good intuitive decisions were, in part, based on input from facts and experience gained over the years, combined and integrated with a well-honed sensitivity or openness to other, more unconscious processes. William G. McGinnis, city manager of Crescent City, California, offered this humorous but wise operating definition of an intuitive decision in a recent article:

> I believe that good intuitive decisions are directly proportional to one's years of challenging experience, plus the number of related and worthwhile years of training and education, all divided by lack of confidence or the fear of being replaced.

MANAGEMENT SITUATIONS AND IMPORTANT DECISIONS IN WHICH INTUITION WAS MOST USEFUL

As a group, respondents were clearly able to identify management situations and important decisions in which they have learned from experience to rely on their intuitive ability most for guidance in how to act. When executives were asked if intuition was most useful in particular circumstances or if they used it freely to help guide all major decisions, they identified the following conditions as those under which intuitive ability seems to function best:

- When a high level of uncertainty exists.
- When little previous precedent exists.
- When variables are less scientifically predictable.
- When "facts" are limited.
- When facts don't clearly point the way to go.
- When analytical data are of little use.
- When several plausible alternative solutions exist to choose from, with good arguments for each.
- When time is limited and there is pressure to come up with the right decision.

When respondents were asked to name examples of very important decisions in which they followed their intuition and the decisions proved to be right, everyone was easily able to do so in detail. Here are some of the more representative examples given that had an impact on both the private and public sectors:

- Recommended not to invest in a $500 million capital project that was supported by our scientific staff, and that we were technically capable of implementing: I questioned its economic value.
- Refused to pull a drug off the market as recommended by the FDA on the basis of adverse animal reactions to tests.
- Decided on a multimillion-dollar production expansion at one of our major plants with a strong quality performance record over another

    plant with lower production costs but a poorer quality performance
    record.
- Supported the regional decentralization of the mental health department statewide over strong internal objections.

These decisions were indeed of strategic magnitude—they involved millions of dollars, impacted the public welfare, and/or
were likely to set a course for the organization in question for years
to come. When viewed as a whole, these decisions also appeared to
be in the context of those circumstances that executives described
as most conducive to intuitive decision making: The decisions
involved a high degree of risk; required a choice among several
plausible options, none of which was clearly favored by the data
available; or involved situations in which data might be inadequate
or the chosen course was even contrary to the direction suggested
by the data at hand.

Let's look at how these executives recall some of their most
important intuitive decisions—first the highly placed respondent
who recommended that his company not invest in a half-billion
dollar capital project. His "feel for the future" proved to be right,
and his company has had to take a substantial loss as a result of not
taking his advice. He said, "My own recommendation was a
judgment call requiring an intuitive feel for future events." At
times, following intuition in the face of "facts" that point in another
direction can mean putting one's own career on the line. The executive who decided not to pull a drug off the market in accordance
with the recommendation of the Food and Drug Administration
said, "I nearly killed myself in the organization on that one."

If we accept the executives' assertions that the intuition-guided
decisions named were in fact successful, this question remains:
How did the respondents know which course to take when faced
with the choices in front of them? These intuitive executives
commonly described the feelings they experienced at the point of
decision: "A sense of excitement—almost euphoric"; "growing
excitement in the pit of my stomach"; "a total sense of commitment"; "a feeling of total harmony"; and "a bolt of lightning or
sudden flash that this is the solution."

Alternatively these executives also seemed to share a common
set of feelings when they sensed an impending decision might be
wrong, that a particular option was inappropriate, or that they
needed to take more time to adequately process the cues they were
receiving to arrive at the best decision possible. At these times,

managers speak of "a sense of anxiety," "mixed signals" being received, "discomfort," "sleepless nights," or an upset stomach.

The situations and types of decisions in which respondents found their intuition to be most useful and the specific cues they received to guide their actions are consistent with the experiences described by many other successful executives and artists. For example, Marilee Zdenek interviewed famous personalities across a wide spectrum of fields for her recent book, *The Right-Brain Experience*. She found that these people were clearly aware that they used intuition to guide their most important decisions, and received cues similar to those described here.

FACTORS THAT IMPEDE THE USE OF INTUITION

Intuitive executives received clear signals that served as guide-posts telling them when they had chosen a workable option, when they had not, and when they needed to take more time before reaching a final decision. But if this was so, why weren't these executives *always* right? The survey also asked executives if they could name important decisions in which they followed their intuition and it proved to be wrong and, if so, if they could pinpoint specific factors in themselves or their surroundings that were present at that time.

Their responses suggested that they indeed made errors, but these errors did not appear to be caused by following their intuition. Rather, faulty decisions often seemed to result from *failing to follow intuition*. That is, judgment errors made by top executives appeared to result, at least in part, from a violation of one or more of the basic principles identified by psychologists working in this field as most effective for using intuition to guide major decisions. Table 10.1 summarizes these principles.

Common errors that executives made included a failure to be honest (facing self-deception and pretense) and to remain nonattached (accepting the way things are rather than trying to make them the way we would like them to be) in reference to themselves and/or the decision they were about to make. Put another way, they engaged in what psychologists commonly refer to as projection, the process by which we distort reality—in this case, intuitive cues. Hence we *project* our own conscious or unconscious process onto a situation and thus transform reality so that it fits with what *we would like to be true* (or what we fear is true). For example, a particular executive can become personally involved with some-

TABLE 10.1

Guidelines for Developing Intuition for Decision Making

Principles	Definitions
Intention	Value intuition and have the intention to develop it.
Time	Devote time to intuition and create a special space for developing it.
Relaxation	Let go of physical and emotional tension.
Silence	Learn to quiet the mind through such techniques as meditation.
Honesty	Face self-deception and be honest with yourself and others.
Receptivity	Learn to be quiet and receptive.
Sensitivity	Tune in to both inner and outer processes.
Nonverbal Play	Produce nonverbal expressions, such as drawings or music, without a specific goal in mind.
Trust	Trust yourself and your experience.
Openness	Be open to all outer and inner experiences.
Courage	Be willing to experience and confront your fears.
Acceptance	Have a nonjudgmental attitude toward things as they are.
Love	Practice love and compassion.
Nonattachment	Be willing to accept things as they are.
Daily Practice	Practice paying daily attention to intuition.
Journal Keeping	Keep a record of intuitive insights.
Support Group	Find friends with whom you can share your intuitive experiences and who do not judge you.
Enjoyment	Find intrinsic satisfaction from expanded consciousness.

SOURCE: Adapted from Frances E. Vaughan's *Awakening Intuition* (Anchor Books, 1979).

one connected with a management decision and thus fail to see the person objectively, or may not be open to intuitive cues because he or she fears that the resulting accurate picture will not fit well with a preconceived notion or preference.

Individual examples of executives' responses are revealing in this regard. One top manager stated:

> I can't recall any wrong decisions where intuition was the final step in the process. I have had situations in which I failed to follow up on a feeling that "things weren't right" and made a decision that really screwed things up. At other times, I ignored the "hard nosed" rational assessment phase and allowed "wishful thinking" to control the decision.

Another highly placed executive vice-president of one of the largest corporations in America spoke of how the president of that same organization sometimes let his own ego involvement cloud his normal ability to make sound decisions: "Sometimes he just gets too ego involved. He wants 100% on an issue when he could

TABLE 10.2
Factors That Impede the Use of Intuition

Projection Mechanisms	*Stress Factors*
Attachment.	Physical/emotional tension.
Dishonesty.	Fatigue, illness.
Time Constraints	*Lack of Confidence*
Rushed to make decision.	Anxiety.
Failed to get necessary background facts.	Fear.
Failed to do homework required.	Confusion.
Acted impulsively.	Feeling of unbalance.
	Accommodation of too many desires/feelings/arguments of others, despite one's own feelings.

get 95% with a lot less grief. I've often had conflicts with him about his tendency to be this way."

Responding executives admitted that effective use of their intuitive ability was impeded when they also made other errors— for example, making critical decisions under time pressures, when they were not relaxed, or when they were not confident (see Table 10.2). Typical statements were: "I've made mistakes when fatigue, boredom, or anger were present"; "My wrong decisions come when physical or emotional stress are present"; "Most things go wrong when I don't listen to myself"; and "When time pressure exists, I make the wrong decision. Supervisors or subordinates often just sit there expecting a decision right now."

Using Intuition in the Decision-Making Process

We have seen thus far that the top executives tested definitely felt they consciously use their intuition to guide their most important decisions. They identified a specific body of cues or indicators employed as guideposts for action, and this process has resulted by their own admission in very successful major decisions. At the same time, they stated that their mistakes resulted primarily from the fact that they failed to use their intuition effectively to guide their decisions. They allowed themselves to get "off course" by letting such factors as ego involvement block the signals normally picked up by their intuitive radar.

What we have identified, then, according to interview data, is a decision-making skill that top executives *believe in and use* to guide their most important decisions. If this is the case, do all executives use their intuitive ability in the same way and at the same stage in their decision-making process, or does the use of this tool vary from executive to executive? To answer this question, the survey asked the executives how they go about using intuition to make their most important decisions.

Their replies revealed that each was conscious of a methodology or system that worked best for them. Many executives shared and used the same or similar systems: They activated intuition in a similar manner and employed it at the same stage in their decision-making process. Nevertheless, several executives in the sample used distinctly different techniques, which varied from executive to executive. In this group, each decision maker had fashioned his or her own particular system (custom-designed to work for them), and each used intuition at different stages in the decision-making process.

Many executives in the sample indicated that they used intuitive ability like *an explorer*. When making decisions about the organization's future, they tried to use intuition to *foresee* the correct path to follow. Under these circumstances, this group of executives was particularly careful to give intuition "free rein," since they were trying to generate unusual possibilities and new options that might not normally emerge from an analysis of past data or traditional ways of doing things. The most effective method for achieving this goal, they found, was *not to adopt* a rigid system or step-by-step method of decision making. What worked was allowing the mind "to flow" where it wanted to go—whether it was sifting past experience or simply playing with concepts and ideas. One executive described the process this way: "The idea of a technique suggests to me a rigidity that chokes off intuition. My own intuition requires freedom that can chew on all sorts of ideas and methods for nourishment."

Another top decision maker explained the intuitive method in this way: "I strive to be independent, nonconformist, and nontraditional in the 'best' sense of these terms. . . . This leads me to consider the possibilities of the unusual—in people and ideas."

On the other hand, a large number of respondents used their intuitive ability quite differently. They had a more structured decision-making system that they routinely employed; it involved specific steps that were regularly followed—often including as the first step the gathering and analyzing of all the relevant data available concerning the problem at hand. For these executives, intuition was used at the back end, not the front end, of the process—not so much as an explorer, but rather as a *synthesizer and integrator*. These executives often insisted on having an adequate amount of time for incubation, or the process of digesting and sifting through the information they have consumed before they would make a final decision. One person described a typical example of this particular approach:

> I establish a clear, concise objective. I gather whatever information is available, digest it and, if time is available, allow a day or two for my intuition to work on it. An acceptable answer, if not "the" answer has always evolved.

The third group of executives (those who had developed their own individual technique or system) might be termed *eclectic*. As mentioned before, the use of intuition to guide decisions varied from individual to individual. For example, one respondent said he used intuition to make early judgments on issues before him *long before* actual decisions were required. But he did not cut off the flow of data he received during the time between his initial assessments and actual decisions. Instead, he consciously cross-checked his initial "intuitive feel" against the data until the actual decision was finally required. He stated, "My initial intuitive decision turns out to be right more than 75% of the time." Another executive in this group used his intuition as a basis for delaying a final decision. He described his process this way:

> When the available options set off an internal signal that cries "wrong," I accept the need to give the decision more time. I start asking logical questions and test my feelings of comfort/discomfort with the answers given.

Techniques Used to Activate/Facilitate Intuition for Decision Making

Whether the respondents used their intuitive ability for exploration or integration, or in an eclectic fashion, as a total group they had in common several specific techniques for activating or facilitating intuition whenever they wished to use it in decision making. When asked how they did this, executives volunteered a long list of techniques they found helpful. (See Table 10.3.)

TABLE 10.3

Techniques and Exercises Used by Executives to Activate
Intuition for Decision Making

Relaxation Techniques	Mental Exercises
Clear mind mentally.	Play freely with ideas without a specific
Seek quiet times.	goal in mind.
Seek solitude.	Practice guided imagery.
Listen to classical music.	Practice tolerating ambiguity and accepting
Sleep on problem.	lack of control.
Fast.	Practice flexibility and openness to
Meditate.	unknowns as they appear.
Pray.	Practice concentration.
Drop problem and return to it later.	Try to think of unique solutions.
Exercise.	Be willing to follow up on points that have
Joke.	no factual justification.

Analytical Exercises

Discuss problem with many colleagues who have different perspectives as well as
   with respected friends.
Concentrate on listening not only to what but also to how one expresses oneself.
Immerse self totally in the issue at hand.
Identify pros and cons; then assess feeling about each option.
Consider problem only when most alert.
Tune into internal reactions to outside stimuli.
Analyze dreams.
Insist on creative pause before reaching decision.
Ask, "What do I want to do, and what is 'right' to do?"

I have summarized these techniques under the headings of
mental exercises, relaxation techniques, and analytical exercises.
What is worthy of note here is that this list corroborates many of
the techniques recommended by experts in the field of intuitional
development. For example, Philip Goldberg, author of *The Intuitive
Edge*, recommends "adopting a certain playfulness and an appreciation of whimsy." This is very similar to the top executives'
practice of "playing freely with ideas without a specific goal in
mind." Goldberg also says that intuition will work more effectively
if the problem to be solved is precisely defined. Goldberg explains
one technique as writing out one's thoughts and another as
"brainstorming with yourself—or allowing intuition to generate
alternatives." Again, these are similar to the techniques that top
executives actually used in decision-making processes when they
practiced the mental and analytical exercises that are listed in
Table 10.3.

KEEPING INTUITIVE ABILITY A SECRET

Expert psychologists working in this field generally agree that one important way to strengthen intuitive ability is to develop a support group—friends and colleagues with whom you can share the experience of intuition. However, executives are in large measure reluctant to engage in such practices. This is so at least in part because management training in recent years has heavily emphasized the use of analytical skills, logic, and other techniques associated with the left brain almost to the total exclusion of other potentially useful skills and methods. Moreover, our organizations and the larger Western culture reinforce this tendency.

It was not surprising, then, to find that nearly half of the respondents, when asked if they tended to keep their use of intuition a secret or felt comfortable sharing this information with others, indicated that they kept it a secret! One top female executive explained that revealing this fact would tend to undermine her effectiveness:

> At work, I work with men, men who tend to regard the use of intuition as suspect, female, and unscientific. . . . If I revealed my "secret," I'd have an even harder time persuading them to accept my suggestions. They wouldn't regard my ideas or decisions as being properly rational. Yet they can justify the worst kind of screw-ups with a chart and a computer printout.

Many intuitive executives—whether male or female—would probably agree that this woman described the kind of organizational environment they often have to endure. As one male manager explained:

> I have tried explanations without success. Also, superiors seem to believe some sort of witchcraft or other dark art is being employed. Better to use it to advantage than go through the hassle of explanation. I've even gotten to the point of telling others I'm just a good guesser.

Because intuitive executives often felt that their colleagues did not or would not understand that intuition can be a reliable basis on which to make important decisions, they often played elaborate games to legitimize the direction they proposed taking. While the decision was actually made on the basis of intuition, the justification used was quite different. One top executive at one of the largest and most successful corporations in America quipped, "Sometimes one must dress up a gut decision in 'data clothes' to make it acceptable or palatable, but this fine tuning is usually after the fact of the decision."

Another typical response is both illuminating and also instructive in that it points out the need for more theory and research on the use of intuition in decision making.

> I share this fact easily with other friendly intuitives, but try to disguise it as careful planning, research, or an intellectual effort around others. This is not a matter of adopting a cunning strategy; those without the willingness/ability to use their own intuition are often frightened by intuitive demonstrations or reject any evidence not fitting their current paradigm. It's hard, however, for anyone to talk about intuition—we lack theory that also fits our rational body of knowledge.

PRACTICING TECHNIQUES TO STRENGTHEN INTUITIVE ABILITY

Numerous experts recommend daily practice of a variety of specific techniques to develop intuitive ability further. But, for all the reasons already mentioned, such practice as a rule is not normally encouraged in organizations today. Even if an executive is aware that he or she has special skills in this area, the person is seldom encouraged to develop the talent further.

It is not surprising then to find even in this sample of highly intuitive executives a certain reluctance to actively embark on a program to further develop this talent. When asked if they regularly practice any technique to this end, only one-third indicated they did. Table 10.4 summarizes these techniques. Once again, this list corroborates the recommendations of experts in the field.

Of course, further empirical research is needed to demonstrate that practicing such techniques actually strengthens intuitive ability. Tentatively, however, one might suggest on the basis of responses received from the two-thirds who practiced no expansive techniques that they might very well benefit from further training. For example, several intuitive executives appeared to believe that practice itself might somehow undercut or hinder their present ability. One manager openly asked, "If I practiced such techniques, would I still be intuitive?" Several executives also admitted that they had never even thought about practicing any expansive techniques before receiving the survey questionnaire. One respondent said, "I do not know how to develop my intuitive ability further," and another exclaimed, "I would probably benefit from a

TABLE 10.4

Techniques Top Executives Regularly Practice to Expand Intuitive Ability

Relaxation Techniques	Mental/Analytical Techniques
Meditating.	Work with I Ching.
Using guided imagery.	Work with mind mapping.
Listening to inner self when relaxed.	Read and attend psychic-related events.
Writing journal.	Expose self to new ideas and situations
Keeping in good physical shape.	outside specialty.
Praying; reading Scripture.	Stay open and flexible.
Fasting once a month.	Read philosophy and philosophy of science.
	Read science fiction.
	Look for patterns where none appear to exist.
	Keep note pad nearby for recording ideas/
	insights before they are forgotten and to
	use for further development.

process that would let me build my effectiveness based on my intuitive sense."

At the very least, executives in this group would probably benefit from workshops on this subject if for no other reasons than to correct many of the misconceptions they currently have about their own intuitive ability and to bring them up to date on the most recent research in this field. It is quite probable that if they were made more aware of some of these techniques in a supportive setting, they could well make great strides in expanding their present capabilities.

Conclusions

The sample of top executives studied strongly believed that intuition was one of the skills they used to guide their most important decisions. They were able to clearly recall examples of such major decisions, their character and type, and the circumstances under which they were made. It also appears that these intuitive executives shared a common body of cues that they use to help make, delay, or not make critical decisions. Many (but not a majority) of executives in the sample regularly practiced a variety of techniques to expand their intuitive skills—exercises that are similar to those recommended as effective by psychologists working in the field for several years now.

Much more research is required on the process of intuitive decision making among top executives before definite conclusions can be reached. Right now, our research suggests that the effective use of intuition could well be a significant factor in increasing managerial productivity in the decade ahead, for several reasons. First, research on how the human brain functions is growing rapidly. Increasingly, processes such as intuition are better understood as are methods for enhancing them. As the mystery and magic of how intuition works is dispelled through hard science research, executives will more likely understand, accept, and use this skill that we all possess to some degree.

Second, the research findings presented here suggest that even among highly intuitive executives, considerable opportunity exists for honing and developing their skills. Executives admitted to frequently making a variety of errors in their decision-making processes, which interfered with the natural flow and effectiveness of their intuitive ability. Further training to help eliminate these errors is likely to increase present productivity. Less than half of the top executives in the sample were willing to share with colleagues the fact that they used intuition to guide their most important decisions. Instead, they spent time and resources "covering up" how they actually made decisions.

No doubt organizational productivity and job satisfaction could be increased if top executives would instead focus their energy in a new and more innovative direction. Specifically, they could adopt a more positive attitude about their own intuitive ability and take an active role in establishing support groups within their organizations in which such skills and techniques could be shared and experimented with. They could also implement research programs whereby intuitive decision-making processes could be quantified objectively and success records could be established. Sharing these findings could help all of us better understand how intuition may best be developed and applied in organizational settings likely to emerge in the decades ahead.

PART IV How to Use Intuition in Decision Making to Increase Productivity

Now that you have a measure of your intuitive ability, you are ready to explore how this skill can be used practically to help increase productivity—both on a personal and an organizational level. Part IV contains three selections that discuss how this can be done in a wide variety of decision-making settings. Case studies are featured here from both major private sector and public sector organizations.

Your attention is called in particular to the Brain Skill Management Program (BSM) outlined in the article on intrapreneurship. A BSM program enables you to identify highly intuitive executives (and/or use your own skills) and sequence their (or your) skills into the proper stage of the decision-making process, with a dramatic increase in productivity as a result.

11

The Intuitive Experience[†]

PHILIP GOLDBERG

When I am, as it were, completely myself, entirely alone, and of good cheer — say, travelling in a carriage, or walking after a good meal, or during the night when I cannot sleep; it is on such occasions that ideas flow best and most abundantly. Whence and how they come, I know not; nor can I force them.

— *Wolfgang Amadeus Mozart*

The quote above, from a letter written by Mozart, elucidates some of the central features of intuition with the impelling economy of one of the composer's quartets. Like other great artists, Mozart not only had uncommonly sharp intuition, but was sensitive to the elusive event itself. As we discuss the when and what of the intuitive experience, much of the material will be drawn from creators.

Although they vary with the circumstances and the individual, there are common elements in intuitive experiences. Your own might not be as dramatic as some of those recounted here, but the basic features probably apply. Understanding the basic themes and your own unique variations will help you become more sensitive to your intuition and take steps to develop it.

Incubation: The Pause That Enlightens

As Mozart's letter suggests, intuitive breakthroughs tend to occur when the creator is away from the work itself. Graham Wallas in his 1929 book, *The Art of Thought*, which outlined the

†SOURCE: "The Intuitive Experience," Philip Goldberg, Jeremy P. Tarcher, Inc., Los Angeles, Copyright © 1983 by Philip Goldberg; used by permission.

stages of the creative process, called this apparently fertile period "incubation." It typically follows sustained preliminary work, which Wallas labeled the "preparation" stage, and is in turn followed by stages of "illumination" (the intuitive breakthrough) and "verification." Mozart mentioned three common incubators: conveyances, solitary walks, and beds. The Poincaré discovery mentioned [in previous chapters] occurred on a bus. The nineteenth-century German physicist Hermann Helmholtz said that his inspirations would come during "the slow ascent of wooded hills on a sunny day." The philosophy of Jean-Jacques Rousseau came to him as a multitude of "truths" in a flash while walking from Paris to Vincennes in 1754. And numerous accounts of innovative thinkers and achievers give the impression that great ideas are as likely to be conceived in bed as children.

The list is long of people who awoke to new knowledge, had it delivered to them in a dream, or were seized by it as they lay about idly. Linus Pauling, for example, realized the shape of the protein molecule when, resting in bed, a string of paper dolls dangled from his hand in the shape of a helix. When Conrad Hilton wanted to buy the Stevens Corporation, which was going to the highest bidder in a closed-bid auction, he submitted a sealed bid for $165,000. But when he awakened the following morning, the number 180,000 was in his head, so he promptly changed the bid. He secured the property, which eventually brought him a $2-million profit, because the next highest bid was $179,800.

Kitchen rituals seem to have a certain fecundity, too. One oil company executive does the family dishes every night even though he has a dishwasher because he has his best ideas at that time. Bathroom ablutions also seem to work. So many inspirations have arisen during shaving (Einstein, for one, remarked on it) that one wonders why artists and scholars keep growing beards. The poet A. E. Housman wrote, "Experience has taught me, when I am shaving of a morning, to keep watch over my thoughts, because if a line of poetry strays into my memory, my skin bristles so that the razor ceases to act."

Psychologists have proposed several theories to explain incubations:

Elimination of fatigue. Like other organisms, we are self-regenerating systems; we normalize ourselves when given the opportunity. Getting away from taxing work might refresh a tired mind just as it rejuvenates tired muscles, thus making it more receptive to intuitive impulses.

Stress reduction. The strain of hard work and the frustration of not having found an answer might cause anxiety. That would work against intuition, which functions most effectively in relaxed conditions. High levels of arousal in the nervous system have been found to inhibit creativity, and at least one study of intuitive problem solving found that subjects placed in a state of anxiety did not do as well as a low-arousal group.

Set breaking. In *The Art of Creation*, Arthur Koestler speculated that incubation allows the mind to discard the "tyranny" of discursive thinking habits: "This rebellion against constraints which are necessary to maintain the order and discipline of conventional thought, but an impediment to the creative leap, is symptomatic both of the genius and the crank; what distinguishes them is the intuitive guidance which only the former enjoys." Innovative thinking can be blocked by habitual ways of viewing a problem. We tend to get into mental ruts. An incubation period might break those patterns, freeing the mind to entertain new possibilities.

Selective forgetting. Psychologist Herbert Simon suggests that in the early stages of problem solving we form a plan, which gets stored in short-term memory. While working we acquire new, pertinent information that we might overlook because our minds are dominated by the original plan. But the new information gets stored in *long-term* memory, Simon believes, and might become activated during an incubation period, when ineffective old ideas are selectively forgotten.

Nonconscious synthesis. Unlike computers, the mind is capable of doing many things at once. While we are sleeping, walking in the woods, washing dishes, or shaving, important work is being done outside our awareness. The factory of the mind continues to work while the manager is out, assembling diverse raw materials and putting them together in unusual ways to create new products. This is what William James meant when he said that we learn to swim in winter and skate in summer.

Incidental input. Nonconscious synthesizing, some psychologists believe, might be aided during incubation by the perception of objects or events that are analogous to the problem under consideration. A scientist who notices similarities between wildly different objects or processes might pursue the metaphor to connections that yield fruitful hypotheses. New products are invented when someone sees a functional link between unrelated phenomena; Gutenberg's mind merged three unlikely elements—the wine press, the process of minting coins, and the stamping of playing cards—to come up with the concept of movable type. And it is said that Mozart thought of a cantata for *Don Giovanni* when he saw an orange, which reminded him of a popular Neapolitan song he'd heard five years earlier.

Each of these theories seems to have validity, and perhaps each process occurs simultaneously during incubation.

Because of a shortage of experimental evidence, however, not all psychologists accept incubation as a necessary prelude to inspiration. Many studies have found no incubation effect at all, and most studies that *have* demonstrated it have never been duplicated.

One reason for this is the unrealistic nature of the testing procedures. Typically, subjects are asked to solve a problem that requires insight. One group is given a break while another works straight through. The results of the two groups are then compared. The subjects are generally given only a short period of time to work on the problem before incubation, and the incubation period itself is brief, perhaps only ten or fifteen minutes. The subjects are told when to incubate, and the type of activity they engage in during the break is determined by the researchers. These activities vary from test to test—waiting in an empty room, doing another demanding task, actively reviewing the problem, and so forth—but they are all artificial and imposed. Then there is the question of the subjects themselves: they are usually college students fulfilling a course requirement or getting a small fee.

As Robert Olton and David Johnson, whose study showed no incubation effect, put it, "'Real life' accounts of the phenomenon describe a profoundly motivated person, a time period that often lasts for days or months, and a task that involves the use of a *well-orchestrated, highly developed repertoire of cognitive skills and abilities* appropriate to a specific body of knowledge."

The anecdotal evidence—not just from great creators but from average people in all walks of life who have come to know the value of "sleeping on it"—is rather compelling. Without exception, the people I interviewed said that their most significant intuitive experiences came when they were away from their work. Despite the lack of experimental proof, a well-timed incubation period seems to be a good bait for intuition, a theme whose practical implications we will return to in later chapters.

However, I have a different objection to the incubation model as it is normally defined: it does not explain all those intuitions that *don't* come during breaks in activity. The intuitive functions we have called evaluative and operative are likely to fall into this category. And sometimes a fertile discovery or creative solution pops into mind when we are busy working on the problem itself. The executive who comes up with unusual decisions in the midst of chaos, the musician who takes off in uncharted directions during a song, the mathematician who suddenly deciphers a puzzle while scribbling symbols on the blackboard, the lover who knows what his or her partner *really* means as they converse, the parent who knows why a child is crying while wiping away tears—all are examples of how intuition can arise during the activity it addresses.

The way we now understand incubation—as an extended period of time away from the relevant activity—will probably be modified. Whatever takes place during those long stretches of time might also occur instantaneously during microscopic diversions of attention. In a meeting, for example, while someone else is speaking, you might miss a word or two. While working intensely on a task, your mind might wander ever so slightly. Such lapses, which we usually deplore, might actually represent momentary incubations, enough of an interlude to set up the right conditions for intuition.

This idea can be taken a step further. The mind can work on several levels simultaneously, although strictly speaking attention is in only one place at a time. Quite possibly, while attending to one aspect of a problem, another part of the mind is, in effect, incubating. For example, the mathematician at the blackboard might be writing down material thought of a moment earlier; while engaged in that sensory-motor activity (which is virtually automatic for him) he might be talking to a colleague or a class. As he writes or speaks, segments of his mind might be otherwise engaged. An instant later a solution might pop into his mind. This isn't quite the incubation that Poincaré had when he went off to military service, but perhaps it works in the same way.

This should not seem at all outrageous, given the fact that we are always doing many things at once. While driving we hum tunes, watch traffic, listen to a companion, and more, simultaneously. And in the midst of all that, we might have an inspired hunch about a work problem or a relationship. If that can happen, why couldn't we be fully involved in a task and have an intuition about another aspect of the same task? Thought always precedes action, and some non-conscious activity must precede thought, so in a sense some component of the mind is always a step ahead of what we are thinking and doing at any given moment. In some cases, the equivalent of a fertile incubation period might be occurring, even though there is no incubation in the usual sense.

Perhaps the truly salient features of incubation are on the psychophysiological level. Incubation should probably be though of as a state of mind or a specific quality of consciousness, the details of which future researchers might be able to discern. Anecdotal reports suggest that a calm inner condition, with low arousal and a low signal-to-noise ratio (meaning that the mind is relatively quiet and free of unnecessary "static"), might constitute the most favorable ground for intuitive experience. Perhaps some forms of incubation, in the traditional sense, produce these physiological conditions. Further, the same or similar conditions might coexist with other states at certain times, enabling intuition to occur during active or more highly aroused periods.

If an incubationlike condition is a necessary prelude to all types of intuition, as I believe it is, then knowing what goes on in the central nervous system at the time might help us free our intuitive faculties. . . . Let's examine the intuitive experience itself.

The Paradoxes of Intuition

"*Whence* and *how* they come, I know not," wrote Mozart, "nor can I force them." Echoed by intuitive people in all fields, this remark suggests the spontaneity and effortlessness of intuition. Intuition comes on its own. Whether a trivial hunch, a pragmatic business decision, or a discovery in a laboratory, it has the same quality that Keats referred to when he wrote, "If poetry comes not naturally as leaves to a tree it had better not come at all." Bach expressed much the same idea in response to a question about where he found his melodies: "The problem is not finding them, it's—when getting up in the morning and getting out of bed—not stepping on them."

You can no more force intuition than you can force someone to fall in love with you. You can prepare yourself for it, invite it, and create attractive conditions to coax it, but you can't say, "Now I shall have an intuition," just as, in Shelley's words, "A man cannot say, 'I will compose poetry.' The greatest poet even cannot say it: for the mind is as a fading coal, which some invisible influence, like an inconstant wind, awakens to transitory brightness."

There is a surprising quality to the experience, as if the intuiter were a magician pulling knowledge out of his own hat, shocking himself. That might be one reason a fortuitous intuition often brings with it a feeling of glee; like children, we love to be tricked. We also like a good joke, and intuition often has the qualities of a punch line. We laugh when the comedian surprises us with an illogical conclusion to a story. Intuition can defy expectation by suddenly veering off in a new direction, rearranging the material we have been working with, or bringing in something that seems entirely out of place.

Not that every intuition has an unanticipated twist. It might suggest a predictable course of action or confirm the choice of a rather ordinary alternative. What might be surprising in such situations is that we feel far more certain than we have any reason to—or that the intuition appeared at all. Intuition can be like one of those friends who shows up a the oddest times, even though all attempts to get him to call ahead or keep an appointment are in vain. Whether it is its content, its degree of certitude, or its timing, something about intuition is usually surprising.

At the same time, just as an absurd punch line somehow "fits" the joke, the content of an intuition may elicit what psychologist Jerome Bruner calls "the shock of recognition," a certain obviousness that, as soon as the surprise wears off, makes us think, "Of course—how could I not have seen it?" From that point on, it might seem absurd that we ever did *not* know what we now know. Mathematicians who wrestle with conundrums for long periods of time say that once the puzzle is solved they cannot remember what it felt like not to know the answer.

A young woman named Terri related a similar experience with a career change: "I had been unsatisfied in my work for three years and felt a strong urge to do something more meaningful. But the only thing I could come up with as an alternative was 'helping people.' That and dancing, which was ridiculous, since my dance training had been suspended ten years earlier, and I wasn't about to resume at age thirty-two. Then it suddenly dawned on me: become a dance therapist! It was a total shock. But from that moment on, it seemed absurd that I ever considered anything else."

In a typical intuitive experience there is a sense of being a recipient as opposed to an initiator. Creative people often describe themselves as "agents" or "channels" for some other source. In a religious context this is known as being an instrument of the Divine, or have God work His will through you. Milton wrote that the Muse "dictated" to him the whole "unpremeditated song" that we know as *Paradise Lost*, and Bach said, "I play the notes in order, as they are written. It is God who makes the music." The more secular-oriented, like Joseph Heller, just say, "I feel that these ideas are floating around in the air and they pick me to settle upon. The ideas come to me; I don't produce them at will."

When the intuitive mind is working with particular fluency, the actions of hands, feet, and tongue seem to occur without deliberation or conscious thought. Athletes and musicians often say they can almost watch themselves perform as if they were in the audience. The great running back Hershel Walker said, "I surprise myself. I don't even know what I'm going to do. I don't have real control. I'll start running and I don't know what's coming next." Try to convince his opponents that Walker doesn't know what he's doing.

Writers often experience what one described as being "part of the typewriter, trying to keep up with whatever is giving the orders." You commonly hear novelists and playwrites say that characters "take over," acting on their own, speaking dialogue, changing the plot irreversibly. Here is Henry James describing how he came up with the plot components of *The Ambassadors*: "These things continued to fall together, as by the neat action of their own weight and form, even while their commentator [James] scratched his head about them; he easily sees now that they were always well in advance of him. As the case completed itself he had, in fact, from a good way behind, to catch up with them, breathless and a little flurried as best he could."

This self-propelling quality of intuition should not be mistaken for the automaticity of habit or physical instinct. Routinely, we act without thinking through the steps, responding mechanically, with well-rehearsed patterns set in motion by an outside stimulus. A driver automatically swerves when a car cuts him off, an editor automatically corrects a spelling error, a mechanic automatically turns the right screw, a dentist automatically diagnoses a toothache. These acts are not the same as the sudden appearance of something new: the driver has a hunch to make a detour and finds a shortcut; the editor gets a great idea for reorganizing the book; the mechanic hits upon why a car won't start when no one else can figure it out; the dentist senses complication beyond the obvious diagnosis.

So it is that a fact might appear to be a message, a decision might seem to be a command, an idea might seem to be a gift. With intuition you, the magician, are surprised by the rabbit, which seems to be in the service of another, superior sorcerer.

Yet—another paradox—it is your hand pulling out the rabbit, and you feel deeply involved in the process. Again, artists embody the dramatic example. They typically report that, in addition to being a "channel," they are so absorbed with the objects of their imagination or the tools of their trade as to feel at one with them.

As William Butler Yeats expressed it, they are "self-possessed in self-surrender" at the moment of revelation.

The attached, involved side of the equation recalls . . . "intimacy," . . . that sense of merging with the object of knowledge. The French philosopher Henri Bergson called intuition a "kind of intellectual sympathy by which one places oneself within an object in order to coincide with what is unique in it and consequently inseparable." By this "entering into" the object, we can know it perfectly and absolutely, Bergson maintained. He contrasted this with intellectual analysis, which he called "translation" and a "representation" in symbols.

Hence the intuitive experience contains contradictions: it is unexpected, but somehow fits; it comes from within, but at the same time from some unnameable *other*; we produce it, but it also seems to happen *to* us; we are involved but uninvolved, absorbed but detached.

The Holistic Nature of Intuition

The word *holistic* has often been ascribed to intuition. It has been taken to mean that intuition gives knowledge of wholes as opposed to just parts. But that can be misleading because it focuses on *what* is known. It is difficult to determine whether something one knows is a whole or a part, since, as systems theory tells us, every part is a whole made up of smaller parts, and every whole is a part of a larger whole (cells are wholes that are parts of organs, which are parts of organisms, and so on). The only object of knowledge that can be called holistic can't really be called an object: the Absolute is wholeness itself; it contains everything and is contained in everything.

The actual holistic quality of intuition has to do with two things. It is axiomatic that a whole is greater than the sum of its parts. The parts and their sum can be discerned through rational analysis, but the *greater* can be apprehended only through intuition. It is experiential rather than conceptual, a realization and a feeling, an intimate identification with the wholeness, not an inference or a fact to be imparted verbally.

The second aspect of intuitive holism has to do with the experience that Mozart seemed to be referring to when he wrote, "Nor do I hear in my imagination the parts *successively* but I hear them, as it were, all at once." We think of intuition as a flash that comes and goes instantaneously. In that instant might be contained an extraordinary amount of information. If a picture is worth a thousand words, then an intuition might be worth a thousand pictures. It is like a train speeding past your field of vision: you don't see any details, just a blur accompanied by sounds—and yet in that instant you know, at the very least, that it was a train. Time seems to be compressed, and so, in some mysterious way, is meaning.

We normally experience and conceive of meaning in a linear fashion, as a sequence of symbols and concepts strung together. An intuitive experience, however, may contain no clear boundaries, no obvious demarcations, no sequential arrangement. It might contain the essence of the knowledge, the way a seed contains the essence of a tree, or it might contain some details; it might be a fragment of the whole, or almost complete. It will usually contain a richness of meaning that will take an eon to articulate compared to the time it took to apprehend.

Flash in the Mind

Intuition is often so concentrated that it flashes by before we can seize it. We have all had the frustrating experience of having a solution dash past our awareness, leaving us to bemoan, "What was that? I had the answer!" It is like trying to capture a snowflake. This sense of loss is what makes artists feel that what they produce is just a drop of water, not a snowflake. Said Shelley, "When composition begins, inspiration is already on the decline, and the most glorious poetry that has ever been communicated to the world is probably a feeble shadow of the original conception of the poet."

But that is not always the case. "The committing to paper is done quickly enough," Mozart's letter continues, "for everything is . . . already finished; and it rarely differs on paper from what it was in my imagination." Perhaps the difference is in the intuiter's ability to sustain the intuitive moment so that its features and its essential message can be clearly apprehended. The impact of an intuition may in some way be related to the clarity with which it is perceived, and the clarity may have something to do with extension in time, or with a kind of *suspension* of time. Look at this part of Mozart's letter: "My subject enlarges itself, becomes methodized and defined, and the whole, though it be long, stands almost complete and finished in my mind, so that I can survey it, like a fine picture or a beautiful statue, at a glance."

Initially, Mozart seems to be describing nothing more than good imagination. But his use of such phrases as "enlarges itself" and "becomes methodized" suggest that he is still an uninvolved witness. Sometimes the intuitive moment can be kept alive undiluted, as if the passing train were to slow down—or time were to stand still—enough for us to appreciate a face in the window or a sign on the side of the locomotive. This would not always be necessary, of course, but at times intuition might contain the germ of further knowledge or richer detail.

It is often advantageous to stretch intuition or hold it still for an instant longer. It is also advantageous to recapture at will the intuitive experience—not just to remember its essential features but to actually reenter the state in which it was captured. Many of us have to get back into the mood of the previous day's work in order to proceed with any continuity. This ability should grow as our intuitive capacities develop.

The Language of Intuition

Like thought in general, intuition can take on different forms. Every sense modality has corresponding mental properties. In fact, Indian philosophy maintains that every thought contains qualities associated with each of the senses, just as any material object could, if our senses were acute enough, be seen, heard, tasted, smelled, and touched.

That the mind can operate in each sensory mode is obvious from the common experience of memory. When recalling a particular event, you might, in your mind, hear a person speaking or a melody played; see a face or a scene; smell the jasmine; taste an apple pie as if it were in your mouth; feel the brush of wind or the touch of a hand on your skin. In the same way, some people can imagine objects they have never actually experienced.

The mind shifts from one modality to another just as we can shift our focus from one sense perception to another. Where the focus rests depends on both the situation and the propensities of the experiencer. We seem to prefer one way of perceiving over another. Painters, for example, might see things in a scene that a musician would not, whereas the musician might be tuned to the sounds around him. In a wooded clearing one person might focus on the feel of the grass underfoot, another on the scent in the air, and still another on the taste of a blackberry.

The same kind of propensities seem to hold in thought as well, and the form our intuition takes will usually correspond to these preferences. Some people tend to think in words, others more visually (these seem to be the predominate modes). There are situational variations, of course. No matter how visual a person normally is, he will think in words when deciding how to address the boss. A verbal person will think in visual images when deciding how to decorate a room.

It is often said that rational thought is verbal and intuition is nonverbal. Like many declarations about intuition, this one has some validity but is overstated. I for one frequently have intuition in linguistic form; when writing, the right word or phrase might pop spontaneously to mind. In routine instances, this might be attributed to memory, as if my mind had scanned some stored vocabulary list. But when the product is an unusual phrase or an imaginative combination of words, it is every bit as intuitive as a business hunch or scientific discovery.

When Samuel Taylor Coleridge awoke with the "distinct recollection of the whole" of "Kubla Khan," the famous unfinished poem that composed itself in a dream, "all the images rose up before him as *things*," he said, speaking of himself in third person. But the words were also there. Coleridge said there was "a parallel production of the correspondent expressions without any sensation or consciousness of effort."

It is not just writers, however, to whom intuition comes in verbal form. Others refer to inner messages as coming to them in explicit language. For example, a psychotherapist said that when working with a particular patient the word "father" kept popping into her mind, although at the time the patient was discussing a problem with her job. Finally the psychologist yielded to the persistent voice and said, "Tell me about your father." It turned out that the patient's boss reminded her of her father, who had raped her when she was a teenager, a crucial bit of suppressed information.

Thus while it is frequently nonverbal, intuition can speak our language without losing its essential character. Similarly, while we normally reason verbally, this is not always the case. Psychological instruments that test reasoning ability often use sequences of pictures, not words. For example, a comic-strip artist or filmmaker works with logical sequences of images. A composer reasons with pure sound. When we manipulate objects in space, including our own bodies, we might be reasoning spatially without verbally constructing each proposition.

On the other hand, intuition will often come in visual images, particularly when the subject matter calls for it, as in art or architecture. An electronics technician said, "On the train home or in the middle of the night I might suddenly see before me in minute detail a wiring diagram that I had been working on that day. Sometimes key connections are moved around, solving a problem that had been driving me crazy." His account is reminiscent of the experiences of Nikola Tesla, the inventor of, among other things, the AC generator and fluorescent lighting. Tesla said that he was capable of such minutely detailed visions that he could actually perform "tests" by mentally running machines for weeks and then looking for signs of wear.

The intuition of scientists can often be as visual as that of poets and painters. One of the most interesting visual intuiters—and one of the more important—was the nineteenth-century British physicist Michael Faraday. Among other things, Faraday developed the first dynamo and electric motor, ideas that originated in his mental vision of the universe as a composite of curved tubes through which energy radiated. Faraday also laid the foundations of modern field theory with ideas that developed out of his images of "lines of forces" surrounding magnets and electric currents.

Other examples of predominantly visual intuitions include that of Mendeleev awakening with the image, virtually in its entirety, of the Periodic Table of Elements that now adorns chemistry classrooms all over the world. And of course there is the famous dream of Friedrich August von Kekulé:

> I turned my chair to the fire and dozed. . . . Again the atoms were gambolling before my eyes. This time the smaller groups kept modestly in the background. My mental eye, rendered more acute by repeated visions of this kind, could now distinguish larger structures, of manifold conformation; long rows, sometimes more closely fitted together; all twining and twisting in snakelike motion. But look! What was that? One of the snakes had seized hold of its own tail, and the form whirled mockingly before my eyes. As if by a flash of lightning, I awoke. . . . Let us learn to dream, gentlemen.

In this way did Kekulé discover a revolutionary idea that was to become a cornerstone of modern chemistry: the molecules of certain organic compounds are not open structures but closed rings.

Kekulé's vision brings up an interesting point: intuition is often symbolic. Carl Jung tells us that a snake biting its own tail is a universal symbol that has taken on different meanings in different cultures. It is not clear how Kekulé knew the snake referred to his laboratory work rather than to something else. Sometimes the meaning is obvious, but at other times it has to be figured out, which might require additional intuitive input as well as analysis. This holds not just for visual images but for any intuitive message. In a remote-viewing test performed at Stanford, subjects in a lab were asked to describe the location of another person. Their hunches were remarkable accurate, but often misinterpreted. For example, they might feel the presence of an "august" or "solemn" building and say it was a library when it was actually a church.

At times the verbal and visual modalities are combined. Coleridge saw the images *and* heard the words to "Kubla Khan." When I had the idea to write this book, what came to me was an image of a bulging file folder filled with an eclectic assortment of notes and clippings. I had been accumulating material for a book, but I could never figure out what the book would be about. When the realization came, I saw that folder, accompanied by some subtle sense of the work *intuition*. I can't even be sure it was a sound, but the meaning was clear.

In a survey of mathematicians, Jacques Hadamard found that most of them think visually—although not necessarily in mathematical symbols—but also kinetically. Einstein's reply was: "The words or the language, as they are written or spoken, do not seem to play any role in my mechanism of thought; the physical entities which seem to serve as elements in thought are certain signs and more or less clear images which can be 'voluntarily' reproduced and combined. . . . The above-mentioned elements are, in my case, of visual and some of muscular type. Conventional words or other signs have to be thought for laboriously only in a secondary stage."

The word *muscular* is clearly an indication of the involvement of a kinesthetic element, which is probably mediated by the sense of touch. Einstein added that vague "combinatory play" with these elements is the "essential feature in productive thought—before there is any connection with logical construction in words or other kinds of signs which can be communicated to others."

As expressions like "I felt it in my bones" and "I had a gut feeling" indicated, physical sensations are often associated with intuition. Often they are global feelings that seem to radiate all over. People describe them as a "glow," a "burning sensation," a "cold chill," "tingling," or "electricity running through me." Sometimes they are localized and can be pinpointed with precision. Describing what happens when a line of poetry comes to him, A.E.

Housman wrote that his skin bristled. He added: "This particular symptom is accompanied by a shiver down the spine: there is another which consists of a constriction in the throat and a precipitation of water to the eyes; and there is a third which I can only describe by borrowing a phrase from one of Keats's last letters, where he says, speaking of Fanny Brawne, 'everything that reminds me of her goes through me like a spear.' The seat of this sensation is the pit of the stomach."

Eugene Gendlin, a psychologist / philosopher whose research on people undergoing psychotherapy led to the technique and book called *Focusing*, found that successful patients were those who were able to derive meaning from what he terms "the felt sense"— what the body knows of a particular situation or problem. This "fuzzy, murky" sense, Gendlin found, seems to occur around the middle of the body, along the central axis, anywhere from the navel to the throat, and most often the stomach. This could possible have something to do with the subtle energy centers call *chakras* that Indian philosophy places at seven points along the spinal column. In any event, the experience of knowing does not seem to be confined to the head. I am reminded of the Zen story in which a monk is asked where he thinks: he points to his stomach.

Physical sensations can interact with intuition in several ways. They might, for example, be raw data that provide information about the body itself. Someone who is sensitive to bodily signals might intuit the presence of a disorder before it can be diagnosed through ordinary methods, or he might know precisely what foods to eat. Here is an example of a good hunch precipitated by the body: A salesman was bothered for some time by a shooting pain in his left leg, especially when he sat. On his way to see a physician, his leg in pain, he had a sudden flash and knew what the problem was: sitting on a wallet bulging with credit cards. The skeptical doctor checked for everything else but found nothing. A switch of pockets was the cure.

As an intermediary between the environment and the intuitive mind, the body might provide behavioral instructions. Sudden muscular tension, a quickened pulse, or a fluttering sensation in the stomach might alert you to a real danger—the equivalent of "Don't believe a word this guy says" or "Get out of this place fast." Quite often there will be no discernible message, just a strong physical urge that is difficult to resist. A female executive tells this story: "I entered the lobby of a building and got on an elevator. A man stepped on behind me. Just before the doors closed, I felt impelled to leave, as if I were being swept back into the lobby by an outside force. I went into a phone booth, and while I was dialing the man stepped out of the same elevator. That was the first time I was consciously suspicious. Sure enough, the guy waited in the lobby until another woman got on an elevator alone. He was apprehended and turned out to have a record."

Physical sensations are not always warnings, of course. They also accompany positive feelings, such as comfort in the presence of a particular person. They might also alert us to an impending intuitive experience. Quite often there is a kind of halo, an intimation that preceeds intuition. Unlike a trumpet-blowing herald, this intimation might be just a faint body sense, some barely perceptible shift in how you feel, like a small child tugging at your sleeve. A receptive person will pay attention instead of trudging on to some other concern and thus missing the intuition entirely. Think of it as hunting: when you pick up the scent of your prey, or hear rustling in the underbrush, you freeze, taking care not to frighten it away.

Bodily sensations might also be part of the feedback loop that helps us evaluate a particular intuition. A decision, a solution, or an operative prompting might be accompanied by a perceptible physiological change. The strength, persistence, and quality of the feeling might be a clue to how seriously to take the mental content. Frances Vaughan quotes physicist Carson Jeffries, who noted that when a sudden spark of insight is true it gives him "a warm, sensual body pleasure." He said he could tell when an idea was good because "it excited me and made me happy."

It would seem that part of becoming more intuitive would be an ability to recognize and decipher the body's messages. This requires a certain sensitivity and a good deal of self-awareness. There are no rules for interpreting bodily sensations in this regard; they are strictly individual matters that can be sorted out with repeated experience. The signals are often quite subtle, reaching awareness only when they exceed a certain threshold of intensity. Also, it is easy to attach too much cognitive significance to them. Much has been made of the connection between intuition and the body, and we have to be wary of overdoing it. Some people go so far as to suggest that intuition *is* body awareness, and that *the* way to be more intuitive is to "get in touch with your body," as if flesh and blood were the exclusive repositories of wisdom. It is important to acknowledge that the body contains information and transmits messages, but we should not elevate every physical impulse to the level of an epiphany.

The verbal, visual, and kinesthetic forms we have discussed are the most common ways intuition is expressed *when it is vivid*. Most of the time, however, it is difficult to categorize the form. People get flustered when pressed for a description and end up saying, "It was just a thought" or "It was a feeling." Typically, such responses seem unsatisfactory; we feel we ought to be able to describe the experience more objectively. But the fact is that intuition *is* thought, and thought is frequently a faint, ephemeral, smoky abstraction that can only be described as a feeling.

There is good reason to believe that thought originates in a more abstract, feelinglike form and takes on concrete, symbolic qualities in a subsequent state of development, particularly when communication is necessary. The feeling level is actually deeper and closer to the source than the more tangible manifestations of sound, sight, and touch. This would seem true of ordinary speech: first you know something, then you find words to convey that meaning, and sometimes there is no way to capture it adequately. A flustered TV character once said of a garbled statement, "You should have heard it before I said it." We might speculate that many intuitions appearing in a specific form, especially a verbal form, are actually adulterated versions of the original, and perhaps some depth of meaning or emotion has thereby been sacrificed.

This is important to keep in mind; often when we have an intimation of intuition, or some faint feeling, we try to force it into a palpable structure, usually a verbal message, even though doing so might create distortions by filtering it through layers of other psychic content. Those faint feelings are actually a deeper, purer level of mind than verbal, visual, or kinetic modes. Part of cultivating intuition, therefore, might entail learning to tune into earlier developmental stages of the impulses. . . .

The Emotions of Knowing

As the use of "feeling" to indicate both an emotion and a physical event suggests, there is a strong connection between the two realms of experience. Perhaps both are mediated by the sense of touch. As with bodily signals, emotions may be the subject matter of intuition (or of rational analysis, for that matter), as when you have an insight into why you have been feeling sad, restless, or sentimental. They might also be clues that feed data about the environment to intuition—you get a positive, happy feeling about a prospective employee and hire him even though he is less qualified than the candidate who made you feel hostile. You can't figure out why you get uncomfortable when you're with a certain person, and you suddenly realize he is keeping something from you. Or an emotion might be a simultaneous expression of an intuition, a clue to its meaning or veracity. That is the context in which we will discuss it here.

Knowing feels good. There is a certain tension created by ignorance, an incompleteness in an unresolved problem. This has physiological and emotional counterparts. When the answer comes, there is a feeling of restoration. Wholeness is restored, and that feels comfortable, like filling in a circle that had a missing section. This might precipitate a sense of exhilaration, joy, or overpowering ecstasy, often accompanied by a burst of energy or heightened sense perception.

In *The Courage to Create*, psychologist Rollo May discusses a sudden breakthrough: "The moment the insight broke through, there was a special transluscence that enveloped the world, and my vision was given a special clarity. . . . The world, both inwardly and outwardly, takes on an intensity that may be momentarily overwhelming." He also writes, "I experience a strange lightness in my step as though a great load were taken off my shoulders, a sense of joy on a deeper level that continues without any relation whatever to the mundane tasks that I may be performing at the time."

They are not always so powerful, of course, but the emotional correlates of accurate and important intuitions seem to center around happiness, harmony, and beauty. It is often said that suffering is necessary in order to create. The fabled cases of suffering artists, however, reveal that anguish and misery came when for one reason or another they could *not* create. It is a dramatic expression of the tension, frustration, and sense of incompleteness that accompanies ignorance. When actually creating, those suffering artists were in bliss, a heightened version of the rapture you or I might feel when we come to a realization about a person or problem. Mozart, who suffered intensely, wrote of the intuitive inspiration, "All this fires my soul," and in the same paragraph, "What a delight this is I cannot tell! All this inventing, this producing, takes place in a pleasing lively dream."

One of the central emotions of intuition, and a major clue to the quality of the revelation, is a sense of esthetic pleasure. As Keats wrote, "Beauty is truth, truth beauty." That sense of beauty and harmony informs artist, scientist, businessman, and lover alike. Something in true intuition elicits the same response as a painting, a song, or the resolution of a well-told tale. It has a certain symmetry and coherence, a sense of balance and inevitability. When an idea doesn't quite fit it is like a dab of the wrong color on a painting or the wrong line of dialogue in a play. It projects dissonance.

When people are asked how they can distinguish the exceptional intuition from the mediocre, it is beauty that comes up consistently. Paul Dirac, who predicted the existence of antimatter two years before it was proven, wrote, "It seems that if one is working from the point of view of getting beauty into one's equations, and if one has really a sound insight, one is on a sure line of progress." Writing in *Newsweek*, Horace Freeland Judson recalls asking Dirac how he recognizes beauty in a theory. "Well—you feel it," Dirac answered. "Just like beauty in a picture or beauty in music. You can't describe it, it's something—and if you don't feel it, you just have to accept that you're not susceptible to it. No one can explain it to you."

Henri Poincaré felt that exceptional mathematicians, those who become creators, are capable of an "intuition of mathematical order that makes us divine hidden harmonies and relations." Like other mathematicians, he spoke of the elegance created by mathematical entities "whose elements are harmoniously disposed so that the mind without effort can embrace their totality."

Despite a great deal of opposition, Johannes Kepler held to his revolutionary astronomy because, he wrote, "I have attested to it as true in my deepest soul and I contemplate its beauty with incredible and ravishing delight." As in art, simplicity seems to be a key to the esthetic of truth. According to the contemporary physicist Richard Feynman, we are able to recognize scientific truth by its simplicity and beauty: "What is it about nature that lets this happen, that it is possible to guess from one part what the rest is going to do? . . . I think it is because nature has a simplicity and therefore a great beauty." For that reason, scientists are trained to look for the simplest hypotheses consistent with the facts.

What is most intriguing about this connection between beauty and knowledge—and its relation to the day-to-day reality of making decision sand solving problems—is that the same qualities are associated with practicality. Rollo May said of psychotherapy, "Insights emerge not chiefly because they are 'rationally true' or even helpful, but because they have certain form, the form that is beautiful because it completes an incomplete Gestalt." Perhaps the executive's declaration of "Beautiful!" when he hears a good idea has something to do the Poincaré's most telling remark about mathematics: "The useful combinations are precisely the most beautiful."

The Transcendental Exemplar

Previously I suggested that illumination, or transcendence, is a prototype of the more familiar varieties of intuition, and that it might serve as an explanatory model. Let's look at it in terms of the characteristics we have discussed in this chapter.

Spiritual disciplines have made a way of life of what we call incubation. Seekers who adopt the path of the recluse renounce worldly affairs for a monastic way, which can be regarded as one long incubation. Those who follow the householder path incorporate periods of incubation into their routines—daily meditations, rituals, secluded retreats. The phase of conscious work that precedes classical incubation can be likened to that portion of the seeker's pursuit when he studies sacred texts, ponders eternal riddles, performs service, listens to learned discourses, and so forth. But it is during the incubatory phases that illumination occurs. Indeed, it could be said that transcendence itself is the ultimate incubation, since it leaves behind even mental activity.

From what we know of the physiology of meditation, transcendence is a state of least excitation, of deep inner silence, along with heightened alertness. This corresponds to the postulated physiology of incubation. And, as the seeker progresses, the core of inner silence is maintained along with thought and action; this is reminiscent of the proposed incubatory state that can coexist with focused mental activity. Perhaps some physiological configuration accounts for the ability to prolong the intuitive moment as well as the range of illumination, which can be experienced as anything from a fleeting glimpse of pure awareness to the permanent awakening of enlightenment.

Despite the arduous discipline associated with mysticism, illumination itself is effortless and spontaneous. As is true with artists, despair is often the lot of seekers, but that is the passionate agony of frustration and restless anticipation. Illumination itself simply occurs, when it occurs, and is described as grace—a divine gift. It arrives like a bud in springtime, but without the predictability, when the seeker is adequately prepared. In fact, as with artistic inspiration and the everyday hunch, transcendence is actually inhibited by too much effort, and seekers are exhorted to "try without trying."

Like ordinary intuition, illumination has a paradoxical quality. It is an "inner" event, and yet it seems to descend like an offering from an outside source. As the seeker advances and the pure, undifferentiated Self is increasingly realized, he might experience the twin sense of being separate from his thoughts and actions—as if silently witnessing them—and at the same time in full control. He will apprehend both the changing, localized self and the universal, boundless Self; he will perceive the world as both part of him and apart from him; he will see reality as the One and the Many. These paradoxes cannot be resolved rationally, but are reconciled by the intuitive experience of illumination.

The holistic quality of intuition—the concentration of vast knowledge into a single instant—and the intimate union with what is known are both exemplified in illumination. There is no *object* of knowledge as such, but in that state the knower is one with all that is. When the experience is vivid, mystics have reported, they feel that they "know everything," and this is accompanied by a sense of perfect simplicity (nothing could be simpler than that which has no duality) along with undiluted certainty. In the *Paradiso*, Dante described it this way: "Within its deep infinity I saw ingathered, and bound by love in one volume, the scattered leaves of all the universe."

Not much can be said about the language of illumination, since transcendence is beyond form, sensation, and symbol. Upon emerging from the experience, however, floods of images and words have been known to erupt, giving us immortal poetry, hymns, sacred books, and other expressions of divine revelation. This sequence from pure, content-free knowing to individuated expression is parallel to ordinary intuition, in which wordless, imageless feelings might quickly translate to form and substance. Illumination is also beyond emotional states. But the surges of ecstasy, happiness, calm, and energy that have been associated with intuitive inspirations of all kinds are reported in stellar form by the illumined. This can be attributed to certain properties of the Absolute, which are variously described as pure and unmanifest energy, concentrated universal love, absolute peace, and *ananda*, or bliss.

Special attention is drawn to these parallels to support the contention that all intuitive experiences can be viewed as microcosms of the highest intuition, that of mystical union. Ordinary intuition is, in some way, a special case of transcendence. . . .

Personal Reflection

To help make the material in this chapter personally meaningful, you might want to reflect on the hallmarks of intuition in light of your own experience. Think back to your most memorable intuitions.

Did they tend to come when you were involved in the subject of the intuition or when you were engaged in something else?
Did they come during restful, relaxed moments?
Did they come spontaneously, as though they were delivered to you?
Were they surprising in content, form, or timing?
Have you ever *tried* to be intuitive? Did it work?
Are your intuitions generally flashes or are they sustained, as in a reverie?
Are they detailed or a patterned sense of a whole?
Do you normally think in words or images? Are most of your intuitions the same?
Can you recall physical sensations and emotions associated with the intuitions?

12

Listen for Those Warning Bells[†]

ROY ROWAN

Wishful thinking is not intuition. Yet it's easy to confuse hope with a hunch. William Agee, as we saw, may have confused his desire to acquire Martin Marietta with the notion that its management would see the synergy of merging with Bendix and surrender. As psychologists warn, "Failure to maintain some degree of pessimism is to be in a state of peril." So don't disregard those nagging voices trying to tell you what you don't want to hear. They may come bearing a career-saving message.

No one is immune to failure. Even the most intuitive executives can cite examples of when they allowed positive hunches to carry them away in the face of a negative forecast—and to a sorry end.

Admittedly, a conflict can arise between the trust it takes to pursue an intuitive flash and the skepticism needed to spurn a flash-in-the-pan idea. At first the two kinds of flashes may seem equally alluring. So listen for the warning bell before you shout, "Eureka!"

There is no faking the Eureka factor. Gut feelings have to be genuine or they aren't worth listening to. However, born losers with an overwhelming need to prove their own brilliance may not know the difference. "Look, I've got this feeling," they'll say, shooting from the hip rather than from the head. Headhunters are frank to admit that the overriding fear in hiring a new CEO today is that he'll turn out to be a hip-shooter.

Professor Eugene Jennings of the Michigan State University Business School, author of *Executive Success*, claims to have found the two most common traits of the failure-prone business leader: the "illusion of mastery of all life's events" and the "illusion of

†SOURCE: From THE INTUITIVE MANAGER by Roy Rowan, Copyright © 1986 by Roy Rowan. By permission of Little, Brown and Company, and the co-publisher, Gower, Hampshire, England.

immunity to bad luck." Operating in concert, those two misconceptions are an obvious duet of disaster.

Jennings has been collecting data since 1969 on success and failure at the corporate pinnacle, particularly keeping tabs on the business life expectancy of chief executive officers and chief operating officers. He reports that today about 25 percent of the two top officers either resign or are fired before reaching retirement age, compared with 5 percent in 1969. "Disagreement over where the company is going and how it should get there," he believes, precipitates many of the early departures. "The conflict is not merely a clash of wills, but a clash of intuition as well," he says.

Almost a third of those CEOs and COOs leaving early, according to Jennings, get caught up in some kind of palace revolt—evidence that ambition or instinct or both lead them astray. But then, today's fast track is known for its dangerous hairpin turns, requiring the hard-driving executive to use superb timing and intuition, along with the usual operating skills. Remember, even the most far-out new idea can be tested against a number of practical criteria.

Do the Facts Support Your Hunch

A good question to ask yourself in trying to decide whether to trust a hunch is: Do facts exist that could perhaps eliminate some of the uncertainty? This is the time to switch on the computers and to let the number-crunchers loose to check on costs and return on investment. Yes, at this stage even the consultants, investment bankers, and market surveyors can be called in for a look-see, as long as they aren't allowed to douse the creative fires.

Gathering facts about the personalities involved in a business gamble is important too. In the case of Bendix's assault on Martin Marietta, one miscalculation admitted later by Agee was the intransigence of opposing CEO Tom Pownall. Anybody in the aerospace business could have told Agee that the former navy officer would never give up the ship. What's more, they could have assured Agee that Pownall would stick to his threat and counterattack by buying Bendix's stock.

Be Prepared to Back Down

Agee could have called off his attack right up until literally the witching hour of midnight when he began buying Martin Marietta stock. Why, then, did he blindly pursue his quarry, destroying Bendix and wrecking his credibility as a CEO? Several books, including one by his wife, Mary, fail to answer that question satisfactorily. One thing is clear. Neither Bill nor Mary—both products of the Harvard Business School—put much faith in their intuition. At the same time, they spurned the advice of Salomon Brothers, Bendix's original investment bankers, as well as the advice of a number of Bendix directors, who urged Agee to back down before it was too late. But Agee totally misjudged the final outcome. "There will be no dismemberment of Bendix," he proclaimed.

Rehearse Your Idea with a Core of Advisers

Repetition in one's mind of the original business objective seems to bolster an intuitive spark. Psychiatrist Abraham Zaleznik, who teaches leadership at the Harvard Business School, explains that continual rehearsing is a crucial part of the verification process. "It becomes a ritual for instinctive business leaders," he says.

Christie Ann Hefner, president and "hare apparent," according to her father, Hugh, the founder of Playboy Enterprises, keeps rehearsing her ideas with a small high-level group. "I try to get them to challenge my hypotheses," says the willowy brunette. Aware that her father supplied the creative genius, she has purposely developed complementary strengths. "Now I am the person managing and leading and making the decisions," she says. "But I can't rely entirely on my own intuition. So I have surrounded myself with a lot of talent."

Joseph McKinney, the Tyler Corporation's intuitive CEO, never lets himself or his fellow officers forget their fallibility. Having gone belly-up in a previous corporate incarnation, he remembers painfully that the most innovative plans sometimes flop. Although Tyler is prospering, he still conducts "stray-bullet drills," as he calls them, "to make sure we can identify all the unlikely bad news." For the same reason he prefers to hire executives who have similarly suffered business reversals. "Bloody noses are great teachers," he says.

Ralph Bahna, president and managing director of the Cunard Line, conducts rehearsals all the time in front of his inner circle of executives. "I'll get a gut feeling and start talking about it," he says. "That way omissions and gaps come to mind. Sometimes it triggers a much bigger idea, or one of the other guys will turn it around and say: 'Hey, fantastic, but why don't we do it this way?'"

He cites the example of the trouble Cunard was having selling Alaska cruises on the *Sagafjord*, a top-rated cruise ship. Another ship, the *Cunard Princess*, was doing very well on the same run. "It's an awareness problem," Bahna kept telling his staff. One of the other executives mentioned that most of the travel agents in the Northwest were young women. "Why don't we give them a free fur coat if they sell a cruise?" he suggested. *Sagafjord* sales picked up immediately.

Listen to the Rumblings from Below

Isolation at the top is a well-known hazard facing chief executives. Subordinates hesitate to knock on the CEO's door, especially if it means being a bearer of bad news. No matter how intuitive they are, smart CEOs keep an ear cocked for what the grapevine in their company is saying. As Professor Jennings points out, the "illusion of immunity to bad luck" can plague a CEO. But sensing the mood of an organization, and slyly tapping the collective intuition of the rest of the employees, can reduce a CEO's chance of being unlucky.

Who will be lucky as a leader and who won't be? Professor Jennings calls this the "greatest guessing game in business." He says that it has always been a gamble how a CEO will fare and that it always will be, "because there's no rung on the way up the corporate ladder that prepares you for the top one."

Men who made their mark as inventors down in the shop sometimes have trouble getting used to the polish of the executive suite. The hip-shooting, gut-feeling entrepreneur, in particular, can find it pretty nerve-frazzling trying to comprehend the subtle chemistry of his own company once it has passed beyond the start-up stage. Edwin Land, for instance, ran Polaroid for the first dozen or so years. When it started growing too fast, he wisely put in place a top management team headed by Tom Wyman, now the CBS chairman, to handle day-to-day operations, and Land stayed in the lab directing research.

Ray Kroc, McDonald's intuitive impresario, remained president until he died. But he sensibly installed a management team to take charge of the Golden Arches and appointed himself the company's "marketing conscience." In that capacity he inspected stores and chatted with customers, relying on his well-tested ability to catch the vibes of the fast-food industry he created.

A number of other founders, like Armand Hammer, Occidental Petroleum's octogenarian chairman, never relax their grip on the company controls. Hammer was trained as a medical doctor. But an intuitive deal-making streak took him into the oil business, and he remains today one of that industry's most incorrigible hunch-players, who is still predicting that oil will hit $100 a barrel before the end of the decade.

Ever questing for new deals, new friends, and new art acquisitions—he picked up Leonardo da Vinci's *Codex Leicester* for $5.2 million in 1979—the good doctor still cavorts around the globe in his Boeing 727 with "1-Oxy" emblazoned on the tail. The plane is outfitted with an office, a master bedroom, three telephones, and in case the aging chairman suffers a heart attack aloft, a cardiac defibrillator. But Hammer does not have a weak heart when it comes to gambling. In 1982 he played his biggest hunch and completed what was then the largest U. S. oil merger ever: the $4 billion takeover of Cities Service.

Hammer still says, "It's the best deal I ever made." But Wall Street analysts claim Oxy is "choking on debt" trying to swallow the domestic oil giant. Since then, struggling for solvency, Hammer has fired a whole string of presidents and suffered a falling-out with Oxy's former number-one stockholder, David Murdock, a takeover genius himself, who boasts of practicing "brain calisthenics." A number of departed Oxy executives think Hammer won't listen anymore, and that his legendary intuition has finally led him astray.

Stay Tuned to Your Intuition

What kind of brain calisthenics does it take to stay tuned in at the top? Just realizing that the mind screens out what it doesn't want to hear is part of the answer. We all know how easy it is to dismiss ideas that don't fit our preconceived notions. Well, it's just as easy to dismiss those nagging voices and queasy sensations accompanying hunches that aren't sitting very well.

The obvious solution is to come up with an intuitive alternative. But that's hard. A hunch being adhered to may be firmly rooted, despite the discomfort it is causing Dr. Eugene Gendlin, the University of Chicago psychologist who developed the technique called focusing for inducing intuition, has also devised a system for dislodging bum steers. Advised Gendlin: "You should say to yourself as if it were true, 'This decision feels fine. The problem is solved, and I feel good about it, don't I?' If you pay attention to your body, you will almost immediately feel a very distinct sense of discomfort."

The next step is to keep reexamining this discomfort, even though you don't know what's causing it. You should search for a single word that epitomizes the problem. "Then wait to hear from your body," he says. If that word doesn't feel right, you pick another, and then another, until you finally hit the right word. "Now," says Gendlin, "you see the whole scene more clearly, and you feel a physical change in your body. The lump comes undone." He equates this sensation with a sort of "instant hindsight." Some CEOs, of course, may think that's hogwash, particularly founders who launched large enterprises on a gut feeling. Understandably, they may believe their intuition is infallible.

Just as intuition can be sharpened and tested with psychological coaching, the verification process can be improved with practice. Here again the psychologists offer some suggestions. CEOs, they say, should consider keeping a record of their important insights and the proven accuracy of these ideas. Knowing that your batting average is good builds confidence in future hunches.

Can the Idea Be Test-Marketed?

Business surveys, unlike the polling done for political candidates, are aimed more at preventing failure than assuring success. But quite often it's possible for CEOs to order up a statistical reconnaissance of the marketplace they are using their intuition to exploit. As one of them says: "We try to put the chart before the course."

Verification of intuition about the marketplace is carried on Star Wars-style these days. Visit the CRT room of Audits & Surveys Inc. in New York City at almost any hour of the day or night and you'll find thirty or more living robots plugged into an automated opinion-gathering system called CATI (Computer Assisted Telephone Interviewing) that is verifying the preferences and prejudices of men, women, and children about everything from a ride on a wide-bodied plane to Coca-Cola's megabrand strategy. A&S conducts more than 2.5 million of these CATI calls a year.

Preprogrammed, randomly selected questions for the surveyors to ask appear magically on the CRT screens. And the tabulated results of the answers can be summoned instantaneously with the punch of a computer key. About the only human element left in this superscientific verification system is the interviewer's voice. Even that is being replaced by speech synthesizers.

Solomon Dutka, the former atomic physicist who founded and runs A&S, points to a major difference between verifying intuition in science and business. "The setting and testing of hypotheses goes on in both fields," he says. "But the hypothesis that is proven in business turns out to be true only for a short time. There ain't no constants in business because people keep changing. Pretty soon you've got to test your hypothesis all over again."

Give Your Ideas Time to Ripen

Cunard's President Bahna explains that when the *QE-2* returned to its transatlantic run after doing a stint as a troopship during the Falkland Islands affair, passenger sales were poor. He was bitterly embroiled in restitution claims against the British government. But the idea suddenly struck him to combine the sale of a *QE-2* ticket to Europe with a free Concorde flight home. "The concept was aimed at executives who didn't have time to sail round-trip," he explains.

Cunard promptly test-marketed the idea, but it bombed. Bahna was baffled and kept telling his associates that Cunard hadn't allowed enough time for the idea to catch on. "Next year we really rolled the dice," he says, "and chartered ten thousand Concorde seats. It was a great financial success." Now Cunard links the *QE-2* trip to Concorde flights all over the world. "The idea's dynamite," says Bahna.

The Proof Is in the Product

In today's unpredictable business environment, it's hard to tell whether even the best hunches will sell. A CEO may come up with an ingenious idea that the board of directors buys but that the public won't accept. Howard Stein, for instance, launched a "moral" mutual fund at Dreyfus composed only of companies that complied strictly with environmental safeguards and fair employment practices. It was the first such fund specifically designed to appeal to universities and nonprofit foundations. "Ironically, this Third Century Fund has outperformed many others," reports Stein, "but the colleges called it a 'do-good attempt' and stuck to traditional investments." The logic behind Stein's concept did not make it succeed.

At the same time, an ingenious new idea that doesn't survive a logical assault isn't necessarily wrong. When Robert Goddard suggested rocket propulsion as the only feasible power source for space travel, critics quite logically, it seemed, scorned the idea, insisting there isn't anything in space for the rocket to push against. But rockets, we know now, work because the momentum of the hot gases rushing backward is matched by the forward momentum of the rocket's shell.

In Goddard's mind the rocket propulsion idea had already survived an internal screening. Even though he couldn't explain exactly why it would work, he could visualize the rocket successfully soaring off into space. Psychologists don't know precisely how this mental screening is carried out. But a subconscious process goes on that constantly weighs new ideas against the mind's accumulated wisdom.

Final verification of intuition's power comes with the new product or concept. But this tangible proof that the Eureka factor works does not depict the sloppy process of discovery. Gazing upon a sparkling new creation, it's impossible to untangle the pieces put together by the original perception, or to tell precisely how or in what order they were assembled. The chances are that development took a haphazard, zigzag course. After percolating in the originator's mind, the separate elements suddenly synthesized into a vision that could not have been predicted. All of the analysis, all of the forecasting, all of the extrapolation from past and current experience could only have provided a sense of feasibility. It was an unrelenting, indefinable inner urge that told the originator to keep on trying.

The extraordinary career of Chester Carlson, the inventor of xerography, illustrates all of these points. Late in life, Carlson and his wife became fascinated with ESP. It was he who funded the precognition experiments conducted by Douglas Dean and John Mihalasky at the New Jersey Institute of Technology.

The son of an itinerant barber, Carlson showed early interest in both chemistry and the graphic arts. In high school he pursued the two fields at once by picking up a discarded printing press and launching a little magazine for amateur chemists. After obtaining a degree in physics from Caltech, he was hired by Bell Labs in New York City. But those were Depression days, and he was soon laid off. Luckily he landed another job with an electrical firm. Attending law school at night, he was put in charge of the company's patents.

Two things quickly became apparent to Carlson. There were never enough carbon copies of the patent specifications around the office. All offices, he decided, needed a machine that could quickly duplicate documents. Just married, he also felt he wasn't getting ahead fast enough.

"I thought the possibility of making an invention might kill two birds with one stone," Carlson said. "It would be a chance to do the world some good and also a chance to do myself some good." At the same time, he was aware of two natural phenomena that might have a bearing on the kind of invention he had in mind: materials of opposite electrical charges are attracted to each other; and certain materials become better conductors of electricity when exposed to light.

Reflecting on early writings about photoconductivity, Carlson later said, "Things don't come to mind readily but all of a sudden, like pulling things out of the air. You have to get your inspiration somewhere, and usually you get it from reading something else."

He began rudimentary experiments in the kitchen of his apartment, then set up a small lab and hired a refugee German physicist to help him. It was above a saloon in Astoria, Queens, that the Xerox process was born on October 22, 1938. But during the next five years more than twenty companies spurned Carlson's invention, refusing to help him develop it. "Some were indifferent," he recalled. "Several expressed mild interest, and one or two were antagonistic. How difficult it was to convince anyone that my tiny plates and rough image held the key to a tremendous new industry." Finally, in 1944, Battelle Memorial Institute, a nonprofit research organization in Columbus, Ohio, signed a royalty-sharing contract with Carlson and began developing the process. Three years later Battelle found a small photo-paper firm called Haloid that would produce a xerographic machine. It wasn't until 1959 that the first practical office copier was unveiled. Able to make copies on plain paper at the touch of a button, it was an instant success.

The Haloid Company evolved into the Xerox Corporation in 1961. Its stock became a hot issue even for those go-go years. So frantically did Xerox try to keep pace with demand that in 1963 every third employee had been hired that year. In the town of Webster, New York, ten miles east of Rochester, a sprawling research and manufacturing complex blossomed on a thousand acres where only apple trees had grown.

The giant corporation has never forgotten the lessons taught by Chester Carlson, who died in 1968. "From this life, we of Xerox have learned much," said Joseph C. Wilson, Haloid's president and the man who gambled on xerography. "First, we will never forget that the individual is the origin of the great creative act. Second, we learned that great rewards come to those who see needs that have not been clearly identified by others, and who have the innovating capacity to devise products and services which fill these needs."

13

Nurturing Executive Intrapreneurship with a Brain-Skill Management Program[†]

WESTON H. AGOR

Organizations across the nation are feverishly searching for new ways to increase productivity. Management expert Gifford Pinchot III recommends that they find and nurture the "intrapreneurs" who are already there.[1] The challenge is to locate this executive talent and provide the management climate necessary for it to flourish.

One technique that helps meet this challenge is a brain-skill management (BMS) program. This program's guiding principle is that intrapreneurship will be enhanced if organizations assign executives to management tasks first and foremost by *brain skills*. The assignments must be made without regard to hierarchical status, responsibility for the problem at hand, or seniority level within a particular organization.[2] This approach breaks through such traditional organizational obstacles to innovation as "group-think" and "analysis paralysis."[3]

This chapter will describe in detail what constitutes a BSM program and outline how this program can be implemented to increase management intrapreneurship. The case study to be used for this purpose is based on a four-day retreat workshop conducted with key management personnel of a major Department of Defense agency in the fall of 1985.

Components of a BSM Program

A BSM program consists of tree major components: diagnostic testing; custom placement based on the situation, problem, or job requirement; and training in overall brain-skill development.[4]

†Source: Reprinted from *Business Horizons* May-June, 1988. Copyright 1988 by the Foundation for the School of Business at Indiana University. Used with permission.

DIAGNOSTIC TESTING

Diagnostic testing can be used when the goal is to locate highly creative and innovative executive talent. Testing can also be used to organize this talent within an organization, facilitating innovation. For example, organizations typically know their personnel by formal job title, responsibility, or years of experience. Seldom do they know which brain skills people possess that can be used to help solve a difficult management problem. Diagnostic testing can help locate the executives with the most innovative brain skills within an organization and introduce these executives to each other.

Extensive research on brain skills indicates that those executives who score highly intuitive on such test instruments as the Myers-Briggs Type Indicator (MBTI) tend to be the most innovative in problem solving. They tend to be more insightful and better at finding new ways of doing things.[5]

CUSTOM PLACEMENT

Custom placement based on brain-skill assessments can advance intrapreneurship and overall organizational productivity in several ways. One way is to segregate decision-making functions by brain skills.

For instance, those executives who score as highly intuitive form the most innovative and creative pool of talent in the organization. They are the intrapreneurs. This talent pool can be best used by grouping these managers together and assigning them the problem-solving tasks for which they are best-suited, such as solving difficult or intractable problems that require brainstorming, or creating new methods of providing governmental services. When grouped together on the same problem or issue at the same time, these executives can make synergistic breakthroughs. This potential exists because intuitive managers tend to use thinking styles that other intuitive people find comfortable to work with (see Figure 13.1.[6]

For example, highly intuitive managers often do not follow a sequential order of reason; instead they bounce around from the front to the back of a problem in no apparent order. These managers also tend to prefer informal styles and settings and often work in bursts of energy that are followed by down periods. When they are forced to work with more traditional managers who follow routine, step-by-step procedures and prefer standard schedules,

Thinking	Intuitive
Style	
Deductive	Inductive
Objective	Subjective
Stress facts	Stress **feelings**
Prefers solving problems by breaking down into parts, and then approaching the problem sequentially using logic.	Prefers solving problems by looking at the whole, then approaching the problem through hunches.

Figure 13.1: Comparison Between the Brain Skills and Styles of Intuitive and Thinking Executives

intrapreneurs often lose interest in the task at hand. They psychologically withdraw their energy from the group to the detriment of organizational productivity. Furthermore, more traditional managers tend to be quick to criticize new ideas proposed by highly intuitive managers, and they often lack the capacity to see how the new proposals might actually work if given a chance. As a result, idea generation is often dampened or scuttled when intuitive managers are forced to work with managers who prefer a thinking style, especially at the early stages of the decision-making process.[7]

TRAINING IN BRAIN SKILLS DEVELOPMENT

Organizations have been slow to develop and use the talents of highly intuitive managers to enhance organizational productivity. Organizations also have been slow to recognize that even the more traditional managers can enhance their intrapreneurial talents through systematic training programs.

There are a number of techniques that can be used to strengthen *any* manager's intrapreneurial skills. A national survey of highly intuitive top managers indicates that these executives regularly use such techniques as guided imagery, self-hypnosis, journal keeping, and lateral styles of thinking to strengthen their intuitive skills, as well as for daily decision making when necessary. Other studies have indicated that the more traditionally thinking manager can also enhance his or her creative skills significantly through these and other right-brain skill-building techniques.[8]

The Department of Defense Case Study

In the fall of 1985, the major components of the BSM program were employed to enhance intrapreurial decision making in a major agency of the U.S. Department of Defense.[9] Fifteen supergrade executives from this agency were transported to a retreat site near their headquarters for a four-day, intensive workshop. There, they were to learn BSM tools and techniques that could be used to help solve a major management problem the agency faced.

The problem exercise selected was, "How do we give the younger generation at work in our agency a sense of mission and dedication?" The problem was particularly appropriate for this agency, because 40 percent of its professional staff had been hired in the previous six years. Training and accommodating this large number of new recruits in such a short time period presented a real challenge to the organization. But is also represented a major growth opportunity, since many of these young professionals have new and different ideas, management styles, and career expectations from those of their predecessors.

The workshop started with BSM testing for each participant. Each executive was tested to see whether he or she was more intuitive or used the more traditional thinking brain skills and styles. As noted earlier, highly intuitive executives tend to be the intrapreneurs or change masters in any organization. Each executive was then charted on a 12-point scale (see Figure 13.2) where 0 represents extreme "left-brain" orientation (thinking) and 12 represented extreme "right-brain" orientation (intuitive).[10]

Thinking 0 ◄——————————————————————————————► 12 Intuitive

Figure 13.2: Scale of Brain-Skill Scores

Table 13.1 displays the scores for each participant. The highly intuitive managers are numbers 2, 6, 8, 9, and 12. Their scores place them in the top 10 percent of intrapreneurial scores achieved in national testing. Their extreme opposites, the highly thinking managers, are numbers 3, 4, and 10. These are the executives that intrapreneurs would find the most difficult to work with on the assigned problem.

The agency executives were then divided into distinct brain-skills groups of like types. The intuitive group was given the task of generating possible solutions to the problem. The list they

TABLE 13.1
Brain-Skill Scores for a Defense Department Agency

Participant Number	Sex	Scale Scores Intuition	Thinking
1	M	8	4
2	M	12	0
3	M	1	11
4	M	3	9
5	M	9	3
6	F	11	1
7	M	5	7
8	M	11	1
9	M	12	0
10	M	3	9
11	M	8	4
12	M	10	2
13	M	7	5
14	M	6	6
15	M	8	4
Total Group Average		7.6	4.4

generated was developed without interference or interruption from the thinking group. The bringing together of intrapreneurs at the same stage in the decision-making process enabled the group to use the thinking style with which they are most comfortable without fear of criticism from their thinking colleagues. Furthermore, this method allowed adequate opportunity for consideration and discussion of proposed solutions. Discussion is often cut short when brain-skill opposites are brought together too early in the process, because thinking managers tend to criticize new ideas even though their biggest weakness is the inability to generate new ideas or proposals of their own.[11]

The next stage of the decision-making process was to have the group of thinking managers review and evaluate the list of proposed solutions generated by the intuitive group. This sequence has certain advantages. For example, the thinking managers' forte is paying attention to precision, detail, and implementation. Accordingly, they are quick to spot items on the intuitive groups' proposal list that are weak and should be eliminated. And by being able to work together as a common group using a similar style, thinking executives have the opportunity to use their analytical skills at the most appropriate stage of the process.[12]

TABLE 13.2

Sample of Proposals Made to Help Instill a Sense of Mission and
Dedication Among Young Professionals in Defense Department Agency

- Identify early key new resource people and then nurture their development.
- Bring new people into the decision-making process with the support of well publicized management directives.
- Provide field tours for interns.
- Rate managers on new hire retentions.
- Have getaway retreats like this one for junior members early in their career.
- Have roundtables within the Agency where upper and middle management make presentations to junior members.
- Have junior level "tiger teams" work on problems throughout the organization.
- Publish a classified newsletter that tells "the story" of recent accomplishments by the Agency.
- Develop open forums for junior level suggestions, feedback, and problem discussion.
- Institute a special program to manage and track progress of this group for the next 10 years.
- Encourage mobility across organizational boundaries.
- Develop an orientation program to show newcomers how they fit into the overall picture.
- Retrain present supervisors to not be so threatened by a young, highly motivated, and intelligent workforce.

Table 13.2 lists the proposals generated by this process. The proposal list is quite long, and all of the executives who participated agreed when formally surveyed that this method of using brain skills helped in the creation of the list. Furthermore, the participating executives also agreed to formally submit the proposal list for consideration by top management when they returned to their headquarters.

The final stage in this BSM program was working with all the executives present to develop each person's intrapreneurial talents more fully. Participants were first introduced to various techniques, such as meditation and guided imagery. They were then assigned a specific problem-solving task to measure their success in using their intuitive skills. Formal post-workshop evaluations conducted by the agency indicated that this stage of the BSM program was very helpful to the participants, especially the thinking managers. Few had been exposed to these mind expansion techniques before the workshop, and most left the retreat committed to using the tools they had learned in their work.

The Institute for Management Studies Case

Another payoff of implementing a BSM program can be seen from the case with the Institute for Management Studies, a consortium of major corporate top executives in the United States. Highly intuitive talent can be identified for the first time and introduced to each other on a personal basis. Each participating company now has in place a new internal network of intuitive talent that can be activated for use on future problems.

As a rule today, organizations do not really know the identity of their intuitive talent, and it is often true that highly intuitive executives do not know each other either—especially across existing departmental lines. Normally, no formal organizational mechanism exists to identify and channel this talent for applied use. This reality exists partly because highly intuitive executives tend to keep their skill a secret for fear of being ostracized by their peers. A BSM program can help overcome these obstacles and channel the talent identified in a more positive and productive way.

Another pay-off of using a BSM program is that the Thinking type executives were able to see and evaluate firsthand the work product of their opposite "intuitive type" colleagues and vice versa. As a result, each group gained greater respect for the other's respective brain skills, which should enhance the way these executives function within their organizations in the future—whether in the private sector enterprise or a city government.

An additional pay-off of implementing a BSM program, aside from those outlined above, is that it enables one to design and implement training programs more productively for corporate or government executives. For example, test results can be used to guide the development of training materials most likely to be effective with one particular set of executives versus another. The latest technology in learning styles indicates that brain skills and styles affect the way we learn. Therefore, test results can be used to enhance the probability of learning by custom-fitting training materials to the particular group at hand.

BSM programs can be used for a variety of training purposes. For example, score results can be used along with other information to create management teams with the greatest probability of working well together. On the other hand, score results can also be used to assess and explain why a particular group may not have worked well together and to identify the type of training that can be used to correct the situation. BSM scores can also help suggest ways to overcome other communication problems internally such as sex, role, and cultural differences. Finally, BSM assessments can be used to guide management development programs. Normally, the higher one's place in an organization, the more the need to integrate both intuitive and thinking brain skills effectively. Frequently, an executive may function very effectively at one level in the organization but have difficulty moving to the next level. Brain skill training can often ease the transition.[13]

Conclusion

One of the very real challenges that organizations face today is finding new and more effective methods of increasing their productivity. These organizations frequently already have the internal capability (in both personnel and brain skills) to increase productivity. What is often lacking is a regular organizational routine or procedure for searching out these resources, combining them in new and creative ways, and applying them to difficult problems. One technique that holds great promise is a brain-skill-management program. This and similar programs may help organizations tap the minds and the intrapreneurial potential of their own employees. This is one of the few remaining resources that can be expanded in the years ahead.

Notes

1. An "intrapreneur" is defined as a dreamer who does, a manager who creates innovation of any kind within an organization. For further details, see Gifford Pinchot III, *Intrapreneuring: Why You Don't Have to Leave the Corporation to Become An Entrepreneur* (New York: Harper & Row, 1985).

2. Weston H. Agor, "Managing Brain Skills to Increase Productivity," in John Matzer, Jr. (ed.), *Productivity Improvement Techniques: Creative Approaches for Local Government* (Washington, D.C.: International City Management Association, 1986), pp. 111-120.

3. "Groupthink" is when only options acceptable to the group are entertained in the decision-making process. "Analysis paralysis" is when an executive or organization unnecessarily delays making a decision to gather more facts, when in fact additional information is not likely to improve the quality of the ultimate decision.

4. For further details, see: Weston H. Agor, *Intuitive Management: Integrating Left and Right Brain Management Skills* (Englewood Cliffs, N.J.: Prentice Hall, 1984); and Weston H. Agor, *The Logic of Intuitive Decision Making: A Research Based Approach for Top Management* (Westport, CT: Greenwood Press, 1986).

5. Weston H. Agor, "The Logic of Intuition: How Successful Executives Make Their Most Important Decisions," *Organizational Dynamics*, Winter 1986, pp. 5-18.

6. Weston H. Agor, "Managing Brain Skills: One Key to Increased Productivity," *Public Management*, August 1987, pp. 20-22.

7. Isabel Briggs Myers and Peter B. Myers, *Gifts Differing* (Palo Alto, Calif.: Consulting Psychologists Press, Inc. 1980).

8. Michael Ray and Rochelle Myers, *Creativity in Business* (Garden City, N.Y.: Doubleday & Co., Inc., 1986).

9. The specific agency in question cannot be named because of restrictions imposed by the granting agency for national-security reasons.

10. For further details on the instrument used and reliability/validity measures, see: Weston H. Agor, *Test Your Intuitive Powers: AIM Survey* (Bryn Mawr, Pa.: Organization Design and Development, 1985); and Weston H. Agor, *AIM Survey Trainer's Manual* (Bryn Mawr, Pa.: Organization Design and Development, 1985).

11. Gordon Lawrence, *People Types and Tiger Stripes: A Practical Guide to Learning Styles*, 2nd ed. (Gainesville, FL.: Center for Application of Psychological Type, Inc. 1982).

12. Weston H. Agor, "Managing Brain Skills to Increase Productivity," *Personnel*, August 1986, pp. 42-66.

13. Weston H. Agor, "Finding and Developing Intuitive Managers," *Training and Development Journal*, March 1988, pp. 68-70.

PART V How to Develop Your Intuitive Powers Further

Now that you have become familiar with the various ways of measuring your intuitive ability and putting the skill to practical use on the job, you are ready to learn how to work on developing your present level of intuitive ability further. Here you will find a variety of methods that you can use toward this end.

The first article outlines methods to help you allow your intuition to work for you, to believe in and trust your skill, and to help cultivate and practice the skill further. The second selection outlines methods that have been introduced successfully in the curriculum at the Stanford University Business School. Pay particular attention to the suggestion in this article that you learn to develop *your own style*. No matter how intuitive a person may be, experience shows that each person must learn their own "technology" for bringing this skill to the surface for applied use in practical settings.

14

How to Use and Develop Your Intuition in Management[†]

WESTON H. AGOR

Broadly speaking, it is true today to say that most management training programs, whether presented in formal academic settings or within organizations, emphasize analytical techniques for making management decisions. We have pointed out, however, that brain skills such as intuition *are also* important resources for decision making. Indeed, we contend that there are certain settings and situations where the use of intuition is either more useful or the only available basis on which to make decisions (for example, in top management, crises, rapid change, and where data are limited).

We have also presented research results to back up our argument based on field testing of over 3,500 managers across the country in a wide variety of organizational settings in both the public and private sectors. Among our most significant findings is the fact that top executives appear to use a management style quite different from their subordinates. Top executives are characterized by an intuitive style. That is, their key decisions are guided by intuition.

It is our contention that intuition is an important leadership and management skill that can be used to increase personal and organizational productivity. Through management testing, we have found that this skill varies significantly by management level, sex, occupational specialization, and ethnic background just as other, more traditional brain skills and capabilities do. It is also our contention that organizations can sharply increase productivity by learning to use *all the brain skills* existing within an organization. We advocate establishing brain skill/management style programs, which should include training programs for the development and

†SOURCE: From INTUITIVE MANAGEMENT by Weston H. Agor, Ph.D. © 1984. Reprinted by permission of the publisher, Prentice-Hall, Inc. Englewood Cliffs, New Jersey 07632.

actual use of these skills in organizational settings, as one of the best vehicles for accomplishing this. In Part IV of this book, we outlined in detail several ways that BSM programs can be used effectively to increase both productivity and job satisfaction.

There are clear signs that several top leaders around the world are already aware of this fact. For example, in Venezuela, brain skill development has become a major national goal under the direction of the minister of education, which has attracted the attention of several other country leaders.[1] A Geneva-based organization, the International Management Institute, has launched a worldwide research project into the nature and potential of intuition in the business world.[2] In this country, a report of the Association of American Colleges in 1985 posits that every baccalaureate degree program should include training that enables a student to "recognize when reason and evidence are not enough, to discover the legitimacy of intuition, to subject inert data to the probing analysis of the mind."[3] A recent conference for senior public executives at the University of Texas at Austin featured the development of intuitive management skills because "we recognize that successful public executives must rely on a mix of intuition and disciplined analysis in their decision making."[4]

In this article, we will outline step by step just how brain skill intuition can be developed so that it can *be relied on* to make leadership and management decisions. We will also show how intuition can be integrated with more traditional sources of information to arrive at decisions that are the best in the context of the options currently available, and to generate new options not yet perceived as available. By doing this, it is our hope that managers will learn that *they can* rely on input—*internally within themselves, within their organizations, and in their relationships with other parts of the world.*

How to Develop Your Intuition

Basically, we all have some intuitive ability at birth. Some of us appear to have more than others—some of us may even be classified as "psychic." Some of us learn to get in touch with this ability, learn how to use the skill most effectively (what medium and under what circumstances), and even learn how to expand our skills further. On the other hand, some of us, for whatever reason (family upbringing and/or life experiences), never do any of these things throughout our lifetime. In fact, some of us may even go so far as to emotionally block the intuitive ability we do have and thereby, seldom or never use our existing ability to its full potential. There are many managers operating in organizations today far below their intuitive potential. If they could learn how to get in touch with their ability, the managers, personally and the organization they work for, would profit enormously.

Sigmund Freud once said, "The mind is like an iceberg. It floats with one-seventh of its bulk above the water."[5] So it is with our intuitive ability. Just how do you go about getting in touch with your intuitive ability, develop it further, and learn to apply it in practical work settings? Basically, any program to develop intuition (whether a personal or organizational effort) should consist of at least these three basic components that address your cognitive, affective, and evaluational attitude about using this skill:[6]

- Methods to help you allow intuition to work.
- Methods to help you believe in it.
- Methods to help you cultivate and practice it.

METHODS TO HELP YOU ALLOW INTUITION TO WORK

There are a number of techniques that are useful to help you allow intuition to work for you in management. First, it is important to learn *cognitively* who you are. This means getting in touch with the level and type of intuitive ability you have and becoming fully aware of the kinds of skills and tasks you can and like to perform. How much you wish to learn about yourself in this regard will determine the tools you use to explore yourself with and also govern just how far you are likely to go in developing your intuitive ability.

Broadly speaking, managers who have a high level of intuitive ability tend to have a set of characteristics. Charles A. Garfield, a psychology professor at the University of California at San Francisco Medical School and head of the Peak Performance Center in Berkeley, has studied more than 1,200 peak performers in various professions during the last 15 years to distill the key elements they have in common. His findings neatly parallel the common characteristics of highly intuitive managers.[7] (See Table 14.1.)

Intuitive managers are particularly good at performing certain kinds of tasks and functions, but they are also characterized by having the potential for certain blind spots or perspectives which need to be watched for. Table 14.2 summarizes these aspects of an intuitive manager's personality.

TABLE 14.1

Characteristics of Highly Intuitive Managers

Good self-image	Prefer informal to formal style
Curious	Focus on solutions rather than problems
Independent	Do not try to be all things to all people
Inner vs. Outer direction	
Prefer action to inaction	
Take risks	

TABLE 14.2

Capabilities of Intuitive Managers

Skills and Tasks They Can Perform	Tendencies to Watch for
Bring up new possibilities	Impatient with routine, details, or repetition
Supply ingenuity to problems	May reach conclusions too quickly and ignore some relevant facts
Read signs of coming change	
See how to prepare for the future	May follow inspiration even when clearly bad
Have enthusiasm	
Watch for new essentials	Frequently make errors of fact
Tackle difficulties with zest	Work in bursts of energy rather than the same rate each day
	Dislike precision details

Beyond these broad characteristics, not all intuitive managers are alike or get their intuitive insights in the same way. As noted earlier, managers also use their intuition to serve different roles and functions depending on the individual and situation involved. More specifically, intuitive managers can be further classified in terms of extroversion and introversion (former Senate majority leader Howard Baker is an example of an extroverted intuitive and Albert Einstein is an example of an introverted intuitive), and also in terms of the medium in which they function most effectively. Some work well in public settings in cooperation with other managers, while others work best primarily alone in more isolated settings. Table 14.3 summarizes their respective management styles.

Intuitive managers also differ according to the most effective medium by which their insights come to them. Some work best when they can touch a person or object before making a decision. Such executives are famous for insisting on a personal interview in such cases. Politicians such as former President Lyndon Baines Johnson are typical in this regard. Other managers work best mentally. They get their insight in isolation totally divorced from

TABLE 14.3

Management Style of Extroverted and Introverted Intuitive Managers

Extroverted Intuitive	Introverted Intuitive
Express self naturally and easily, works easily with others	Find self-expression difficult, prefer to work more alone
Most effective in the promotion and initiation of new enterprises	Most effective in promoting understanding and interpreting life experiences
Use inner awareness to understand how to approach a situation	Use a situation to get better inner understanding
Enthusiastic at outset, but sometimes fails to follow through on activities or details	Have difficulty persuading others to see clear answers or to implement them practically
Insight comes through personal interaction and/or touch	Insight comes through mental processes

the stimulation of other people or outside objects. Jonas Salk, the inventor of the polio vaccine, is a good example here.

One of the best ways to get in touch cognitively with how much intuitive ability you have is to take one of the tests available that can measure it. For a quick general picture, use the *AIM Survey* described earlier in the book. This instrument will tell you whether you score very high or very low in intuitive ability, and whether it is your strongest resource for making decisions as compared to relying primarily on facts to do so. The test will also give you a picture of whether or not you *actually* appear to be using your intuitive ability for making on the job decisions. So, you will have some sense whether or not you are working in the most productive manner *vis-à-vis* your underlying ability or whether you appear to be pushing water upstream instead. You can also use the test results to compare yourself with your co-workers and/or get a picture of the creative potential existing within your organization. The higher the score on intuition, the greater the creative potential is within your organization.

If you wish to learn not only how much intuitive ability you have but also what type of intuitive manager you are, other instruments such as the MBTI will give you a good reading. From the test scores, you will he able to determine the level of intuitive ability you have in much greater depth than the *AIM Survey* told you. In addition, you will be able to learn whether and to what degree you are an extrovert or introvert intuitive. Finally, you will also be able to get a measure of other aspects of your personality (for example, whether you are extremely judgmental) that can affect your capacity to use the intuitive ability you have to make on the job decisions.[8]

Getting in touch with your intuitive ability in this manner can be one powerful way of putting it to use not only for yourself but also for your organization. Two executives (one from the public sector and the other from the private sector) put it this way after having the experience:

> I now believe that this focus . . . is extremely important in improving one's ability to manage people, not the least of which is oneself . . . extensive effort must be devoted to developing and teaching the techniques of application to managers and would-be managers.[9]

> I would like further information on the availability of the two tests taken . . . and to discuss with you in greater depth what the potential would be for a company such as ours to use these skills.[10]

Should you wish to go still further and explore your other psychic skills such as precognition (ability to see the future), many other instruments are available for use. Several authors such as Keith Haray and Alan Vaughan have also developed a software computer game for use with the Apple micro computer that measures your precognitive ability as opposed to chance scores.[11]

Besides these tests, begin to examine the process and means by which intuitive insights come to you. There are several ways to do this. One is to begin to keep a systematic record of your insights in a journal. Include such information as how and when they come, by what means (for example, dreams), and keep a record of their accuracy (see Table 14.4). Doing this will help you to get a better understanding of how you function best. It will also give you a record to discuss with other professionally trained people to help you develop your ability further. This record will also give you an overall picture showing whether you in fact seek to implement the intuitive insights you receive or whether you have adopted the style of simply ignoring them. It will also give you clues as to how you might actually be blocking your intuitive ability from coming through to serve you.

Another way to help get in touch with your intuitive ability is *to share* your experience with others—whether it be friends, family members, or coworkers. Simply taking the risk of sharing the experiences you are having with others is a useful tool for unlocking this ability and developing it further. Psychologists will tell you that a pattern that recurs over and over in therapy is that the patient is afraid to share their experiences—whether good or

TABLE 14.4

What to Record in Your Intuition Journal

Level of Intuitive Experience
- Physical
- Emotional
- Mental
- Spiritual

Accurate Intuitive Experiences
- Examples
- Level used
- Conditions/circumstances (e.g., time events, people involved, own emotional state, and so on)

"Inaccurate" Intuitive Experiences
- Examples
- Level used
- Conditions/circumstances (same as above)
- Record other possible factors operating that might have interrupted intuitive flow (e.g., projection, ego involvement)

Other Experiences
- Sharing with support group members
- Success/failure with practice techniques

---

bad—because they believe they alone are having them. One of the keys to solving personal problems—or to unlocking new doors—is to recognize this and share the experience with others. This sharing can be accomplished on a formal or informal basis. One step you might find helpful is to form a group of peers and/or friends that meets regularly to share intuitive experiences and work to develop them further. You might even take a problem you are trying to solve at work or in your personal life as a group project and make it the central concern of your intuitive work group for resolution. This experience will not only serve to give you support, it will help to teach you new ways of getting in touch with your intuitive ability. Another approach might be to have a regular time with your family in which each member can share his own experiences—such as sharing dreams from the night before at breakfast time.

Reading about the experiences of others who have gone before you in this field is another safe way to learn about yourself. You will be surprised to find that what is happening to you has already happened to others many times. You will also learn to profit from their experiences—to find other ways to recognize and tap into your ability, and learn to apply it day to day to help guide your decisions. Recent research has shown, for example, that one of the major obstacles to developing psychic ability among children is the fact that neither they, their teachers, or their parents understood or knew how to handle the process when it was unfolding.[12] Recently, medical research among schizophrenics has indicated that not all were ill. Instead some were gifted psychics whose intuitive insights were not understood by the world around them, rather than the other way around.[13]

An important way that organizations *can learn to benefit* from the potential intuitive ability of their managers is to create a personal/organizational environment in which these skills are supported, valued, and practiced in day-to-day life to make decisions. Frequently, we reject new and different ways of solving problems because we become accustomed to a particular way of doing things. Often, it is only in a crisis (business failure, loss of health or loved ones) that we reach for alternative ways of doing things or allow our inherent intuitive skills to surface and be of assistance to us. As Woody Allen says, "If you're not failing every now and again, it's a sign you're not being very innovative in what you're doing." Put another way, making mistakes simply means you are learning faster.

Essentially, it is a productivity question. Organizations and the managers that lead them can use the right brain skill intuition to increase productivity by simply *allowing it to happen*. Roger Von Oech, president of Creative Think in Menlo Park, California talks of it this way:

> I think the most important motive for coming up with new ideas is fun. Creative thinking is a lot of fun. I like to think of creative thinking as the sex of your mental lives.[14]

Ed Everett, an assistant county manager in Nevada, talks about the practical benefit that organizations can derive by allowing intuitive skills to function effectively:

> With shrinking revenues and demands to maintain service levels, why should you, as a manager, devote time, effort, or money to something as esoteric as creativity? For many organizations the human mind and the creative potential of the employee are one of the few remaining resources which can still be expanded. Not using this resource is the same as turning your back on a new revenue source.[15]

Besides recognizing and accepting that intuitive ability can be used to increase organizational productivity, it is important to *eliminate the interference that interrupts its flow*. This means tension, anxiety, fear, desire, or other similar blocks. *One's own mental attitude* is important. You must have a relaxed positive attitude about letting it happen. Research shows clearly that those people who feel they are creative are, while those who are not felt they were not. Von Oech has identified seven mental locks that managers impose on themselves and others that work to interrupt realizing their own and their organization's full creative potential: everything is fine, follow the rules, to err is wrong, playing is frivolous, that's not my area, be practical, and I'm not creative.[16] One manager describes what his personnel learned by working with exercises to expand their mental capital.

> We learned most by examining our inabilities to solve certain problems, a process that gave us insight on what each of us does to block creative solutions. Defining the problem too narrowly, making unnecessary assumptions that restrict thinking, and assuming all problems should be solved using only our left brain were some of the blocks we discovered.[17]

There are a wide variety of tools and techniques that can be used both on a personal and organizational level to help unblock our intuitive ability. Among those that have been used effectively in various settings in both the eastern and western world are hypnosis, meditation, guided imagery, dream analysis, and related holistic health applications such as diet and lifestyles analysis (for example, stress and biofeedback). The pattern of office design, seating, colors, music, and interpersonal communication can also play a very important part in facilitating the flow of right brain input to solve organizational problems.

More specifically, these techniques have been used practically in the following ways depending on the organization and problem at hand. Where appropriate, functioning with a very open, flexible technique or no meeting agenda has proved to be a means by which intuitive input is encouraged. Another useful technique is to segment meetings into creative open times rather than structured times. During these open periods, evaluation of proposed ideas (particularly by left brain managers) is held in abeyance. Experience has shown that these techniques are productive because intuitive managers tend to prefer being given a problem to solve, but resent being told *how* to solve it.

Creating a relaxed, informal, fun-type tone is also helpful. Intuitive types tend to prefer this method of addressing problems over a highly structured work format or methodology. Informal clothing and seating patterns is also normally preferred. Musical backgrounds including the use of formal meditation exercises before beginning to work on a specific problem also appears to facilitate generating creative input. Intuitive managers often prefer a warm environment in which to work—both in terms of colors and interpersonal communication. They appear to function best when they *feel* their input is truly solicited and given careful consideration. This is particularly so when totally new problems are being addressed where standard operating procedures have not yet been established. Emphasis on cooperative vs. competitive ways of solving problems appears to generate the most right brain input possible.

One highly successful company that regularly uses these techniques is Hawthorne/Stone, a San Francisco real estate firm. The founders of the company became millionaires in three years. Six of the firm's 34 staff members each earn over $200,000 per year. Marshall Thurber, William F. Raymond, and Rob Cassil, founders of the firm, explain, "The true purpose of our real estate company is to create and play games together, transcending the economic limitations in a satisfying environment." Thurber goes on saying, "I felt that if I could set up an organization that comes from choosing to play rather than having to work to make a living, then we could create miracles."[18] There are no regular hours for the staff at H/S. The office decor is warm and homey. One of the staff tells about how she felt when she was hired. "When I came for my first interview, everyone was very positive, very friendly, very interested in who I was and where I was coming from."[19]

METHODS TO HELP YOU BELIEVE IN INTUITION

The pioneering research of Douglas Dean and John Mihalasky, authors of the book *Executive ESP*, showed that executives who scored highest on ability to use ESP and had the highest profit record also had one other important characteristic—*they believed in ESP!*[20] Mentally, how we think and what we are willing to accept or entertain as possible has an effect on what is possible. *We create our own reality!* Another term for this process is *negative power*—when we narrow the range of possible options simply by what we are willing to entertain as possible.

Frances Vaughan, the psychologist and author of the book, *Awakening Intuition*, found that many of her adult patients felt they were more intuitive as children, and that they learned to keep their intuitive perceptions to themselves after encountering skepticism or ridicule from adults.[21] What you need to learn to do is keep an open mind about the possibility that intuitive experiences are within your grasp and that your ability can be expanded further. As Jean Piaget, author and child psychologist, says, "If you want to be creative, stay in part a child with the creativity and invention that characterize children before they are deformed by adult society."[22]

Laurence R. Sprecher, Senior Associate of Public Management Associates in Beaverton, Oregon, notes that people often presume a vast gap exists between logic and intuition. He asks:

> What if intuitive thinking was merely a subspecies of logical thinking—one in which the steps of the process were hidden in the subconscious portions of the brain? What if intuition was in reality a series of subconscious programs stored in the cerebrum and passed on from generation to generation? We know that, in other species, important information like migration patterns and survival reactions is passed on genetically. If we accepted the intuitive as an extension of the logical, wouldn't we be more comfortable using it? By treating intuition as something mysterious . . . do we not make it more difficult for most managers . . . to use it?[23]

Sprecher argues what is needed is an application of administrative androgyny that would allow us all to be both rational and intuitive, cognitive and emotional, competitive and nurturing—depending on what is appropriate for the situation at hand.

Examine your emotional state. Research shows that tension and anxiety interfere with learning of any kind. Examine your existing attitudes and beliefs about intuition. Become conscious of the fact that your own thoughts can work to create your own state of consciousness—learn to take responsibility for that! Suspend judgment for a moment—particularly if you scored high on being judgmental on the MBTI instrument mentioned earlier. Entertain at least the possibility that intuition exists as a skill that you can use to make decisions on the job. Learn to listen to yourself—and to others. Well developed intuition is a clear and accurate perception of reality, both inner and outer. In order to get clear perception of reality, you must learn to distinguish between yourself (ego) and reality. Often when we become too ego-involved with a situation or person, we project. This is the unconscious process whereby we see in another person something we do not wish to acknowledge or accept in ourselves—either positively or negatively.

> The potentials of the mind are awesome. Sometimes one feels lazy, frightened, and uncertain in the quest for self-knowledge. Sometimes

it seems easier to play old games, to maintain old images, unsatisfactory as they may be, than to risk stripping away the facade and seeing who one really is. Because of this, the commitment to awakening intuition requires relentless courage and a continuing willingness to face the unknown.[24]

I am reminded of experiences I have had on military bases across the country where I have trained officers in management skills. One of the exercises I have used to help increase participants' awareness of each other's skills and abilities including intuition is the synergistic game called Desert Survival produced by Human Synergistics in Plymouth, Michigan.[25] The purpose of the game is to show how individuals working together openly in a synergistic manner will result in better organizational decisions. The way the game works is that you are given a list of 20 objects and told to prioritize them in the order you would discard them so that you could survive on the desert. First, each individual works on the exercise alone and makes their choices. Then teams are formed, group decisions made, and then the scores compared for each individual and each team. Invariably, the group scores are better than the individual scores as a whole. But, certain individuals can score higher than the group did—or they come closest on an individual basis to beating the group score. They are called the key resource persons in each group.

The power of previous learning and conditioning to thwart the use of intuition in this exercise is amazing. Frequently, I find that female officers in the group *with no formal desert survival training at all* achieve the highest scores on the exercise—they have an intuitive sense of how to survive. You will note that this is consistent with our own national testing which showed that women managers on the average scored higher than men did. But, several factors often function to prevent women or other key resource people from using their intuitive knowledge to improve the decision of the total group. One factor is their own reluctance or inability to argue their case. Frequently, this is due to the fact that women are conditioned (or have allowed themselves to be conditioned) to take on more passive roles. In this case, women will often automatically adopt or willingly accept instructions to serve as recorder or secretary of the group rather than the role of a more active participant. On the other hand, male officers are more likely to try to take command of the group and seek to lead it—particularly if they have had desert survival training. It is significant to note that they often *are not* the key resource person in the group. They,

TABLE 14.5

Steps to Learning About Your Intuitive Ability

Step	Method to Use	Exercises to Practice
1. *Quiet the mind*	Learn to relax. Don't try too hard. Develop sense of alert awareness.	Any form of meditation, open focus.
2. *Concentrate*	Focus your attention, visualize your mind as a lazer beam.	Self-hypnosis tapes, word association and problem-solving exercises.
3. *Be receptive*	Suspend judgment, be aware of yourself physically, mentally, and emotionally; listen to yourself and others accurately by holding ego in abeyance and avoiding projection.	Exercises such as "Who am I?", "Who Are You?", and "What Does Our Organization Stand For?"

more than anyone, are amazed when they find out *who is*, because it is often the person *they totally discounted*—and also the person that *discounted themselves*!

The moral of the story is that one of the keys to unlocking intuitive ability is our own mind set about the subject itself, and the role we assign to it and ourselves in making decisions in our lives. Communication is in part a relationship between the sender and the receiver. What we each believe to be so will affect what is so. Following the completion of this game, both the senders and the receivers in the group normally have had their awareness level so altered and expanded that they will never again be able to function at the same consciousness level as in the past.

Learning to believe in your intuitive ability, and that of others, means learning to take the basic steps outlined in Table 14.5.

There are numerous exercises that you can try on a personal basis or in your organization to help you learn to believe in intuition. I will share a few with you here and refer you to the bibliography in the back of the book for other suggestions. One that I have found effective in workshop settings is to hand out a brief questionnaire where only the participants see their responses. It is an exercise designed to get them in a space where they will dialogue with themselves. It is designed to help them observe themselves without deception so that they can be honest with themselves. By focusing their attention on their responses to the questionnaire, it helps them to stop, take a moment in their active lives (perhaps the first time they have done so in years), and to focus their minds. The process gets them in touch with their intuitive ability. *They learn to know what they already know!*

The stage is first set by taking a brief break from the normal workshop activities. When the participants return, they are instructed to relax and get in a comfortable position. A meditation tape, including music, is played, and then the questionnaire is distributed. Each participant is told that he is free to share or not to share his responses with the other workshop participants as he wishes. Then begins the self-dialogue exercise. I ask these ten basic questions.

SELF DIALOGUE EXERCISE

1. *I believe on faith in ESP.*
   (a) True
   (b) False
2. *I have had psychic experiences.*
   (a) Yes
   (b) No
3. *I have had occasions when I saw what was going to happen before it actually did happen.*
   (a) Yes
   (b) No
   If yes, describe the one you remember the most.
4. *Have you had a major trauma in your life in the last five years* (illness, lost a key job, got a divorce, lost a loved one, etc.)?
   (a) Yes
   (b) No
   If yes, what do you remember about your feelings *the day* you felt the worst?
5. *Have you had an idea recently at work (in the last year) that you feel is good for your organization, proposed it, but failed thus far to get it implemented?*
   (a) Yes
   (b) No
   If yes, list *one to three* examples *most* important to you.
6. *Do you like your present job?*
   (a) Yes
   (b) No
   Why? (Be specific.)
7. *Do you like the organization you are presently working for?*
   (a) Yes
   (b) No
   Why? (Be specific.)

8. *Are you really happy with the person you are living with? Or, if you are not living with anyone, are you happy about it?*
   (a) Yes
   (b) No
   Why? (Be specific.)

9. *If the answer is no, what does that tell you about yourself? (In each of all of questions 6 to 8).*

10. *Write down whatever is on your mind right now!*

There is no question that such an exercise has tremendous power. Participants during or after the workshop will come up and relate insights that have come to them ranging all the way from business problems to their own personal lives. The energy in the room in that moment is unmistakably higher. They have tapped into an energy source they had not been fully aware of before. A president of one large west coast firm wrote, "I applaud your work and hope you will continue to pursue it."[26] Another southwestern insurance partner with John Hancock later said, "Your recent seminar was excellent, and the thought occurred to me that you might be of some help to us in our agency."[27] Typical comments on evaluation forms later were, "I answered questions about myself that I was afraid to ask"; "The seminar helped me to see my potential and realize ways to develop it"; and "The seminar is a new beginning for the advancement of business."[28]

Imagery in various forms is another way to tap into your intuition. It can be exercised on several different levels:

* Affective—use dreams, fantasy, imagination as tools.
* Auditory—sounds, music.
* Kinesthetic—body movement, dance.
* Olfactory—smell.

One exercise you may wish to practice here is word concentration. Ask managers to simply reflect on what the word *intuition* means to them. Another technique is to sit across from a fellow manager you do not know. Imagine that this person is an animal. Describe the characteristics you see. Reverse the process and exchange with your partner, members of the group, and then seek the input of members who know this manager well. You will be amazed how accurate your perceptions are.

Practice similar exercises in an organizational context to get a sense of how intuitive insights can be practically applied to make management decisions. For example, start a business meeting differently than usual. Ask your staff to relax and sit in a comfortable position. Ask them to close their eyes and to imagine that they are surrounded by a warm white light. Ask them to think warmly of the things they like about their co-staff members, their job, and organization. Then ask them to slowly focus again to the present moment and ask them to try to solve a particular problem you are facing in the organization at that moment. Michael Ray and Rochelle Myers, professors at Stanford University Business School, are experimentally using such techniques at their classes there. One business student related after the experience, "It was one of the most valuable courses I have taken here. I hope the skills I learned in the course will stay with me for the rest of my life."[29]

METHODS TO HELP YOU PRACTICE INTUITION

The third major step to take in developing your intuition is to cultivate and practice it daily. *Practice makes perfect!* Learn to take the risk of using your intuition to make decisions and learn from the process. Seek outside verification and then learn from your mistakes. Hone your ability to the point that you can clearly distinguish between your own ego and reality. We all possess the ability to use intuition to make decisions. Frequently, the primary reason we fail to develop our ability to the fullest is that we are simply lazy. It is analogous to the blind person who develops his or her other inherent senses to the point that color can be seen through touch. If a blind person can develop his or her other senses to this degree, why can't we develop our intuitive ability in the same way?

Frequently, we fail to make full use of our intuitive ability because we are afraid to give up methods of making decisions that we are used to or comfortable with—whether they are really effective or not. Getting in touch with and using your intuition may mean that you have to learn to *take the risk* of giving up old ways of thinking and doing things—in a word, *changing.*

> Imagination is the vehicle whereby intuition finds expression in life. Many of the constraints and limitations in one's life can be attributed to lack of imagination.[30]

Intuition does not evaluate. It indicates possibilities and provides insight into the nature of things. Ask yourself how many times you have had an inspiration or insight on how to solve a problem and then failed to follow up on it? Are you aware of how you close off the possible use of your intuition—and that of others in your organization?

Arthur Hastings, parapsychologist and management consultant, helps businessmen do this in workshops and on-sight settings by getting them to first learn to relax more by employing some of the techniques we have already discussed. He finds that creative solutions to problems that have been elusive come into focus.[31] Try this exercise yourself. Take a problem that is facing you in your organization or personal life that has you preoccupied. Work on defining the problem as clearly as possible. Even go so far as to write it down. Now, go through some of the steps outlined earlier that were used in workshops before the Dialogue with Self questionnaire was answered. Relax by playing soft music, travel your body from head to foot slowly relaxing the tension you feel anywhere at all. Once you are completely relaxed, imagine that you are in the woods. It is a warm sunny day. You can hear the wind rustling in the trees. You can hear a bird chirp here or there, and water is slowly rolling down a hill over rocks in a stream. You are sitting on the front porch of your lodge. You feel comfortable, strong, and at peace in this moment. You look out over the valley and see the sun reflecting against the mountains in the background. Your mind again turns to the problem that preoccupies you. . . . The solutions are coming to you now, and you see clearly what your next step should be.

Here are some steps to take in practicing the use of your intuition. Keep an idea journal. Whenever a flash of insight comes to you, write it down. This usually happens at times when you are in some sort of relaxed state such as after awakening from a dream, driving across the desert, watching the sun go down at night, or showering in the morning. Reflect on how you process the insight. Are you receptive, do you cut it off, ignore it, or follow up on implementing it? Reflect on key turning points in your life. What did you rely on then to make your key decisions? Was it only facts or were there important intuitive feelings involved? When a problem is concerning you, learn to sleep on it. Say to yourself, "I will put this problem to rest. I will sleep on it, and it will be solved in the morning." Keep a record of the decisions you make based on intuition. Be objective, and evaluate how often you are right or wrong. Analyze from time to time the ingredients that were involved *within yourself* in each case, and learn to eliminate or reduce the causes for error. Each day, consume a philosophical food whether it be a meditation tape, a book on Zen, a conversation about universal knowledge, or a weekend retreat to sit alone in the woods.

Perhaps a personal illustration from my own work will help clarify the importance of daily practice. The *AIM Survey* you completed earlier I send to every manager I test. On that form, I not only score the two parts of the test which measure intuitive ability, but I also write in long hand whatever comes to me about the person at that time. Frequently, I will write whole paragraphs and get quite specific about patterns of behavior they exhibit and steps that they need to take in their management or personal lives. I follow the same practice in workshops, except that rather than writing down my perceptions on a response form, I give feedback that I receive verbally. I have found that personal hand touch will also give me impressions or pictures about the individual. Usually I will express whatever comes to me at the moment and then seek verification for accuracy.

The results are sometimes amazing. Recently, I received this letter from the wife of a CEO who herself is a president of a public relations and marketing firm.

> Just a few minutes ago, my husband shared with me the results of the management style test which you mailed to him recently. Needless to say, I was so impressed with your comments that I decided to follow up with you for two reasons:
>> Would it be possible to mail me a questionnaire or test so that I may complete it accordingly?
>> Considering the results of Pantin's test, which are surprisingly accurate, do you recommend or suggest any existing publications or management tool that could help someone develop existing capabilities to the fullest?[32]

Another respondent wrote, "I want to tell you how much I appreciated your letter last spring with the analysis of my management style. I must say you were very accurate in the between-the-lines vibrations you picked up about me."[33] Now, this does not mean that I am always on target about everyone I practice this technique with (anymore than data-based decision making is 100% accurate all the time), and some people are easier to pick up cues from than others. But, I am learning to be more accurate day by day with practice, and as others become more open with me in workshops, we find that intuition can be used as one effective guide for making decisions.

CASE EXAMPLES OF ORGANIZATIONS AND INDIVIDUALS USING INTUITION TO INCREASE PRODUCTIVITY

There are a number of ways that you and your organization can make the use of intuition an integral part of day-to-day decision making. Practiced regularly, it will serve you as a reliable resource. Joseph McKinney, chairman and CEO of Tyler Corporation in Dallas, Texas, uses a technique called "the stray bullet drill." "When everything is going great, we try to imagine what combination of circumstances could constitute a serious threat to us."[34] Before McKinney begins this exercise, they start each staff meeting on Monday with prayer—one form of meditation. Their approach there is to try to tap into the spiritual level of intuition. In essence, what they do is acknowledge that there is a higher source of energy than themselves—in this case, God. McKinney says, "We recognize in that prayer that we can't do anything without God's help, and we also take great confidence from the knowledge that with His help we can do anything." They also practice guided imagery.

> When I was working on the C & H Trucking acquisition, I sat there and imagined the contract and the scratching of the pen on the paper, and I could see the half-chewed cigar in the other man's mouth, the suit he was wearing, the suit I was wearing, and the pressure of his handshake as we agreed on the deal.[35]

The work environment is also flexible and somewhat less formally structured than is the case in many business settings. McKinney explains his management style this way:

> We really believe in results around here and not in efforts. . . I don't really hold any of my people to a high standard of long hours or worry about how hard they work. There are a lot of people who are so busy preparing to do a tremendous job they never get around to doing it. We operate and compensate on the principle that results count.[36]

The product is a positive work environment supportive of the creative exploration of new ways of doing things—one in which right brain processes like intuition can flourish. As a result, Tyler Corporation is regarded as one of the top five best managed companies in the Southwest. McKinney sums up his philosophy this way, "Just because something has not been done doesn't mean it can't be done. There are no limits."[37]

Government managers have also found that practicing the use of intuition on a regular basis can be helpful in guiding decisions in a whole range of situations—from planning for the future development of a city to putting out the daily fires that come up at city hall. Francis T. Fox, city manager of San Jose, California, relies on intuition as one technique as he tries to guide the development of a grand strategy for the development of the city for the year 2000. Trying to predict the future has become a monumental challenge for city managers. The rate of change has accelerated and there has never been more instability in society. Biophysicist John Platt suggests that there have been more profound changes in the past 40 years than in the previous 600 years combined. In San Jose, the Planning Department, city officials, and a blue ribbon committee of industrial and commercial leaders are trying to meet this challenge through a future planning process called Horizon 2000. Their goal is to avoid the threats of overdevelopment while providing the necessary services to their residents.

City manager Fox describes how he uses intuition integratively with facts to develop the plan for the future.

Good management of human beings involves inspiration and supervision. Under the heading of inspiration comes the intuitive approach to management. It is based upon the major judgment, the past experience, the gut feeling, and more importantly, on the reflective thinking of the manager of a major operation such as the city of San Jose. Albert Einstein acknowledged the importance of this factor in these words, "I believe in intuition and inspiration. Imagination is more important than knowledge, for knowledge is limited whereas imagination embraces the entire world, stimulating progress, giving birth to evaluation. It is strictly speaking a real factor in scientific research."[38]

Randolph J. Forrester, city manager of Wyoming, Ohio, uses a free association technique to tap into his intuitive ability and encourage that of his staff. Essentially, he avoids a logical step-by-step approach to analyzing a given problem. Instead, he approaches any given situation with the attitude that he is willing to try anything and a presumption that there is not a 100% right way to do anything forever. When a creative idea doesn't work, he goes back to the old way or tries another approach. This method, Forrester finds, helps employees feel that they are not stuck with a new idea that doesn't work and yet a positive environment remains in which to keep trying new ideas. Intuitive thinking, he finds, is not only practical in the sense of being a problem-resolution technique, but it is also fun and one of the more psychologically rewarding aspects of management. To see a new approach or idea become a successful, better way to accomplish something is very satisfying.

> This approach has worked for me, and has resulted in a number of unique solutions and approaches. These range from women's intern programs and combined meter reader/animal warden positions to self-insured dental/optical/savings accounts.[39]

William G. McGinnis, city manager of Crescent City, California, believes that the difference between good managers and great managers is their relative ability to make correct decisions in tense or emergency situations. He sees the ability to use intuition to guide decisions under these circumstances as the key factor that separates the good from the best. McGinnis' formula for intuitive decision making is both colorful and succinct.

> I believe that good intuitive decisions are directly proportional to one's years of challenging experience, plus the number of related and worthwhile years of training and education, all divided by lack of confidence or the fear of being replaced.[40]

In emergency situations, he uses only his intuition. There is not time or information to do otherwise. McGinnis finds in these situations the best decisions are made when he is able to step back from the action for a moment and redirect the adrenaline from his body to his brain.

Washoe County, Nevada, has been seeking to develop and use the creative potential in their governmental unit by experimenting with a number of the tools and techniques we have outlined above. Ed Everett, assistant county manager, puts it this way:

> Many of us feel that creativity is something only a few exceptional people like poets, musicians, and scientists have. Hence, we passively accept our noncreative lot in life—our cocoon. Quite the contrary is true however. All of us have the potential to be more creative—we just need practice and training.[41]

The approach they have found to be successful is to start with a small group of ten employees initially composed of department and division heads, a first-line supervisor, an administrative assistant, public health nurse, and the assistant county manager. No agenda was set, and no particular methodology was initially adopted on how to go about improving the creativity of the county government.

At first the group began by focusing on developing their own intuitive skills with the eventual goal of transferring what they learned to the governmental units they worked for. There were some false starts and delays, but in the end after two years of work they find they are much more creative than when they started. Through monthly meetings and weekend retreats, the group started working on puzzles found in such materials as Eugene Raudsepp's series of books on creative growth. By working on the puzzles and sharing their solutions, they gained insight into how each group member often blocks creative solutions to problems.

Next, they moved from the puzzles to rigorous brainstorming on hypothetical problems and eventually to actual problems within the county government. They also turned to an outside consultant to assist in this process. Relaxation techniques such as music, art exercises, self-hypnosis, and guided imagery were introduced. They also discussed holistic health and the necessary relationship between mind, body, and spirit. They also examined the science or art of knowledge, acupuncture, reflexology, and iridology. They came to realize that to be truly creative required an integration of both the left and right side of the brain.

The group now believes strongly that creativity is a major skill needed to prevent their county from becoming obsolete. They have learned to look beyond traditionally accepted solutions and not to become trapped in the negative power of group think. Now they also hope to effectively change the total county organization of 1400 employees by forming separate groups of ten, each led initially by members of the original ten.[42]

RESOURCES TO HELP YOU DEVELOP YOUR INTUITION

There are a number of resources that you will find useful in helping you develop your own intuitive ability as well as that of your organization. These include books, audio- and videotapes, tests, and exercises. There is also a worldwide "intuition network" that has been formed that is designed to facilitate the exchange of tools and techniques that have proven useful for developing intuitive skills for applied use in management settings. You may obtain further details by contacting me personally or completing the form contained in the Appendix of this book.

First, to develop your cognitive awareness about intuition and your own personal intuitive ability, as well as that of your total organization, I suggest becoming familiar with and taking the various test instruments outlined earlier (*AIM Survey*, Myers-Briggs Type Indicator, computer assessments). I encourage you to study your results and compare them with your friends' and colleagues'. A similar exercise in your organization would be highly useful at this point. Other indicators of intuitive ability, as well as measures of other brain skills, are also available, including handwriting analysis.[43] For example, examine the work of Charlotte P. Leibel, author of *Change Your Handwriting, Change Your Life*, and the *Journal of Graphoanalysis* published by the International Graphoanalysis Society in Chicago. Having your own handwriting analyzed is strongly recommended.

You now have a snapshot picture of who you are, how you think, and whether you use your strong suit on the job to make decisions. You should take a look at your tension levels and health statistics at this point. What does it tell you? Are you well aligned personally and on the job? Or, do you have some repair work to do? A complete physical examination using some of the modern health assessment techniques would also be ideal at this stage.

One of the things that constantly amazes me is that individuals and organizations seldom stop to spend this kind of time or effort on self-assessment when it appears to have such a high potential for productivity improvement as well as job satisfaction. Even in those rare cases where some kind of testing or assessment has been completed by an organization, frequently the orientation is really more like a spot oil check than a necessary check for ongoing maintenance and development of our most important resource—human capital.

To help you get an even better handle on who you are, your ability to use intuition to make decisions, and your future potential, it is recommended at this stage that you examine some of the materials available that describe intuitive personalities in greater detail, their different types, characteristics, strengths and weaknesses, and how they can potentially function best in organizational settings. Especially recommended is *People Types and Tiger Stripes: A Practical Guide to Learning Styles*, Gordon Lawrence; *Gifts Differing*, Isabel Briggs Myers and Peter B. Myers; *Please Understand Me: An Essay on Temperament Styles*, David Kinsey and Marilyn Bates; and *Facing Your Type*, George J. Schemel and James A. Borbely.

It is now time to examine your immediate career goals and work. Are the goals realistic? Does the job seem to fit you. What kinds of changes (if any) are required, and how might you go about making them? At this point, you might wish to complete the Self Dialogue exercise outlined above. This should help you to get further in touch with *your internal processes* and the role you have played up to now to get you where you are presently—or where you are not *vis-à-vis* your own goals. Now is a good time to pause and reflect again on what you have learned about yourself so far. Relax. Let what you have learned come to your cognitive awareness.

Now go on to the next step in the process of developing your cognitive knowledge about intuition and your ability to use it to make decisions. Review some of the existing literature on intuition, ESP, and psychic phenomena. You will be surprised to learn in the process how many managers use this skill and openly admit doing so. You will also begin to get clues on how other people have learned to work with and develop their intuitive ability further. You may wish to begin with Douglas Dean and John Mihalasky's book called *Executive ESP*. This book outlines how top CEO's of major corporations scored on tests for ESP, and how this skill is linked to a higher profit record. Frances E. Vaughan's book, *Awakening Intuition,* is an excellent and inexpensive paperback book that will give you a firm background on how to develop and use your intuitive ability. You will now probably find it instructive to read Chapter 4, "Zen and the Art of Management" in the bestseller, *The Art of Japanese Management: Applications for American Executives* by Richard Pascale and Anthony Athos, who are faculty members in the business schools of Stanford and Harvard respectively. I also recommend *The Book of Five Rings: The Real Art of Japanese Management* by Miyamoto Musashi.

There are many other books that could be recommended here for a general background and to build your cognitive knowledge. Just a few are *Mind-Reach: Scientists Look at Psychic Ability*, Russel Targ and Harold Puthoff; *Psychic Discoveries Behind the Iron Curtain*, Sheila Ostrander and Lynn Schroeder; *Edgar Cayce on ESP*, Doris Agee, and *Jung, Synchronicity and Human Destiny*, Ira Progoff. If you wish to get a little more far out exposure to psychic phenomena, look at *Beyond the Body*, Sandra Gibson; *Ahead of Myself: Confessions of a Professional Psychic*, Shawn Robbins; and *Psychics*, which contains in-depth interviews with several well known psychics.

Now you are ready to work on developing your own intuitive skills further. There are mounds of resources to help you in this process. Games and exercises abound in the three book series by Eugene Raudsepp on *Creative Growth*. Jean Houston, the author of *Mind Games*, published a book in 1982 entitled *The Possible Human*, which is, in effect, a course on extending your physical, mental, and creative abilities further. Martin Gardner's book, *Aha!*, contains puzzles to exercise and improve your ability to solve problems. The short book by Mark A. Thurston entitled *Understand and Develop Your ESP* focuses on this dimension of your intuitive ability. *Using Your Head* by Stuart B. Litvak explores in some detail how you can develop the brain skills you presently allow to lie dormant. Chapter 11 is devoted exclusively to intuition.

There are a number of other books and resources that outline techniques that you can use to help unlock your intuitive ability. This includes everything from meditation to guided imagery to dream analysis. A best seller by a doctor is Brugh Joy's *Joy's Way*. Another recommended book is *Exploring Inner Space: Awareness Games for all Ages*, Christopher Hills and Deborah Rozman. Meditation exercises for young and old are contained in such books as *Meditation for Children, Joy in the Classroom*, and *Into Meditation Now*, all released by the University of the Trees in Boulder Creek, California. Betty Edward's recent book, *Drawing on the Right Side of the Brain*, outlines techniques for enhancing creative artwork. The techniques she outlines have direct application to style of management as well.

Audiovisual aids also abound, but few are directly linked to applications in management settings. However, recently, a few have been produced that help fill this void.[44]

Finally, you may wish to consider attending a weekend retreat or seminar to work on developing your intuitive ability. Around the country, such programs are regularly offered and recommended selectively as a way to accelerate your own personal development. If you have difficulty locating one satisfactory to you, consult your phone book for a local parapsychological association which should be up to date on current activities. If that is not possible, call the Psychology Department of the nearest university in your area. Usually at least one faculty member is active or aware of such events.

Practicing Your Intuition at Work

Here are a few hands on games you can try at work as you are developing your intuitive ability further. It might be more fun to try this with some of your coworkers or managers too and keep a record of your successes and failures over time. Meet periodically to discuss how each of you did. Try to identify within yourself those factors that seem to lead to successful predictions and those that do not. Try to strengthen the former and eliminate the latter.

MONTHLY FORECASTS

Whatever your organization, take an activity or performance objective that is considered an important measure of success and that is also reported on a monthly basis. Now, try to predict what that figure will be 1 month out, 2 months out, and so on up to one year. Play this game following these rules:

1. Think of what the figure will be before you go to sleep. Be relaxed about it—just put it in your mind for a moment, toss it around lightly.

2. Play a short meditation tape or engage in some other form of relaxing exercise.

3. If you awaken during the night with a figure, write it down. If not, don't worry about it.

4. When you awaken in the morning, see if you have a figure then. If so, write it down. If not, don't worry about it.

5. Engage in a short meditation exercise before eating breakfast. After doing so, see if you have a figure in your mind. If so, record it. If not, again, don't worry about it.

6. Sometime during the day that is convenient within your work schedule (or just after work), meet with your team partners. Practice a short relaxation exercise and then jot down whatever number "feels" right. Share it with your team. Based on this exchange, either keep that number or change it.

7. Practice these steps every day but don't do it on the weekends unless you really feel comfortable doing so.

8. At the end of the month before the actual monthly figures are released, rescan the numbers you have recorded at various times. Again, pick the *one number* from your series of predictions that feels right to you *right then!*

9. Put it in an envelope and seal it.

10. Meet with your team members at the time you normally do each day—or just before lunch. Exchange sealed envelopes. Try now to *predict* the number given to you that is inside the envelope handed to you by a team member. Put it in an envelope and seal it. Now go to lunch, and open the envelopes. Whoever is closest to the *actual monthly forecast* and who is most accurate in predicting a team member's own prediction gets the free lunch or some other prize.

11. Keep a record of successes and failures for six months or so. Now, sit down seriously one day at work and exchange all the available information each of you has such as MBTI test data, techniques used to predict, personal exercises followed, things each of you has

learned about your own feelings. This process should give you concrete clues as to why some members in the group are *consistently*
more accurate in their predictions than other members. This will
help you and your organization in several practical ways: to identify
those managers who should be assigned to problem-solving matters
where intuitive skills would be particularly valued; to identify specific work-related exercises that can be used to help you and other
managers develop your right brain skills more effectively; and to
assist everyone in learning how to build team skills more effectively
which, together, are most likely to lead to greater productivity overall.

SUPERVISOR-SUBORDINATE

Take people who are presently working in some form of regular
day-to-day supervisor-and-subordinate relationship (examples are
doctor-nurse, boss-secretary, president-district manager, foreman-
assembly line worker). Follow these steps identified as an "experimental exercise" within your organization, but administered
by a person inside or outside the formal setting competent to act as
a facilitator.

1. Start with 30-minute exchanges made up of 15 minutes each.
2. Ask each of the two participants to sit facing each other. Tell them to
   hold hands and close their eyes. Now ask them to think of words like
   cooperation, support, help, and *assistance.*
3. Start with the supervisor asking the subordinate the simple question,
   "How do you feel I can do my job more effectively?" You record the
   answers while the supervisor listens.
4. Now reverse the process with the subordinate asking the same question. Again, record in the same manner.
5. When this process has been completed, ask each person to thank the
   other person for his suggestions. Ask each of them to acknowledge
   that he will reflect on what was said and report back next time.
6. Use the next session for an exchange where each person can freely
   outline what he has accepted or rejected and why. Again, at the end
   of the session, ask each person to thank the other for his input.
7. After this process has been completed at least twice, spend one
   session where you ask each person separately and then jointly what
   he has learned *about himself first,* and *then about* the other person.
8. Clear, precise, and measurable indicators should be now available
   showing that the process is not only productive, but should be
   implemented throughout your organization. If you think it would be
   helpful, you might also wish to consider awarding some kind of

prize or giving some form of personal recognition for the suggestions which had the greatest impact on organizational and/or personal productivity.

CREATE YOUR OWN GAME

One of the best exercises you can use to practice developing your intuition for use at work is to create your own game related to management problem solving.

Think about the organizational and personal goals that you have at work. Think about the work environment you would like to experience in reality that would be conducive to achieving them. Ask a coworker or management team to do the same. Then share your respective lists. Next, create your own playfair games for yourself and your colleagues to help bring you to the *actual place you want to be together*.

Notes

1. For the details on this country's effort and that of others, see "Tarrytown Meeting," *Leading Edge Bulletin*, (vol. 4, no. 14, June 4, 1984), p. 3.
2. "Swiss Management Institute to Study Intuition's Role in Business," *Brain-Mind Bulletin* (vol. 14, no. 4, January, 1989), p. 1.
3. *Integrity in the College Curriculum: A Report to the Academic Community* (Washington, D.C.: Association of American Colleges, 1985), p. 15.
4. "New Times, New Strategies," paper given at the Public Executive Institute, University of Texas at Austin (Austin, Tx., July 12-20, 1985).
5. Cited in the brochure of Psychic Enterprises, Inc., Los Angeles, California.
6. Cognitive orientations refer to your factual knowledge about a subject. Affective orientation refers to how you feel about a subject—positive or negative. You can have very strong feelings about a subject about which you know very little. Evaluational orientations refers to what you decide to act on based on the product of your cognitive knowledge and affective feelings about a subject. What is important here is the interplay between facts and their impact on your feelings about a subject and vice versa.
7. Beverly Stephen, "Search Aims for Secrets of Success" (Tribune Company Syndicate, 1982).
8. Research has shown that one's own skepticism influences ESP scores. Also personality is a factor. Cold and rigid personalities (more likely to be left brain in management style) tend to block the ability they may have. For a discussion of this issue, see Alan Vaughan, "The Time Disbeliever," *Reincarnation Report* (March, 1983), pp. 10-11 and 45.
9. Letters to the author on May 18, 1982, and June 3, 1982, from Thomas H. Bush, deputy director, Department of the Treasury, State of New Jersey, Trenton, N.J. Reprinted with permission.

10. Letter to the author on March 19, 1983, from Harry W. Anderson, president of Tri-State Wholesale Associated Grocers, Inc. Reprinted with permission.

11. Press release of Alan Vaughan. The floppy disk for this game, entitled Psychic Defender, is available by writing Vaughan, 3223 Madera Ave., Los Angeles, CA 90039.

12. Frances E. Vaughan, *Awakening Intuition* (Garden City, N.Y.: Anchor Books, 1979), p. 62.

13. Stanley R. Dean, M.D., president of the American Association for Social Psychiatry, is doing work in this area. He is also particularly active in efforts to bridge the gap between medical science and psychic research.

14. Roger Von Oech, "The Mind as a Management Tool," *Public Management* (January, 1982), p. 7. Copyright 1982 by International City Management Association. Reprinted by permission of *Public Management* and The International City Management Association.

15. Contained in "Editor's Notes," *Public Management* (February, 1983), back of front cover. Copyright 1983 by International City Management Association. Reprinted by permission of *Public Management* and the International City Management Association.

16. Roger Von Oech, op. cit., pp. 7-9.

17. Ed Everett, "Improving Creativity—One Organization's Approach," *Public Management* (February, 1983), p. 7. Copyright 1983 by International City Management Association. Reprinted by permission of *Public Management* and the International City Management Association.

18. David F. Brown, "Consciousness in Business," *New Realities* (vol. 1, no. 3, 1977), p. 17. Copyright 1977, and reprinted by permission of *New Realities* and by Hawthorne/Stone Real Estate & Investments.

19. Ibid., p. 21. Marshall Thurber, one of the founders of the firm, has since left and gone into business for himself in San Diego.

20. Douglas Dean and John Mihalasky, *Executive ESP* (Englewood Cliffs, N.J.: Prentice-Hall, Inc., 1974).

21. Frances E. Vaughan, op. cit.

22. "Editor's Notes" citation, *Public Management* (February, 1983), back of front cover. Copyright 1983 by International City Management Association. Reprinted by permission of *Public Management* and The International City Management Association.

23. Cited in Commentary Section of *Public Management* (February, 1983), p. 18. This was a special issue devoted to creativity in the public sector. Copyright 1983 by International City Management Association. Reprinted by permission of *Public Management* and The International City Management Association.

24. Frances E. Vaughan, op. cit., p. 183. Excerpt from *Awakening Intuition* by Frances Vaughan, copyright 1979 by Frances Vaughan, reprinted by permission of Doubleday & Co., Inc.

25. J. Clayton Lafferty and Alonzo W. Pond, "The Desert Survival Situation: A Group Decision Making Experience for Examining and Increasing Individual and Team Effectiveness" (Plymouth, Mich.: Human Synergistics, 1974).

26. Letter to the author from George Boyadjieff, president of Varco Intl., Inc., Orange, Calif., dated May 11, 1982. Reprinted with permission.

27. Letter to the author from Leonard A. Goodman, Jr., General Agent for John Hancock dated January 28, 1983. Reprinted with permission.

28. Evaluations dated February 1, 1983, and March 3, 1983, conducted by the Center for Professional Development, University of Texas, El Paso, which is located in the College of Business.

29. See Michael Ray and Rochelle Myers, *Creativity in Business* (Garden City, New York: Doubleday & Co., 1986).

30. Frances E. Vaughan, op. cit., p. 185. Excerpt from *Awakening Intuition* by Frances Vaughan, copyright 1979 by Frances Vaughan, reprinted by permission of Doubleday & Co., Inc.

31. Cited in Frances E. Vaughan, op. cit., p. 154.

32. Letter to the author from Maria Elena Toraño, president of META, Miami, Fla., dated March 15, 1982.

33. Letter to the author from Jean Mathison, Associate Regional Director, Area Health Education Center, University of Southern California School of Medicine, Los Angeles, Calif., dated February 24, 1983.

34. "An Interview with Joseph McKinney, chairman and CEO, Tyler Corporation" in *Travelhost Prosperity Series*, February 28, 1982. Copyright 1982, reprinted by permission of Travelhost, Inc.

35. Ibid.

36. Ibid.

37. Ibid.

38. Cited in Commentary Section of *Public Management* (February, 1983), pp. 18-19. Reprinted by permission of *Public Management* and The International City Management Association.

39. Cited in Commentary Section of *Public Management*, op. cit., p. 17. Reprinted by permission of *Public Management* and The International City Management Association.

40. Ibid. Reprinted by permission of *Public Management* and The International City Management Association.

41. Everett, op. cit., p. 7. Reprinted by permission of *Public Management* and The International City Management Association.

42. Ibid. Reprinted by permission of *Public Management* and The International City Management Association.

43. David L. Kurtz, C. Patrick Fleenor, Louis E. Boone, and Virginia M. Rider, "CEO's: A Handwriting Analysis," *Business Horizons* (January-February, 1989), pp. 41-43.

44. A catalogue is available from ENFP Enterprises, 5525 N. Stanton St., #18-D, El Paso, TX 79912.

15

Practical Intuition[†]

MICHAEL RAY
and
ROCHELLE MYERS

To some people the phrase "practical intuition" seems to be an oxymoron: two contradictory words in a single phrase. They consider intuition highly impractical, something to be left to psychics, unliberated women, and those without the training or intellect to reason things out. But many successful people operate with their intuition, although in the past some didn't talk much about it.

It took editor James Bolen two years—from 1972 to 1974—to get together a special magazine issue on "ESP in Business." What took so long? Bolen said that it was hard to get people to talk about how they used intuition. They seemed embarrassed.

> For example, Alexander M. Poniatoff, founder and chairman of the board, emeritus, of Ampex Corporation, revealed to me that previously he wouldn't admit to anyone, specifically business people, why his decisions sometimes were contrary to any logical judgment. But when he learned of others who follow intuition, he didn't mind talking about it.

By the eighties, many business people acknowledged that intuition is an obvious cornerstone of business. In reviewing a book about business by two nonbusiness authors, Robert Lubar of *Fortune* says:

> In this connection the authors have also discovered and made much of a phenomenon that most executives become aware of early in their

†SOURCE: From CREATIVITY IN BUSINESS by Michael Ray and Rochelle Myers. Copyright © 1986 by Michael L. Ray and Rochelle Myers. Reprinted by permission of Doubleday, a division of Bantam, Doubleday, Dell Publishing Group, Inc.

careers. They learn that rationality has its limits. . . . When it comes to the crunch, the numbers and the analysis go out the window and gut feelings take over. Solman and Friedman quote the ruminations of a former IBM executive about an important investment decision he once had to make: "Ultimately it's a gut call."

At first, in spite of the emphasis on intuition in our course, we (Rochelle and Michael) felt a bit sheepish when our students asked our speakers leading questions about meditation or other intuition-awakening techniques, and about their use of intuition itself. We soon outgrew embarrassment as the questions hit the spot. Almost every speaker had his own idiosyncratic approach to tapping his creative resources, including intuition. Even somewhat conservative speakers like Raychem's Paul Cook and Alumax's Robert Marcus answered directly in the affirmative when they were asked about intuition. Cook said:

> Strangely enough, the company has made two or three big mistakes that it never would have made if I'd followed my intuition faithfully. I would not let that happen anymore. I've learned to trust my intuition. I really have. It's made a big difference.

When Marcus was asked whether they relied a lot on intuition at Alumax, he got a big laugh when he said, "I think so, yeah, we probably do. That's one of my big jobs. It doesn't require a lot of work." Perhaps we laughed because executives aren't supposed to admit that they do something that doesn't require a lot of work. Or perhaps we laughed in the delight of hearing that creative ability comes forth in such an effortless way in the form of intuition.

The Truth About Intuition

Intuition can be practical and effortless for you too. Once you understand more about the nature of intuition, you'll know what you have to do to bring it into your life. Here are some golden truths.

Intuition is a gift that must be developed. Because experiences with intuition so often seem to come out of the blue, you might assume that it is strictly a sometime thing, a matter of come-and-go lightning. It is equally easy to assume that intuition is the province of the gifted few or, less charitably, of oddballs—that it is an innate talent that you either have or don't have. Not so; this kind of debunking from the VOJ can divert you from using your own intuition.

Instead, as a quality of Essence, intuition is a skill that everyone can develop. In fact, as with any gift from your source, you have a responsibility to accept, develop, and perfect intuition.

Intuition complements reason. Blaise Pascal, the great French philosopher, mathematician, and physicist, says:

We know the truth, not only by reason but also by the heart.

Psychologist Carl Jung said:

The term [intuition] does not denote something contrary to reason, but something outside the province of reason.

Jonas Salk, the discoverer of polio vaccine, has recently been investigating the roots of creativity. Salk told *Time* correspondent Peter Stoler in an interview in *Psychology Today*:

I'm saying that we should trust our intuition. I believe that the principles of universal evolution are revealed to us through our intuition. And I think that if we combine our intuition and our reason, we can respond in an evolutionary sound way to our problems . . .

In business the stories go way back. Andrew Carnegie carried a deck of cards and played solitaire to calm his mind before making a decision. And when Conrad Hilton was bidding for the Stevens Hotel in Chicago, a number popped into his head. He used the number and purchased the world's largest hotel with a bid that won by just two hundred dollars.

But you don't have to go back decades to see the practicality of intuition in business. Every day you have to make decisions without complete data or with what seems to be contradictory information. What do you do? You use what you might call guesswork, insight, hunch, speculation, imagination, judgment (not the blame and criticism kind), gut feel, sixth sense, a feeling in the bones, good guesses—intuition.

Fairly solid evidence indicates that those who rely on intuition in their decision-making make more profitable decisions than do others. Engineers John Mihalasky and E. Douglas Dean at the New Jersey Institute of Technology found that eighty percent of those company leaders who had doubled their companies' profits in a five-year period had above-average precognitive powers (intuition). And when Weston Agor of the University of Texas at El Paso applied his test for intuitive ability to over two thousand managers he found that top managers scored higher than others.

Of course this research alone doesn't prove that all successful executives actually make decisions in a yes/no fashion, but the link is there.

No one is suggesting that decisions should be made solely on the basis of intuition. It is the combination of experience, information, reason, *and* intuition that is so powerful. Psychologist Arthur Reber of Brooklyn College, who has shown the superiority of intuitive over analytical approaches, maintains that "A blending of the two modes . . . is still preferable to the use of only one or the other."

Intuition is unemotional. You might mistrust intuition on the grounds that it springs from emotion as opposed to reason. But intuition does not come from emotion. In fact fear, anxiety, pride of authorship, wishful thinking—the entire VOJ gamut—get in the way of the clear operation of your intuition, which flows from an empty cup.

Arthur Hastings, dean of faculty at the Institute of Transpersonal Psychology, brings this home. In a talk on "ESP and Intuition in Business and Management," he described a hypnotist who led people to yes/no decisions from their subconscious.

> He tried this with women who were pregnant, because he figured the subconscious mind ought to know whether the baby is going to be male or female. He asked them under hypnosis, "Are you going to have a boy or a girl?" And they would answer, "It's a boy" or "It's a girl." Well, they were right exactly fifty percent of the time. (Laughter) Pretty accurate but no more accurate than if they had flipped a coin! So he changed his procedure and asked. "Would you *like* to have a boy or a girl?" and he got an answer to that question. Then he asked, "Is the baby going to be a boy or a girl?" and he got an answer to that question. And once he'd allowed them to express their emotional feeling, its power was discharged, and he got eighty-five percent accuracy on that time, the second time. So, let go of your emotional needs first, as much as you can, and be willing to accept whatever the answer is.

Listening to intuition is not the act of concentrating on what you think you want. It is not hedonism, a move toward the most pleasurable short-term alternative. It is not giving vent to the inner emotional child left over from your infancy. It is simply paying clear attention, without mind chatter and emotions, to the most appropriate alternative that comes from the creative Essence.

Our speakers seem to tell us that intuition kicks in precisely when they move through the stress and the frustration to a calm, clear state beyond. At that moment, the appropriate action appears almost as a solid conviction: Take the case of Robert Medearis. Instead of emotion, he prefers to talk about energy:

> I think everybody has a certain amount of energy about them. And I think that one of the critically important things is to allow that energy to take place. Don't be afraid of it, don't try to channel it. Let it emerge. Because that energy is the source, it's the food for the idea. . . . Allow it to ferment, allow it to come out, allow it to bubble up if you will even though you might think that it's somewhat negative in origin. Allow it to manifest.

Notice in the following example how Medearis moved very quickly from rage into popping ideas for a totally new venture.

> Silicon Valley Bank was started because I was pissed off at my bank. I was flying on a plane down from Calgary, and I'd been turned down on an income-tax loan and I was furious. They had changed their organizational structure so that I couldn't talk to the local manager. I don't know what happened, but I was just plain pissed. The more I thought about it the madder I got. And I don't think that was negative energy. I think it was my body sort of starting to ferment some ideas and let them come out. So I started playing around with some names. Silicon Valley has a terrific identification, so I got off the airplane—true story—I got off the airplane and I immediately went to a phone called my attorney, and said, "Would you check the name Silicon Valley Bank and see if there is any registration of that kind of name? I'm heading down to my office right now; call me after you get a run on it." So he called me and said that nobody had registered it. I said "Register it, because I think it's a good name."

> Lesson: Listen to your body, listen to your gut, allow the intuition to come forth. Because your subconscious is probably a better guide than your conscious when it comes to gut feeling. You know what they mean when they talk about gut feel decisions? They're talking about your subconscious. They're talking about listening to your body, about letting the energy come out. So listen to your intuition and believe it. You have it, but you've got to learn to believe it.

Dansk founder Ted Nierenberg dislikes the emotional term "gut feel" but speaks about an extra recognition—the kind of recognition that led him to sell his late father's business ("The fastest decision I've ever made") and get married less than a week after meeting his wife ("The best decision I ever made in my life").

Recognition, which literally means "to know again," is probably as good a synonym as any for intuition. When you have worked diligently and built upon experience in any area of business, the right decision comes instantly as a sort of emotionless recognition. Venture capitalist Wayne Van Dyck has this to say about his intuitive breakthroughs:

> In business, most of the ideas that you get come out of the blue. They come only from looking at the problem and saying, "Hey, I think there is something that needs to be done." Getting down and starting to work with it. Not necessarily knowing where the answer's going to come from or even, in most cases, what the answer will be. For example when I started Windfarms, I had this idea of what I wanted to do in terms of demonstrating that the large-scale technology could work, but I couldn't figure out what to do about it. Here was one little guy, and out there were these massive organizations. What could I do? But I kept very clear in my mind that there had to be a way to achieve the result that I wanted.
>
> Then one day I was sitting with a friend down in Los Angeles and it happened. I can remember because it was like a photographic slide flashing on. I got this picture of what Windfarms should be. And once anything becomes really clear, you can make it happen. Then it's only a matter of doing it.

Intuition demands action. R. Buckminster Fuller said:

> I call intuition cosmic fishing. You feel a nibble, then you've got to hook the fish.

Too often you get the nibble of an idea or a yes/no leap, and you don't follow through to solidly hook the opportunity. To do this you have to unite intuition with all the other aspects of Essence—will, joy, strength, and compassion.

People who have followed through make it sound easy. They use words like "just" and "only." Perhaps their follow-through seems easy only in hindsight. Or perhaps their decisions were so powerful that they were propelled forward into implementation. But the fact remains that if you don't follow through, your decision or idea dies.

Certainly those people who identify intuition as luck always caution that hard work is also necessary. Dana's Rene McPherson says that you can be lucky, but "You don't get to be a slobby dog." Tandem's Jim Treybig argues that creative success in business comes from luck *and* hard work.

Follow-through in business is more than just hard work. It is *timely* hard work. Remember that Bob Medearis called his lawyer about Silicon Valley Bank right after getting off the airplane—and that wasn't the end of it. Within days he conferred with a banker to learn all that he could about the business, drove around the area and commissioned a market study to determine the best location, worked with knowledgeable people to discover the bank's market niche, and put together a blue-ribbon founders group of one hundred individuals who could provide capital, credibility, and publicity for the bank.

If there is one characteristic that signals creativity in business, it might be follow-through. For instance, Nolan Bushnell is only one of the people who could be credited for fathering the video game, but he often gets the credit because he was the first to bring any to market in a big way. He says:

> After the creative moment I thought, "Gee, anybody should be able to make a business out of it." As it turned out anybody could. I had twenty-seven competitors so fast! (Laughter)

But timely action isn't necessarily the same thing as immediate action. Charles Schwab told us that many of the ideas for his discount brokerage appeared over a twenty-year period. But when it was time to implement them, he did so with dispatch.

Heidi Roizen, president of T/Maker Corporation, had come to such an appropriate moment when the first MacIntosh computers came out. Everybody in her office played constantly with the MacPaint art option on the new computer, but most were disappointed in the results of drawing with the computer. Was it possible, she wondered, that a computer-program version of the clip-art services available to commercial artists could fill an important need in the market? Was the idea a yes or a no?

There were at least four negative arguments. First, such a program would require a completely different distribution system than did the company's main product, a business software system. Second, the project would mean turning vital resources away from industrial to consumer markets where costs were greater and competition was fierce. Third, the twenty-five thousand dollars needed to develop and launch the program represented about eighty percent of the small company's quarterly budget, and was already needed desperately for T/Maker's established product.

Fourth, the product idea was so obvious and good that other marketers were probably already producing it.

So how did ClickArt become a yes? Heidi Roizen tells us what happened.

> I was sitting in a restaurant with a co-worker before going to see the movie *Gorky Park*. We were talking about this new art program idea for the MacIntosh. I said, "Wouldn't it be neat if you had a set of images of household furniture and appliances that you could call up?" Furniture was actually the first thing we thought of. Instead of actually having to go move your furniture, you could have these little things on the screen. Then we said, "Wouldn't it be neat to have cars and animals and people." We wrote this list down on a napkin. And I sat through the whole movie, and I couldn't keep my mind on it because I was so fired up by this product idea. When we came out of the movie, I said, "You know something is going on when I can't pay attention to a whole movie."

> For me, though, it was enough satisfaction just to have thought of the idea. But not for my co-worker. He sat me down a week later and said, "You haven't done a goddam thing. I think it's a good idea, and I'm going to do it. Are you going to help me or not?" He was really right. If he hadn't been this real-world person saying, "Do it, you're going to get something out of it," it would probably have been one of those ideas that I would have seen someone else advertising a month later.

Follow through, Heidi Roizen did, and ClickArt became a bestseller that sold over twenty times the break-even level in the first year. Her small group got the product on the market in only eight weeks, faced off six competitors to become the number one seller, brought out a special version of the product for publication work in another twelve weeks, and a third version of the product in twelve more weeks. The line of ClickArt products brought in fifty percent of the company's revenues in the first year.

Intuition is mistake-free. Will you always make the right decision if you use yes/no and intuition? Isn't there a danger in making a yes or no decision when the situation is still only at the maybe stage? If you make a decision intuitively, how do you explain it to your family, your boss, the people who are going to implement it, your directors or stockholders? How do you defend yourself if it goes wrong?

It's not unusual to have doubts like these about bringing intuition into your decision-making. Reason, analysis, and logic seem solid and familiar; you have imbibed them well over the years. They are something that can be computerized, put on paper, discussed. And there is something mysterious about intuition.

If using intuition to make decisions is worrying you, ask yourself what part of you this worry is coming from. Remember what Ken Oshman said, . . . to the effect that searching for "right" is wrong. And, remind yourself that, since good reasons usually support both sides of any argument, you'll probably have no trouble explaining your intuitive decision on a logical basis.

Claude Rosenberg of Rosenberg Capital Management banishes the fear of making mistakes by what he calls "dealing with the Y in the road."

> A very learned man said to me once, "The most serious thing is to get stuck at the Y in the road. You don't know which way to go, and you stay at the Y." I think that's really true. It has to do with creativity and change. You come to the Y in the road and you think for a minute. If your instinct doesn't tell you which way to go, don't stay there and muddle muddle muddle. Think it through, but then you've got to go down one of the forks. And once you go down that fork, you will find that you've gone the "wrong" way or the "right" way and you might come back, but that's the learning experience.

Rosenberg reached a major fork in the road in 1970. He had been with the investment banking firm of J. Barth and Company for fifteen years. During that time he had become a research partner, published two books on investing, developed the largest investment research department in the western U.S., and pioneered formalized regional investment research. But now, during a downturn in the market, he seemed to be ready to go out on his own. Was it a yes or a no?

> It wasn't that there was anything wrong with J. Barth and Company. I had wanted to leave and do my own thing for a number of years, but I had stayed there out of an exaggerated sense of loyalty, despite feeling that I wanted to do my own thing and that I was tired and frustrated by not controlling my destiny myself.
>
> I remember when I told my senior partner (who remained a good friend until he died) that I was going to leave and start my own firm. The market was terrible and the investment business looked bad. He said "Do you want my reaction?" and I said, "Yes." He said, "I think you're nuts." I went out of his office thinking, "Now there's a guy with good judgment." Normally he did have it, but he didn't in this case. It could have been foolhardy, but I was lucky. I was in the right place at the right time when we opened our business.

Today Rosenberg's independent investment counseling firm manages over four billion dollars of fixed-income and equity assets. In addition, in 1975 he formed RREEF Corporation, which purchases high quality, income-producing real estate for tax-exempt clients. RREEF is the third largest corporation of its kind with well over a billion dollars under management. An amateur musical comedy lyricist, Rosenberg gives a lot of the credit for his success in both his business and personal life to making decisions with intuition.

If you never do anything about these ideas, then you will be part of something that I don't think will do you very much good. I read an interesting article once that said that the most dangerous word or phrase was "should" or "should have." I think that's really true, so I've written a song about it called "Shoulda Coulda Woulda." I'll read some of it to you, because I think it means something. It goes.

Life's filled with options, those forks in the road,
Requiring adoptions that change living modes.
My problems, my choices, once set in concrete,
Incite bleeding voices that seem to repeat:
I shoulda done this, I coulda stood pat
I just can't dismiss how I coulda changed that.

And then it goes on, but the singer is really saying: "I don't want to take it that one step further. I don't want to take my creativity the next step and do something about something." What I'm saying is that you've got to find the creative things that fit with what you can do, and then do them. One conduit to happiness is this ability to keep the enthusiasm going, and to create, and to have a positive attitude toward change, which I think is really the secret to what differentiates successful people within their business experience and in their own personal lives.

Living with yes/no develops a positive attitude about change. At its base, procrastinating about decisions because of fear of making mistakes is really an attempt to avoid change. In contrast, love of change characterizes successful business people, even the change that comes from what others might think of as a mistake.

When we asked Nolan Bushnell to tell us about a time when he lost a game in life, he mentioned his having to sell Atari to Warner for twenty-eight million dollars. It was a loss to him, because he couldn't move his company into retail consumer sales fast enough. But he made the decision with reason and intuition and went on to build other companies. At the time he visited our class, video games and his old company Atari were riding high with billions in sales. But conditions have changed since then, and so has Bushnell. His name now comes up often as a backer of successful new technology.

When conditions change, creative people make new decisions. We've already reported how Ed Zschau decided not to run for the U.S. Senate. But seven months later he became convinced that the candidates planning to run against the incumbent were not going to win. So he changed his decision. He began to explore possible support for a Senate race.

Many of our speakers echo Rosenberg's positive attitude towards change. When Jim Benham quit Merrill Lynch to start one of the first money market funds, he left so quickly that he lost benefits money and had no income for three years. Mistake? Not to Benham, mainly because Capital Preservation Fund has opened up to him whole new worlds of challenge, opportunity, and reward.

Remarkably, Benham and the others don't really see the possibility of a mistake, even in a clear failure. Most people rationalize a failure when it is clearly apparent, but these creative business people use failures as learning experiences, and come back even stronger.

Not all people put the same kind of confidence, energy, and commitment into their personal decisions that they put into their business ones. But in personal life, too, you must be willing to make decisions, not worrying about making mistakes, and realizing that it is better to go down a fork in the road than to stay stuck at the Y.

Tricks of the Trade

Decisions are conscious ("I want vanilla ice cream"), and unconscious ("I want to fail in my new job"). It's the unconscious decisions that too often rule daily behavior. Bringing unconscious material to conscious knowledge is the primary movement in effective decision-making. The best way to do this is to flex the intuition muscle by consciously making many decisions into yes/no ones every day—starting with today. Here are some tricks of this essential trade.

Develop your own style. When nineteenth-century composer Anton Bruckner was asked how, when, and where he thought of the motif for his Ninth Symphony, he replied:

Well, it was like this, I walked up the Kahlenberg, and when it got hot and I got hungry, I sat down by a little brook and unpacked my Swiss cheese. And just as I open the greasy paper, that darn tune pops into my head.

Stories like that belie the work and preparation that led to that moment. No one else could have walked up the Kahlenberg on that particular day and have that "darn tune" (which some have called divine) pop into his head. Nor can anyone else have your unique ideas. Because of your experiences and work, you have the idea or decision already within you, but you must make the choice of whether to heed it or not.

How do you know whether you have enough information, enough experience? Advice on this varies widely. R. Buckminster Fuller said, "When in doubt, don't." Songwriter and pop recording star Harry Chapin said, "When in doubt, do something." And former Belgian prime minister Achille Van Ackere used to say, "I act first, then I think about it."

The answer is to develop your own style; only you know what is right for you in each situation. Each time you experience your own creative resource makes it easier to experience it again. The more you make decisions from Essence, the quieter your VOJ. And the quieter your VOJ, the sharper your observation; you begin to pay attention without worry or mind chatter, and you begin to build up the wisdom to make good decisions. And the more sharply you observe, the more profound your questions. Either you find the problem or it finds you.

You can develop your decision-making style and your ability to make creative decisions by starting with small decisions and by paying attention to what happens. Notice the conditions in which ideas occur to you. Is it in the shower, in doing something physical or athletic, in silence, in discussions with co-workers in the heat of battle, in getting away from it all, in meditation, in using some fifties creativity technique, in dreams, or in toughing it out until the idea or decision occurs? Use whatever works for you.

Replace frustration with simulation. As you pay attention to what happens with yes/no, you'll increasingly see ways to get to your intuition quickly, without the long frustrating periods of beating your head against a wall. Meanwhile, you might want to try the following four-step simulation based on some remarks by Dean Arthur Hastings. We recommend that you approach it as a meditation: sit comfortably, with your eyes closed.

First, diffuse emotional desires. Allow yourself to accept whatever outcome your intuition gives you. Our students find that reminding themselves that there is really no right or wrong way to go—that "This isn't for keeps," that the decision isn't really important in a cosmic sense or even in terms of their whole life—helps them to divest themselves of any emotional wishes or desires.

Second, clear and calm your mind. This usually means relaxing physically or using a meditation technique.

Third, put the question into your mind. Don't try to work on it or strive for an answer. Have no expectations. See the question in your mind's eye. Hear it inside. Wait for your answer.

Fourth, observe. What is the answer? What are your reactions to the answer? Imagine the outcome of the decision that comes.

When you finish with the simulation, after you have opened your eyes, act on the answer, even if it is just to write it down or to mentally affirm it. This is not a frivolous game. It is a process by which you can develop your most valuable decision-making tool. What you want to develop is the ability (which you inherently have) to make good decisions quickly and efficiently as soon as you need them, without going through any four-step technique, even in the heat of controversy and pressure.

Flip a coin and pay attention to your feelings. Since most decision situations add up, pro and con, to about fifty-fifty on an analytic basis, you might as well flip a coin. But unlike the superstitious ancients who practiced sortilege (the drawing of lots), you can still override the coin's answer with the one your Essence gives you. Sense your body. How does it feel if the coin comes up with a yes? Are you uncomfortable with it? Do you want to try two out of three? Then it is probably a no for you.

Follow the gnawing feeling. A variation of the coin-flip occurs when you sound out ideas or decisions before you fully act upon them. James Cook, president of L. G. Balfour, was reported in the *Wall Street Journal* to differentiate between "gut and guess" by observing his own reactions when his colleagues shoot down his ideas. If his feeling persists—"and gnaws and gnaws"—he is more likely to stay with his idea.

Nolan Bushnell told about presenting the idea for the video game "Breakout" to a group at Atari, where people were encouraged to be frank about others' ideas. He got an overwhelmingly negative response. But the gnawing went on and:

> The common wisdom in the game companies at that time was that games with paddles were passé. But I just knew in my mind that the

game was going to be fun. I hired a consultant who developed a prototype of the game. Once everyone played it, they said, "Oh yeah! Why didn't you say this in the first place?"

There is a caution implicit in Bushnell's story, however. People very often confuse habit ("It worked before") with a message from their Essence. That could have been the case here since Bushnell started the video game revolution with a paddle game. Fortunately he had the check of reactions of others in his company. You can benefit from the same kind of check.

Stimulate your whole brain with a breathing exercise. Recent research indicates that our breathing is intimately related to patterns of brain hemisphere action. When you breathe predominantly through the left nostril, your right brain is more active, and vice versa.

Given what we know about right brain versus left brain, it wasn't long before researchers asked the obvious question: Is it possible to activate one side of the brain or the other by selective nostril breathing? The answer is yes, which probably explains why a centuries-old hatha yoga breathing exercise works so well in relaxing people and in opening up their inner creative resources.

You can do this exercise right where you are now, since it involves nothing more than alternating breaths across nostrils. It can clear and direct your mind while you are making a decision.

The alternate nostril breathing rhythm goes as follows: Pinch your nose as if you smell something, putting the first finger of your right hand on your left nostril and the thumb on your right nostril. Then lift your thumb and inhale easily and deeply into the right nostril. After inhaling all the way, close the right nostril with your thumb, lift the first finger, and first exhale out of and then inhale into the left nostril. Then close the left nostril and open and breathe out and into the right. Continue alternate breathing for as long as it feels comfortable, remembering to shift nostrils after each deep inhalation.

Concentrate intensely on one activity. You probably often get insights and make good decisions when you are involved in something that is unrelated to the problem. You can achieve the same effect by concentrating intensely and silently on any activity, such as eating. Simply eat alone and pay total attention to the tastes, temperature, colors, odors, sounds, and textures of the food, and to your bodily and emotional reactions to it. Don't read, watch TV, or think about anything but the food.

The sensing, looking, and listening exercise of the last chapter can do the same thing wherever you are. Whatever you concentrate on, don't *expect* anything. Just see what happens, especially when you get back to your decision problem. You might be surprised.

Cherish your revelations. As you live with the yes/no heuristic, many small revelations will occur. These came from our students:

Food seems to taste better when it is chosen by yes/no.

Yes/no saves time.

No decision is forever.

You never seem to be able to compile enough facts to be able to make a decision based solely on them.

There doesn't have to be a rational reason for your decision.

Big decisions are usually made by yes/no already.

You can do a yes to a no as long as you know it is a no (and also vice versa).

Revelations like these (you will have your own) are validation that the intuition is operating. You can keep the process going by writing down your findings and acknowledging your successes.

Ask yourself if it's a yes or a no. Surprise. We have come full circle to the trick of the trade that is the very basis of this chapter. It is truly a powerful little idea for revolutionizing your decision-making. If you're diligent in applying it, observing and even writing down your experiences, you are well on your way to making creative decisions consistently in all parts of your life.

PART VI Future Research Agenda

This concluding article is a call for interdisciplinary research on the role of intuition in leadership and management worldwide. Gaps in the present literature are identified, and hypotheses are proposed for future field testing. The piece also describes new, emerging research programs that have been recently started toward this end, including the author's own.

16

The Logic of Intuitive Decision Making
An Agenda for Future Research

WESTON H. AGOR

The role and importance of intuition in decision making have been acknowledged throughout the ages of man.[1] In more modern times, many practicing executives and scholars alike have posited that intuition is not only a brain skill that is partially inherited but also one that can be trained and expanded for applied use in management.[2] Despite this fact, it is startling to find that there is little in the way of applied research on this subject.[3] Putting aside many of the more popularized treatments of intuition in the literature today,[4] there are only a handful of serious scholarly works on the subject. Of these, the majority are essentially theoretical in nature and tend to be produced almost exclusively by psychologists or psychophysiologists.[5] Interdisciplinary research on intuition is virtually nonexistent, and field research in applied management settings is still quite sparse.[6]

Of the studies that do exist, the very design and focus of them are equally disconcerting. As a rule, for example, the researchers who carry out this work often give their studies such titles as "paranormal" or "non-rational processes."[7] What this really means is that the "hard scientists" who have taken up this subject for research cannot yet explain or measure successfully the precise process by which intuition works—even though there is at the same time a ready amount of hard evidence to indicate that the process itself does exist.[8] Rather than admit this fact—and thereby the very limits of hard science technology itself at this point in its development—nonneutral labels are assigned to work on this subject instead. This tends to discourage serious research on intuition and/or acceptability in the scientific community even when significant findings are actually presented.[9]

The very design of several of these research studies also makes it difficult to obtain reliable results that are acceptable to the broader scientific community and/or that satisfy the demands from potential financial supporters for evidence of the practical usefulness of this work. For example, a large body of research has involved asking subjects to demonstrate greater-than-chance ability to read card numbers and colors that another subject is looking at—or other similar repetitive tasks.[10] Much of this work has been conducted under highly controlled laboratory conditions. The problem with this design is that the experimental subject quickly loses interest in such repetitive and routine tasks, and his or her record of success correspondingly declines. Potential government and private sector research sponsors ask how this rather antiseptically designed work can be used in some practical way to justify its support to watchful members of Congress or stockholders.[11]

At the very same time, we are on the threshold of achieving major advances in our understanding of how the human brain functions. Already, replication of some of the more elementary and routine functions of the brain has spawned a whole new field known as "artificial intelligence," which is working with some success to develop ways of putting research findings to practical and applied use.[12] These and other new breakthroughs that can be expected in the next decade all suggest that an investment in developing practical ways for using and increasing our human brain skills to the fullest for applied decision making is likely to pay high dividends.

This is so in large part because we know so little at the moment about how our brain in fact functions and how particular processes like intuition take place and can be encouraged to take place. Unfolding technological advances applied to such a virgin field all suggest enormous upside potential. As one public executive put it recently, the mind and the creative potential of employees represent one of the few remaining resources that can be expanded. Not using these resources is the same as turning your back on a new revenue source.[13]

An Agenda for Future Research

For the last eight years, I have conducted extensive research on the subject of intuition and how managers use this brain skill to make their most important decisions.[14] This research should thus far be regarded as exploratory. An exploratory study is one done in an area in which little or no previous research exists. Often, the findings are tentative and could well be later modified through subsequent research. In fact, one of the objectives of my research is to encourage both academic scholars and practicing executives alike to devote more time and resources to this systematic study of intuitive decision making—preferably in more applied and inter-disciplinary settings than in the past.

For those who are interested in making such a commitment, I have several thoughts and suggestions for you to consider before proceeding. First, I suggest that you adopt this "going-in mind-set" about the subject of intuition. Take as your working hypothesis that intuition is simply a rational and logical brain skill that can be used to help guide decision making. It is not paranormal. Allow your mind to imagine the possibility that hard science has not yet developed the ability to quantify step-by-step how this process in fact works, but that this capability will be developed sometime during the balance of this century. In the meantime, assume that the process by which intuition works is a highly complex one. Assume that this process involves a series of input sources. Assume that one of these is a series of programs that are hidden in the brain and passed on from generation to generation, something analo-gous to the migration programs for birds and the survival instincts of other animals.[15]

Assume that other input sources can include either factual and/or feeling cues experienced during this particular lifetime that can also potentially serve as one possible basis for future-genera-tion brain programming. Assume that the degree to which input from any or all of these potential sources is actually experienced will depend in part on how we process our life (or lives) through the filters of our own personal and cultural/societal egos.[16] Hence, for example, our definition of "reality" may well depend not only on reality itself as it truly exists but, at least in part, on our own perception of reality and/or our willingness to accept what is in fact so—either about ourselves or about the organizations in which we work. The more receptive and open we are to the potential cues that exist on all these levels (i.e., factual, feeling, preprogrammed), the greater our "consciousness" is of reality. The greater this con-sciousness is, the greater is our potential intuitive ability. Whether we "actualize" this potential ability on any or all of the levels of intuition[17] will also depend on whether we learn to "actualize" or bring it "on-line" on command. This takes practice. Some of the ways to achieve this facility appear to be through the techniques outlined in my previous research on this topic—on both an individual and a group level.[18] Other avenues are yet to be discovered.

Quantitative hard science research concerning how the intuitive process in fact works step-by-step will take a major effort spanning several years. For research of such magnitude to be both meaningful and supported by potential funding sources, it will have to demonstrate practical and applied results in both the short and the long term. In order to accomplish this goal, several suggestions seem plausible. First, the effort should be global and interdisciplinary in scope. The very best minds in all the various disciplines will be required to unravel one of the brain's greatest puzzles, and the nature of intuition itself also demands an interdisciplinary understanding. Second, the establishment of a global "intuition network" to facilitate this process would also seem to be a highly productive step to take. This network would have several advantages. The latest findings could be instantaneously transmitted worldwide by such means as computer or satellite hookups. Unnecessary duplication and overlap of studies could be avoided, while the network would also help to ensure that research is designed to build upon earlier work that has already been successfully completed. Some of the destructive potential applications of intuitive brain skills could, it is hoped, be minimized through such an open sharing process as well.[19]

Finally, efforts should be made to enlist the participation and support of successful highly intuitive executives around the world for the establishment of this intuition network. No single step will generate more support—whether financial or otherwise. For example, if some of these executives could be encouraged to speak out openly about their intuitive ability and how they use their ability to make decisions, others would be encouraged to do likewise. A major global resource would thereby be developed for more systematic study and development. If these executives would also be willing to be studied more carefully by interdisciplinary teams of researchers, we could well more effectively learn about how the intuitive process in fact works by the level of its application. Similarly, if organizations themselves through their own efforts would adopt internal programs designed to assess and evaluate the intuitive processes of their management staff and report to the network regularly on their successes and failures, general financial support for ongoing research from traditional funding sources would probably soon be forthcoming.

It is also recommended that before scholars or laboratory scientists begin to carry out their proposed study designs on this subject, they solicit the review and comment of a panel of these highly intuitive executives who are willing to participate in this manner. This process could well focus research efforts more effectively to help ensure immediate short-term payoffs in the form of findings that can be used practically by their organizations, which in turn will help to generate further support for more extensive long-term projects. Another outcome of this review process could be that totally new directions in research will be suggested that are highly plausible but never thought of by the scientists concerned (or pursued even when so)—quite possibly because these scientists tend to be predominantly analytical-type thinkers who are themselves less prone to appreciate and understand intuitive thinking processes.

Some thought should also be given to whether research on intuitive processes should not also include in the study design young children and students in private and public sector management programs at the university level in addition to practicing intuitive executives. There has been a growing body of research to suggest, for example, that young children are far more intuitive than adults but soon learn to suppress and/or "unlearn" this ability as a result of our current model of classroom instruction as well as through societal pressures.[20] Longitudinal study designs encompassing these different age groups might unlock other clues to our understanding of how the intuitive process works and can be developed further. Similarly, the study of gifted children in this regard might provide still other clues. For example, some of the recent research by Howard Gardner and D. N. Perkins suggests that our traditional notions about human intelligence and how it is acquired are at best only "partial glimpses" of reality.[21] One might well speculate whether precocious children's early ability is really one manifestation of the fact that man does have some form of programmed knowledge at birth that complements knowledge acquired by more traditional means during this lifetime. Or, do the newer theories of quantum physics suggest still other explanations for ways we can learn to "tap into" our intuitive pool of knowledge more systematically.[22]

Other pieces to understanding the intuitive puzzle may well be found through the study of how our brain stores and forgets accumulated information—including genetically from generation to generation. The latest research available on this process, for example, suggests that some of the previous scientific notions about it held by such famous psychologists as Sigmund Freud are at least partially incorrect.[23] When it comes right down to it, at this very moment we know that the brain has the capacity to create totally new synaptic connections as a result of electrical impulses generated through outside stimuli from life experiences. These synaptic connections become our new knowledge, awareness, or extended capabilities beyond those that we started with when this process began.[24] How this all works precisely step-by-step or can be facilitated is still largely an unfolding mystery.[25]

In addition to the global "intuition network" that you may join by completing the form contained in the Appendix of this book, another new global research effort has been established. Under the direction of Jagdish Parikh—a native of India who has received management training in the West at Harvard University—the International Management Institute of Geneva in 1988 conducted a research roundtable, "The Role of Intuition in Business Vision and Decisions."[26] Regional sites throughout the world are in the process of being formed to coordinate and support ongoing research including various countries in Europe, Asia, and the United States.

I think it is safe to say that you will witness in this next decade a crescendo of research on the use of intuition in organizational leadership and management around the world. I predict that over this next decade we will come to understand a good bit more about the "logic" and the "technology" of the human intuitive process. I believe we will also see a concerted effort to "mainstream" the use of this brain skill. By this I mean that coordinated efforts will be made to practically apply intuition to improve our strategic decision making within organizations and our global understanding among all peoples. Some of this "mainstreaming" will be a by-product of the artificial intelligence efforts to replicate the brain's processes. I fully expect that a decade from now we will have not only a handful of articles and research projects on intuition to report about—which we have today—but also a whole array of studies and practical uses that will help to demystify this brain skill and harness it for the well-being of all mankind.

Notes

1. For a discussion of this fact, see the recent article by Nobel Prize winner Herbert A. Simon, "Making Management Decisions: The Role of Intuition and Emotion," *The Academy of Management Executive* (February, 1987), pp. 57-64.

2. See, for example, Frances Vaughan, *Awakening Intuition* (Garden City, N.Y.: Anchor Books, 1979); John Naisbitt and Patricia Aburdene, *Reinventing the Corporation* (New York: Warner Books, 1985).

3. One example is Milton Fisher, *Intuition: How to Use It for Success and Happiness* (New York: E. P. Dutton, 1981).

4. See, for example, Roy Rowan, *The Intuitive Manager* (Boston, Ma.: Little, Brown & Co., 1986).

5. See, for example, Malcolm Westcott, *Toward a Contemporary Psychology of Intuition: A Historical, Theoretical, and Empirical Approach* (New York: Holt, Rinehart & Winston, 1968).

6. One exception is Daniel J. Isenberg, "How Senior Managers Think," *Harvard Business Review* (November-December, 1984), pp. 81-90.

7. A recent title of a serious research study in a series of many at Princeton University's School of Engineering is titled "On the Quantum Mechanics of Consciousness with Applications to Anomalies Phenomena" (Princeton, N.J.: Princeton University, June, 1984, revision). The very title of the laboratory where this research is being conducted is an illustration of what I mean.

8. Duke University conducted research for years. More recently, Russell Targ, Harold Puthoff, and Keith Harary in northern California and Stephen Schwartz and Rand De Mattei in southern California have been active. A recently published paper in a respected hard science outlet on this subject is Robert G. Jahn, "The Persistent Paradox of Psychic Phenomena: An Engineering Perspective," *Proceedings of the IEEE* (vol. 70, no. 2, February, 1982), pp. 136-170. For another summary in policy circles, see Christopher H. Dodge, "Research into 'Psi' Phenomena: Current Status and Trends of Congressional Concern" (Washington, D.C.: Library of Congress, Congressional Research Service, June 2, 1983).

9. For example, see Russell Targ and Keith Haray, *The Mind Race: Understanding and Using Psychic Abilities* (New York: Villard Books, 1984).

10. Much of the research conducted by J. B. Rhine at Duke University was of this type for years.

11. Some of the U.S. government support for the Stanford Research Institute research fell into hard times for this very reason.

12. For a recent discussion of this topic, see Hubert L. Dreyfus and Stuart E. Dreyfus, *Mind Over Machine: The Power of Human Intuition and Expertise in the Era of the Computer* (New York: Free Press, 1986).

13. Ed Everett, "Improving Creativity—One Organization's Approach," *Public Management* (vol. 65, no. 2, February, 1983), p. 8.

14. See my two major books, Weston H. Agor, *The Logic of Intuitive Decision Making: A Research Based Approach for Top Management* (Westport, Ct.: Greenwood Press, 1986), and Weston H. Agor, *Intuitive Management: Integrating Left and Right Brain Management Skills* (Englewood Cliffs, N.J.: Prentice-Hall Press, 1984).

15. Laurence R. Sprecher, a consultant with Public Management Associates in Oregon has suggested this view of intuition in a letter to the editor in *Public Management* (vol. 65, no. 2, February, 1983), p. 18.

16. For an extensive treatment of this particular orientational model of the subject of intuition, see several selections in Roger N. Walsh and Frances Vaughan, eds., *Beyond Ego: Transpersonal Dimensions in Psychology* (Los Angeles: J. P. Tarcher, 1980).

17. For a discussion of the levels of intuition, see Vaughan, *Awakening Intuition.*

18. Weston H. Agor, *How to Use and Develop Your Intuitive Powers for Increased Productivity* (Bryn Mawr, Pa.: Organization Design and Development, 1987).

19. For a discussion of some of the potentially destructive aspects, see Targ and Harary, *The Mind Race*, pp. 247-260.

20. See Alex Tanous and Katherine Fair Donnelly, *Is Your Child Psychic? A Guide for Creative Parents and Teachers* (New York: Macmillan, 1979).

21. See Howard Gardner, *Frames of Mind: The Theory of Multiple Intelligences* (New York: Basic Books, 1983), and D. N. Perkins, *The Mind's Best Work* (Cambridge, Ma.: Harvard University Press, 1981).

22. Fritzof Capra, *The Tao of Physics*, 2nd ed. (Boulder, Co.: Shambhala, 1983); Fred Alan Wolf, *Star Wave: Mind, Consciousness, and Quantum Physics* (New York: Macmillan, 1984).

23. See the public television program "Learning and Memory" in the series on the brain produced with the support of the Annenberg Foundation in 1984. This program presents research that questions Freud's notion that childhood memories cannot be recalled simply because they are painful. Another probability is that one normal process of the brain is "to forget" unimportant information in order to allow space for new, more important information necessary for survival. How this same process might relate to remembering or forgetting earlier life experiences and regression therapy is intriguing and could well provide some of the explanations we are looking for on how intuition works.

24. *Ibid.*

25. Equally relevant to our understanding might be to learn how it is that human beings (and animals) learn "to calibrate" to each other over time, and why sibling pairs seem to have greater ability to communicate with each other than the average brother or sister.

26. For details, see "Report of the IMI Intuition Network Roundtable Meeting on the Role of Intuition in Business Vision and Decisions," held in Divonne, France, April 19-21, 1988.

Appendix:
Global Intuition Network:
Individual and Organization Registration Form

The purpose of the "Global Intuition Network" is simple: to promote the applied use of intuition in decision making; to share new knowledge on how to use this brain skill as it becomes known; and to promote ongoing research on intuitive processes for practical use in organizations. Once fully established it is anticipated that a computer exchange network will be used to facilitate this process and regular conferences will also be held for this purpose.

Once you have completed and mailed me the following form, I will return a contact list for your area and also a brochure describing materials that are available for using and developing your intuition for practical decision making in organizations today.

Please type or print the information requested below. Mail this form to: Weston H. Agor, University of Texas at El Paso, P.O. Box 614, University Station, El Paso, TX 79968. If you have any questions, you may also call 915-747-5227.

Name: _____

Address: _____

_____

_____

Phone Number: (___) _____

Preference (Indicate One):
  Join Network in my area ___
  Organize Network in my area ___
  Register my Organizational Network Already Established ___

Index

About the Contributors

Weston H. Agor is Professor of Public Administration at the University of Texas at El Paso, and president of ENFP Enterprises, a management consulting firm specializing in intuitive management skills. He is the author of *The Logic of Intuitive Decision Making: A Research Based Approach for Top Management* and also *Intuitive Management: Integrating Left and Right Brain Management Skills*. His books have been translated into several foreign languages, including German and Japanese, and are being used by the leading management schools in the United States including Harvard, Stanford, and Yale and in several other universities in many countries worldwide.

Philip Goldberg is the author of *The Intuitive Edge: Understanding and Developing Intuition*. He holds a degree in industrial psychology and is a consultant to business and research organizations. He currently resides in Los Angeles.

Stephen C. Harper is Professor in the Department of Management and Marketing at the University of North Carolina—Wilmington. He is the author of *Entrepreneurial Blueprint*.

Daniel J. Isenberg is Assistant Professor of Business Administration at the Harvard Graduate School of Business Administration. He is currently completing a study on the thinking processes of major corporate leaders.

Rochelle Myers is coauthor of *Creativity in Business* and the founder of the Art and Growth Studio and the Myers Institute for Creative Studies in San Francisco.

Michael Ray is Professor of Marketing and Communications at Stanford University's Graduate School of Business and coauthor of the book *Creativity in Business*.

Roy Rowan is a former member of the board of editors of *Fortune* magazine and author of *The Intuitive Manager*.

Herbert A. Simon is Richard King Mellon University Professor of Computer Science and Psychology at Carnegie-Mellon University.

He has received the Alfred Nobel Memorial Prize in Economics and the National Medal of Science. He has published over 600 papers and 20 books and monographs.

Frances E. Vaughan is a Ph.D. graduate from Stanford University and the author of *Awakening Intuition*. She has a private psychotherapy practice in Mill Valley, California, and is past president of the Association for Transpersonal Psychology.

NOTES

NOTES

NOTES